Peter Barnes

Plays: 2

Red Noses, The Spirit of Man,
Nobody Here But Us Chickens, Sunsets and Glories,
Bye Bye Columbus

'Peter Barnes is a colossus whose returns to the stage serve as a salutary reminder that there is more to it than two men and a dog.' *Financial Times*

A comedy about the Black Death, 'Peter Barnes' *Red Noses* is a brilliant play. He has written a tremendous life-affirming piece that celebrates the human spirit while deriding those who would tyrannise and encase it.' *Guardian*

'*The Spirit of Man*, an ingenious triple-bill exploring Man's need for faith through three short satires, based in medieval France, Protectorate England and nineteenth-century Eastern Europe . . . A bold and unusual screenplay by a first-rate writer.' *Independent*

Nobody Here But Us Chickens, a linked trilogy of short plays, is 'one of the funniest plays of the century'. Bernard F. Dukore, *Barnstorm*

Set in medieval Italy during a crisis in the Church, *Sunsets and Glories* is 'a work of the highest and most thrilling theatrical energy'. *Independent on Sunday*

Bye Bye Columbus was televised in 1992: 'Wildly entertaining'. *Guardian*

Peter Barnes is a writer and director whose work includes *The Ruling Class* (Nottingham and Piccadilly Theatre, London 1968), *Leonardo's Last Supper* and *Noonday Demons* (Open Space Theatre, London 1969), *The Bewitched* (Royal Shakespeare Company at the Aldwych Theatre, London 1974), *Laughter!* (Royal Court Theatre, London 1978), *Red Noses* (RSC, Barbican, London 1985) and *Sunsets and Glories* (West Yorkshire Playhouse, Leeds 1990). He has won the *Evening Standard* Award and the John Whiting Award 1969; Laurence Olivier Award 1985; Sony Best Radio Play Award 1981; Royal Television Society Award for Best TV Play 1987; and was nominated for an Oscar in 1993.

by the same author

Peter Barnes Plays: 1
(The Ruling Class, Leonardo's Last Supper, Noonday Demons,
The Bewitched, Laughter!, Barnes' People: Eight Monologues)

Peter Barnes Plays: 3
(Clap Hands Here Comes Charlie, Heaven's Blessings,
Revolutionary Witness)

Revolutionary Witness &
Nobody Here But Us Chickens

The Spirit of Man &
More Barnes' People

Sunsets and Glories

PETER BARNES

Plays: 2

Red Noses
The Spirit of Man
Nobody Here But Us Chickens
Sunsets and Glories
Bye Bye Columbus

Introduced by the author

Methuen Drama

METHUEN DRAMA CONTEMPORARY DRAMATISTS

This edition first published in Great Britain in 1993
Reissued in this series in 1996
by Methuen Drama

ISBN 0 413 68030 4

A CIP catalogue record for this book is available at the British Library

Typeset by Hewer Text Composition Services, Edinburgh
Transferred to digital printing 2002

Contents

A Chronology   vii

Introduction   ix

Author's Note   xiii

RED NOSES   1

THE SPIRIT OF MAN   121
I   A Hand Witch of the Second Stage   123
II   From Sleep and Shadow   141
III The Night of the Sinhat Torah   159

NOBODY HERE BUT US CHICKENS   171
I   Nobody Here But Us Chickens   175
II   More Than a Touch of Zen   189
III Not As Bad As They Seem   203

SUNSETS AND GLORIES   219

BYE BYE COLUMBUS   309

A Chronology

of First Performances

1965 *Sclerosis*, Aldwych Theatre, London

1968 *The Ruling Class*, Nottingham Playhouse and Piccadilly Theatre, London

1969 *Leonardo's Last Supper*, Open Space, London

1969 *Noonday Demons*, Open Space, London

1970 *Lulu*, Nottingham Playhouse, Royal Court and Apollo Theatre, London, adaptation of *Earth Spirit* and *Pandora's Box* by Frank Wedekind

1974 *The Bewitched*, Royal Shakespeare Company at the Aldwych Theatre, London

1978 *Laughter!*, Royal Court Theatre, London

1985 *Red Noses*, Royal Shakespeare Company at the Barbican Theatre, London

1990 *Sunsets and Glories* at the West Yorkshire Playhouse

Introduction

Oh, oh, oh, that's four 'ohs' coming and going. No, only going. Coming, it's four ho, ho, ho, hos.

If you didn't know me you'd think I was a stranger. Moving effortlessly from half-asleep to half-awake, wondering why this isn't Thursday, I've been ripening on the wrong side of the hill for too many years. Just look at fellow workers in the vineyards.

The Russian poetess, Marina Tsvetayeva, whose vast compassion encompassed the Universe, left her youngest daughter tied to a chair in her freezing flat for hours. The child finally died, aged two. Bartók, on the other hand, liked to dress his wife up as a duck when they made love.

I should've remembered the advice: don't write anything you can phone, don't phone anything you can talk, don't talk anything you can whisper, don't whisper anything you can smile, don't smile anything you can nod, don't nod anything you can wink. It would have been a lot easier winking my way through life.

But some problems are without solutions. My profile remains as bright as an out-of-order phone box. If your work isn't regarded or understood then you resign yourself to try again and look to the future to soothe wounded pride. I haven't quite cured myself of the vanity of thinking about posthumous fame. But interpreting the present from the perspective of a future ideal is a pathological condition. Obsessive artistic striving conforms to the textbook definition of madness: 'an internally consistent, but fundamentally mistaken understanding of the nature of the external world and a determination to preserve this vision at all costs despite its evident harmfulness.' At a guess, that definition fits most artists and all politicians, those stunned mullets who think they are born to rule us.

'My job is to do the best for my country!'
'Resign then.'

Thoughts escape from my head and I'm always trying to find them again. They're all around in the form of butterflies, coloured according to subject: black, gold, pink and murderous red. But, then, I knew one man who believed he was the youngest son of the Virgin Mary and planted twigs in the ground to grow as his sons and daughters, and another, who was bald and had been sleeping with his neighbour's wife. The neighbour knew about it because there were no hairs on the pillow.

The English have learned, over the years, to fall on their knees, touch their forelocks and sit up and beg, all at the same time. They like to call it stoicism rather than servility but just listen to those enamelled voices making skin crawl at thirty paces, listen to those proprietorial vowels flattened and stretched by centuries of boss living, listen to them giving orders, and worse, watch the way the rest of the country grovels. Louis XIV once said in sincere amazement, 'I almost had to wait.'

On the other hand, Islam is full of vile injustice, poverty and ignorance, where every action, good or bad, is committed in the name of God the Merciful, God the Compassionate.

If you get too depressed think of John Henderson and Zoe D'Arcy who were fined £50 each for a post-coital cigarette in a non-smoking carriage after fellow passengers had ignored them having oral sex in a first-class compartment.

That helps, confronted with the Medusa face of life when the whole history of the world can't show one single instance of oppression being ended by the humility of the oppressed. I'd like to see the wheat grow tall and an immediate increase in the number of black-footed ferrets, but the monsters are real and hungry. That is why I find myself salting the clouds, spoiling the picnic.

It's pretty obvious I wasn't born in Poona where whisky-swigging Colonels used to spend their time falling off polo ponies, but I would've liked a catered life and been able to polish off a great novel in a weekend, write a Gershwin tune (how about you?), sculpt Rodin to shame, and scrape my own teeth, amid the river mists of Kew.

As it happens I was born in Bow, within the sound of Bow Bells, though I never heard them ring. I grew up in a downmarket seaside resort on the east coast, where my parents worked in amusement arcades on the pier and later owned two cafes on the seafront, along with the cockles and whelks stalls, the deck chairs, Punch & Judy booth and sand artists, who would draw, with a pointed stick, elegant pictures in the wet sand, usually of a patriotic nature, Union Jacks and lions rampant.

One of the games on the pier, operated by my father, consisted of a wooden railway sleeper with large nails. The customer paid sixpence and had three chances to knock the nail in, so the nailhead was flush with the wooden surface. This is more difficult than it sounds. The blows have to be exact as well as strong, otherwise the nail goes in crooked. The game was popular, and the spectacle of men paying sixpence for the privilege of frenziedly knocking a nail into a block of wood, with a prize they would never have bought in the first place, remains a potent image of human futility and cupidity.

Or rather it's an image of the writer forever banging away at a nail, and always missing. You have to hit it just right to win a prize and when you do you know the prize will turn out to be disappointing.

Much could be made of this colourful background as an explanation of the carnival aspect of my plays, with their mixture of songs, dances, jokes and comic routines. It fits into one of those pigeon-holes that help to make sense of the messy inconsistencies of artists who, like everyone else, are rarely all of a piece in their work or lives. Men and women always act out of character, those in drama rarely, which is why they are never 'real' and shouldn't aim to be.

The problem with my carnival background is that it's both true and untrue. Those sights and sounds of the sea and arcades, donkey rides, ice-cream vendors, dodgem rides, speedboats, sailing boats, and hot-dog stalls, were all around and about me, sight and sound, raucous and pungent. That is me, trying to capture a world gone, as if it were true.

I tried to ignore this world of seafront photographers charging for snaps of day-trippers, when there was no film in the camera, of weatherbeaten fishermen selling high-priced freshly caught fish, which they had bought earlier that morning at the local fishmongers, and the cries of the passengers high on the helter-skelter mingling with the screeches of 'You are Lobby Lud, and I claim my £10 reward'.

This outside world of a seaside resort in summer was always dim. I'm conjuring it up more vividly now than I experienced it then.

The winter picture of the place is stronger, grey sea and deserted seafront, white mist, long forgotten romances behind empty kiosks and the snow falling on forsaken putting greens.

I don't know how real this is, or was. I've felt, more strongly as I've grown older, that reality's always somewhere else. You can't take reality in your hand, it's a perfume and it's everywhere. But I've never been able to find out where it comes from, so I'm left wondering, is it real?

Author's Note

There is always a problem in publishing the text of a play.

Do you publish the text as written by the playwright before rehearsals, or do you use the one after rehearsals, or a combination of the two?

There is the added complication that the publishers want to publish as soon as possible, before the opening night.

I publish the fullest texts possible, complete with all the rehearsal additions and alterations. I expect the texts for all the major plays, with the possible exception of *The Ruling Class*, to be cut. But the cuts for each new production will be different, depending on the strengths and weaknesses of the particular company.

Red Noses

Red Noses was written in 1978. It took seven years for it to be produced, which is the same time it took Solomon to build his temple. The time lapse is not surprising. The reaction to *The Bewitched*, the last play of mine produced by the Royal Shakespeare Company, ranged roughly from 'someone should take an axe to the author for writing it', to 'someone should take the subsidy from the Company for producing it'. Of course I have selected two of the more favourable comments.

But it is all perfectly natural. I am in no way complaining, merely providing necessary information. For if *Red Noses* were written today – 1985 – it would be much less optimistic. The world has moved on in seven years, and not towards the light. Men and women can still be overcome by a sudden wave of compassion for the poor and sick but they quickly get over it, while the majority, it seems, find something deeply offensive about any transaction in which money does not change hands.

Red Noses is a letter from a transfigured world, much like ours, where statues come to life and human beings turn to stone. It's a letter wishing you good thoughts, but chiefly, good feelings.

Peter Barnes
1985

Characters

Viennet

Moncriff

Evaline

Bonville

Madame Bonville

Dr Antrechau

Flote

Grez

Scarron

Druce

Sonnerie

Archbishop Monselet

Father Toulon

First Attendant

Mistral

Brodin

Rochfort

Marguerite

Lefranc

Pellico

Camille

Marie

Le Grue

Bembo

Frapper

Boutros Brothers

Vasques

Bigod

Sabine

Patris

Mother Metz

Papal Herald

Pope Clement VI

Flagellants, Peasants, Artisans, Pedlars, Lepers, Monks, Attendants and Guards

Red Noses was first performed by the Royal Shakespeare Company at the Barbican Theatre on 2 July 1985. The cast included:

Mother Metz/	
Mme Bonville	Yvonne Coulette
Marguerite	Polly James
Camille	Rowena Roberts
Marie	Katharine Rogers
Sabine	Cathy Tyson
Pope Clement VI	Christopher Benjamin
Archbishop Monselet	Raymond Bowers
Bembo	Derek Crewe
Rochfort	Richard Easton
Father Toulon	Peter Eyre
Grez	Nicholas Farrell
Lefranc	Norman Henry
Sonnerie	Jim Hooper
Le Grue	Bernard Horsfall
Pellico	Don McKillop
Boutros One	Charles Millham
Scarron	Brian Parr
Brodin	Pete Postlethwaite
Flote	Antony Sher
Patris	Peter Theedom
Boutros Two	David Whitaker
Frapper	Nicholas Woodeson
Druce	Jimmy Yuill
Other parts played by:	Nicholas Bell
	Phillip Dupuy
	James Newall
	Steve Swinscoe
Director	Terry Hands
Designer	Farrah
Music	Stephen Deutsch
Choreographer	Ben Benison
Lighting	Terry Hands and
	Clive Morris

Act One

Scene One

Auxerre, France. 1348. White mist. A bell tolls and a **Voice** *calls,* 'Bring out your dead!' *Five plague victims stagger on Upstage Centre.* **Moncriff** *manically sniffs scent boxes,* **Viennet** *tries to wrap himself in a winding sheet,* **Evaline** *moans and* **Bonville** *beats a tiny drum for* **Madame Bonville** *as she dances weakly.*

Viennet Out. Tear out these scabs. (*He tries to tear off the scabs on his arms.*) No pain here, pain's a sure sign of the pestilence.

Moncriff Monday: wormwood, rosemary, marjoram. Tuesday: valerian, alant, juniper. Wednesday: red-fern, milfoil, lavender. They cure the plague if you sniff. I know, I've spent money.

Viennet I plead. *Durante bene placito.* In life, lawyers dress in black ready for the Diet of Worms.

Evaline Day's gone, night's here. Kneeled out my life asking forgiveness. A dead, dry branch.

Bonville You served me old meat, Madame, that brings on the plague. Go dance and die.

Madame Bonville Drum, Maurice, drum. He's playing games with my bones. Run fast, run soon, return late is the only certain plague cure.

They collapse Upstage Centre as **Dr Antrechau** *enters Upstage Left carrying a long stick and a document, which he reads aloud.*

Dr Antrechau The College of Physicians of Paris hereby make known the cause of pestilence, the scourge of God, known as the Black Death. It arose in India when the sun sucked up, *whoosh*, the Great Sea, in the form of white mist which turned corrupt. 'Twill continue as long as the sun's in the sign of Leo, they say.

Bonville Help us, Dr Antrechau, Dr Antrechau.

The five crawl towards him. He holds them off with his stick.

Dr Antrechau Stay back eight metres, else I catch the pestilence.

Viennet You read us the cause, read us the cure!

Dr Antrechau I prescribe wine and they die, no wine and they die, exercise and they die, abstinence and they die, debauchery and they die, cold meat and they die, hot meat and they die, no meat and they die, sleep on the right side and they die, left side, ditto. I've a hundred per cent record of failure. All turn black and stinking.

A line of four cowled **Monks** *enters Downstage Right moaning rhythmically. As they cross to exit Stage Right the last one,* **Marcel Flote,** *starts jerking convulsively and falls on his knees.*

Flote *Aa-ooh-aah,* light my way, Lord, show me what I must do. Trees wither, fixed stars fall, darkness swallows the world and the dead are no longer counted. Infection's everywhere and the people cry, 'O wicked God.' It came October last in the year of Our Saviour 1347. Twelve Genoese ships fleeing from Kaffa entered Messina carrying the buboes of the Black Death. Mercy, Lord. One third of Christendom now lies under sod. Men waking healthy are dead before noon, stripped and dragged to plague pits where they lie pickled like game in a barrel, quicklimed instead of salted. There's no pity, faith or love left, when the breath, touch or look of a loved one's pestilential, and suckling babies drink up death instead of mother's milk. Let me be chosen, Lord, to mend it. You came to me, Lord, in a street in Auxerre. Like Paul I was afflicted. I cried out *aa-ooh-aah. (He jerks violently.)* You spoke in my inner ear saying, 'I have work for thee, Marcel – wait.' I still wait, waiting, Lord, for a sign so I may begin. What would you have me do, Lord? I thirst for it. Speak, Lord, let me hear again the voice of Him who made the world, *aa-ooh-aah.*

Whips are heard cracking loudly as two **Flagellants** *enter Downstage Right, hitting themselves with clubs. They are half naked, with iron bands round their waists and foreheads.* **Grez,** *the Master of Flagellants, in a black coat with a red cross, walks alongside.*

Flagellants *(chanting)* 'Pain, pain, pain. Our journey's done in holy name. Christ himself to Calvary came. Pain, pain, pain. Mary's honour free from stain. Repent and do not sin again. Pain, pain, pain.'

Grez Ave Maria, sweet Mother Mary, hear the plea of thy servant Grez, Master of Flagellants. Have pity on us. Rise, O Heaven, let Christ's black anger for our sins be appeased by this bloody sacrifice. Let our penitential scourging take away God's pestilential wrath. We feel Christ's thorns, whips, nails and spear, that we may be freed of sin and death. Join us, Brother. Join us on this painful pilgrimage.

Flote I come, Brother, *aa-ooh-aah.*

He gets up, jerking, and crosses to **Grez,** *who hands him a club.*

Grez Welcome to the Brotherhood of Pain, Brother.

Flote *Aa-ooh-aah.*

Jerking violently, he inadvertently cracks the club down on **Grez**'*s head.* **Grez** *groans and falls to his knees.*

Grez No, Brother, you hit yourself for Christ's sake, not me.

Flote *Aa–ooh-aah.*

Flote *has another spasm and hits* **Grez** *again as he tries to get up. Grunting with pain,* **Grez** *deliberately takes a club from his waist, rises slowly and hammers* **Flote** *over the head with it.*

Grez And *aa–oohh-aah* to you too.

Flote *grunts and clubs* **Grez** *back. The two hit each other with increasing fury, as they slowly sink to their knees. Suddenly* **Flote** *holds up his hand.* **Grez** *stops hitting him. They both listen to an unaccustomed sound: the* **Flagellants** *are actually laughing at them. As they scramble up,* **Flote** *becomes entangled in* **Grez**'s *cloak. More laughter; even the* **Plague Victims** *upstage manage to smile.* **Grez** *finally untangles himself, cursing. He signals furiously to the* **Flagellants**. *They exit Stage Right laughing with* **Dr Antrechau**. **Flote** *looks after them, then falls on his knees.*

Flote I hear you loud, Lord, in the sound of their laughter. I hear and obey. I now know what I must do. Heaven's to be had with my humiliation. God wants peacocks not ravens, bright stars not sad comets, red noses not black death. He wants joy. I'll not shrink from the burden, Lord. Only turn away thy wrath. Give us hope.

He rises and crosses to the **Plague Victims**.

Evaline The light is dying! They take away the light, the light of the world.

Viennet (*drinking from a bottle*) This water's dead. This is dead water.

Moncriff I begin to ooze.

Madame Bonville Lord've mercy, what night is this night?

Bonville I rake my ashes.

Moncriff I hear worms.

Flote *touches the crouching* **Moncriff** *who topples over dead.*

Flote So . . . so . . . (*He gently closes* **Moncriff**'*s eyes.*) *In nomine Patris* . . .

Viennet Aren't you frightened?

Flote I'm so frightened the water on my knee's splashing. I feel like Philip the Fair's new jester, Bosco Gide. 'Make me laugh, Bosco, or I'll rack and bastinade you,' said Philip. 'Sire, sire, my wife's dying, my six children're starving, my house's burnt down and I've lost all my money. I've nothing left. Spare me! Spare me!' 'Heee-heeee-hee, that's very good, Bosco, you're hired,' spluttered Philip. (*He puts on a clown's bulbous red nose and sings.*) 'Don't make it serious. Life's too mysterious. You work, you pray, you worry so. But you can't take your gold when you go, go, go . . .' Did you know your navel is a useful place to keep salt when you're eating celery in bed? (*Singing.*) 'So keep repeating it's the berries. The strongest oak must fall. The sweet things in life to you were just loaned.' . . . Simon went to heaven. 'How did you get here?' asked St Peter. Simon sneezed and said, 'Flu . . .'

Viennet Flu! The final degradation, to face life's supreme test surrounded by an incompetent clown.

Flote I know. But tell me, Master Viennet, is it true lawyers believe all men innocent till proved penniless?

Viennet *stares at him, lets out a thin, whinnying laugh and dies.* **Evaline** *clutches at* **Flote,** *who takes her hand.*

Evaline Are there still young men outside? Is it wrong to love?

Flote The commandment is, love thy neighbour only don't get caught doing it. (**Evaline** *smiles and falls back.* **Flote** *singing.*) 'Life is just a bowl of cherries . . .'

Madame Bonville Father, Father!

Flote Did you hear about old Dubois? He told the marriage broker he wouldn't marry the girl without a sample of her sexual powers. 'No samples,' said the girl, 'but references he can have . . .' (*Singing.*) 'So live and laugh at it all.'

Madame Bonville *stops dancing, shakes with laughter and collapses.*

Bonville She's dead. There's nothing I wouldn't have done for her and nothing she wouldn't have done for me. So we ended up doing nothing for each other.

Flote But swallows always fly in pairs and mandarin ducks never roost apart.

Bonville My thanks, Father Flote, it's easy finding someone to share your life, but who'll share your death?

He curls up, coughs and dies. **Flote** *makes the sign of the cross over the dead.*

Flote The immortal souls of men and women who dwelled on land, change into birds after death they say. Fly, fly my sweet souls, fly, fly to heaven. And I must fly too to see the Bishop, if he's still to be found in Auxerre. (*Singing softly.*) 'Yes, life is just a bowl of cherries, so love and laugh at it all.'

Two corpse-bearers, **Scarron** *and* **Druce**, *dressed in black hoods and smocks painted with white crosses and carrying long, forked poles, enter Stage Left, 'cawing' harshly.* **Druce** *puts on gloves to search the bodies before they use their poles to slide them off, Stage Right.*

Scarron Run, spit-gobs, run. The corpse-bearers, the Black Ravens have come, *caw-caw.*

Druce These mouldering scrag ends got nothing worth stealing.

Scarron *takes out two small bottles and hands one to* **Druce**.

Scarron There's always something worth stealing. The boils, the wet plague boils are worth stealing. Squeeze. Squeeze 'em.

As they squeeze the pus from the boils on the corpses and into the bottles, **Flote** *joins them.*

Flote What are you doing, friends?

Scarron We need more plague pus. Plague pus mixed with aconite and napellum makes the best killing grease.

Druce Tonight we grease silver spoons, brass door handles, jewelled crucifixes, anything lace-soft fingers touch, full lips kiss.

Scarron As their lives were made easy with riches, so their deaths're made easy with grease.

Flote But they are still men like you.

Scarron No, we're not men, we're Black Ravens – corpse-bearers. And before that galley slaves and before that serfs. We've always been poor, never men. Don't call us men now because it suits.

Flote But why do you grease?

Druce Every one we grease dead means . . . Jesu, this old 'un's still breathing . . . (*He takes a small cudgel from his belt and kills* **Madame Bonville**.) . . . an extra two denari plus pickings. The rich are the richest pickings, so we grease the rich.

Scarron That's not it at all. We grease for a higher purpose, to wipe the slate clean, turn the world underside up, crack the Universe. We grease because we hate. I travelled through my life in the world's bowels like Jonah in the dark fish. Now I'll stride into sunlight palaces. Grease the fat bellies out.

Druce (*examining* **Evaline**'*s body*) Here's a fine white ewe, swan-necked and soft all down. Lookee, she's flashing dead eyes at me. She's got thighs.

Scarron War, famine, pestilence, the world's dying only to be born again. Just as the seed corn rots in order to sprout and bear good fruit, so mankind must stink to flower in glory. Salvation's built on putre-faction. Plague time heralds a new dawn sun rising in the West. But we must seize the day not the nearest piece of tit-and-arse Hell-bait.

Flote I'll pray for you.

Scarron Don't. We are the darkness.

Flote Poor darkness. I've always felt sorry for the darkness.

Scarron *Caw-caw.*

As they slide **Evaline**'s *body off and exit after it Stage Right,* **Druce** *sings sweetly.*

Druce (*singing*) 'Stay lady, stay, join lips to mine as pigeons do. Thy body's marble-white but soft to touch and sweet to view. Death cannot take thee, let him wait. For thy sweeter smiling grace. I suck thee back, on thy flat belly roam. And plunder thy full honeycomb.'

Flote Lord, I have not begun yet and am already cast down. I know the real sin of the Israelites in the desert was not their rebellion against God but their despair. (*He kneels.*) Lord, I kneel and stand upright, dance and remain motionless, shout and am silent all at the same time. But still I tremble at the burden. I dreamed I was leaning on a cane near a river and the river was a river of tears, tears of all the people suffering and dying everywhere. Must I cross the river alone? Solitude is welcome but loneliness is hard to bear. I'm on the road, Lord. Speak to me again. Blind me even as you did Paul, shake the earth, crush it in thunder, split it with raging fire . . . I look, I listen . . . (*There is the sound of tiny bells.*) Bells? Who asked for bells? Since when did God speak with bells? (**Sonnerie** *enters Upstage Right, his costume covered with tiny silver bells which ring gently.*

He crosses to **Flote** *and bows gracefully.*) And good day
to you too. (*He rises.*) I am sorry I was talking to God.
(**Sonnerie** *shakes his right leg.*) Yes, it is quite common
nowadays . . . I'm Father Flote. Who are you?
(**Sonnerie** *jumps, shaking his left leg.*) Ah yes, a
beautiful name, most fitting . . . (**Sonnerie** *shakes his
right arm.)* No, I haven't heard of you before. I'm sorry
but I have been busy – the plague . . . (**Sonnerie**
improvises a little dance; **Flote** *laughs.*) Yes indeed . . .
Very wittily put . . . Master Sonnerie, I am a fool! I
mean, I am a fool for not seeing it before. You are the
sign sent by God. Christ can use you, sweet Sonn.
(**Sonnerie** *shakes his body.*) No, I offer nothing except
humility's tears. Peter cried, 'Oh thou shall never wash
my feet,' and Christ answered, 'If I wash thee not thou
hast no part of me.' There's no reward except laughter
for His name's sake. Do you wish to join me, Master
Bells, sweet Master Bells?

Sonnerie *looks at him for a moment, then suddenly leaps
into the air, shaking arms, legs and body.* **Flote** *laughs
delightedly. They embrace and* **Flote** *presents him with a
clown's red nose.* **Sonnerie** *bows, as* **Archbishop
Monselet** *rushes in Upstage Centre, accompanied by*
Father Toulon *with papers and a* **First Attendant**
carrying a bowl of vinegar.

Monselet I'm leaving, Father Toulon, eternity's
growing on my flesh. The rim and centre's breaking.
Seven Cardinals, including the noble Giovanni
Colunna, and one hundred and five bishops're already
plague-pitted, plague-dead. So in return they hang two
scrawny Jews. Those were the only two left for
slaughter. That's the size of the problem.

Toulon *dips a parchment into the bowl of vinegar and
hands it, dripping wet, to* **Monselet**, *who reads it with
difficulty.*

Toulon Live Jews haven't caused it, dead Jews can't
cure it. The plague's but the inflammation of our sins –

greed, wantonness, pride, blasphemy, despair, doing evil
because it is evil. We die only to live in Hell's
devouring flames.

Monselet You're such a comfort, Father. (*He stuffs the
wet parchment into the* **First Attendant**'s *pouch as*
Toulon *dips another document into the vinegar and hands
it to him.*) Wet it! Wet, wet with vinegar! Vinegar's a
protection against infection. Kills off the winged plague
worms. (*He whips out a wooden fly-swatter and hits the
air.*) Plague worms! Plague worms! Is it any wonder we
sin? God sleeps and Satan's a mighty Prince, ever
active. He grows. Have I chosen the wrong side? The
losing side.

Flote *and* **Sonnerie** *approach.*

Flote Reverend Father, I've come to see you.

Monselet Stay back! You haven't been vinegared. Back
eight metres. (*He hits out with his swatter.*) I see wingy
plague worms.

Flote Most Reverend Father, I'm Father Flote and this
is . . .

Sonnerie *shakes his right leg.*

Monselet God be with you, Master Bells.

Flote Forgive me if I stand amazed, Reverend Father.
Everyone expected you to flee with the rest of the
clergy.

Monselet *Arrrx*, you hear that, Toulon? Everyone
expected me to flee. You said everyone expected me to
stay. I risk buboes and plague worms for you. (*He hits*
Toulon *savagely with his swatter.*) Zealot. Fanatic. It's
no good giving you a penance. You enjoy doing without
things. Damnable conscience keeper. If I die, I'll kill
you. What do you want of me?

Flote Only your approval, Reverend Father. I've been
chosen to go out to cheer the hearts of men with gibs,
jibes and jabber jinks. On the Octave of the Epiphany

we hold the Feast of Fools when the Mass is brayed and
water poured over the clergy at Vespers. I'll hold a
daily Fools' Feast. With thy blessing others'll join.
We'll form a brotherhood of joy, Christ's Clowns,
God's Zanies – that's us, the Red Noses of Auxerre.

Sonnerie *rings the bells on his right and left arm at*
Monselet.

Monselet So, Master Bells, you say he heard God
speak. But nowadays every Tommy Tom-Turd man
hears God booming out of every stunted bush and
passing cloud. There are too many footloose clerics
about like you, Father Flote, preaching indiscriminate
Christianity. It's natural with whole congregations dead
and the . . . DEAD, you hear me? I could be dying
even as I say this! Dead before I end this speech! Kill
the plague worms! Vinegar the air! Yet Flote's Noses
could be useful to the Church. The people'd see there's
no panic in the Temple of God. But the Holy Father,
Pope Clement, must give formal confirmation.

Toulon Most Reverend Father, is this wise?

Monselet I don't have to be wise, just decisive.

Toulon But laughter's the very pip of Eve's green
apple. We must suffer to be saved and dare not weaken
God's anger, die soft. (*He produces a Bible.*) There are
no laughs in this book, 'cept God's *haaa-haaa* roaring
in His triumph, *haaa-haaa.* 'The Lord shall laugh at
him for he seeth His day coming!' Psalm 37. Not the
laughter of fools, cackling thorns under the pot *eeee-
heee-heee.* But God's bloody laughter *haaa-haaa* roaring
in his triumph, *haaa-haaa* not *heee-heee.*

First Attendant *Hoo-hooo-ooooh.* (*He pours the bowl of
vinegar over his head and shrieks.*) I've got the boils, the
black buboes! I'm stricken. (*The others shrink back.*)
Mother of God, I'm not ready. I've only just been born
and now I have to die. All the fault of writers – cock-
pimping scribblers. They've prepared the way. Always

writing stories where some characters are important and others just disposable stock – First Attendant, Second Peasant, Third Guard. Stories're easier when 'tisn't possible to care for everyone equal. That's how itty-bitty-bit people like me come to be butchered on battlefields, die in droves on a *hoo-hooo-ooooh*. But we First Attendants are important too. We've lives. I've lodged in the chaffinch, lived in the flower, seen the sun coming up. I've discovered unbelievable things. I'm an extraordinary person. I'll tell you a secret . . .

He dies. **Scarron** *and* **Druce** *enter quickly Upstage Centre and hook him off with them whilst* **Monselet** *tries to grab* **Toulon** *round the throat to strangle him.*

Monselet Judas priest, because of you I'm exposed to that! Flote, you've my permission to continue and multiply. I don't care if you collect red noses or black buboes.

Toulon Your Grace, this fatuous Father could endanger the Church like the heretical Beghards, Beguines and buggering Bogomils who've been taken in Cambrai, Paris and Orléans. Now here in Auxerre I see another heresy being born – Flotism, the damnable heresy of happiness!

Monselet It's why you're staying, Father, to see he doesn't fall from orthodoxy into snout-deep error. Obey and suffer. You're to be one of Flote's Noses, *hee-hee-hee*.

Toulon Crush, whip, scourge, crucify, only spare me this shame.

Monselet Not here to discuss. The plague worms won't survive snowy peaks so I'll go to the mountains, St-Jean or Montrecon.

Flote I hate mountains, they spoil the view.

Toulon *grabs* **Monselet** *round his legs and is dragged across the floor.*

Toulon I can't let you go, you betray Christ with this cowardice.

Monselet Peter betrayed him thrice *cock-a-doodle-do, cock-a-doodle-do, cock-a-do-doodle*. My cowardice is transformed from inside by being practised with a religious fervour. Nothingness is at my back!

He kicks **Toulon** *off and exits quickly, ducking and weaving, Stage Right.* **Toulon** *gets up.*

Toulon The first duty of a Priest is obedience. So I must become a Nose. (**Flote** *shakes his head.*) Don't shake your head at me in that tone of voice. (**Sonnerie** *gently waves his arm in front of* **Flote**'s *ear.*) Why are you whispering?

Flote Before you can join Christ's Clowns, Father, you must prove of use.

Toulon Use? A man of my moral inflexibility would be welcomed with open arms in any religious community.

Flote First we must ask, can you play a tune on your head like Sasha Gelen, 'the man with the musical skull', or by rubbing your knees together like Perri Rouve, the Human Grasshopper? Can you play the hubble-bubble buffoon, the capering roach and simkin? Can you make them roar with a quip that brings the roses back to their elbows?

Toulon Insolent priest, I only smiled once in my life and then my face slipped. No, I can't play a tune on my head, rub my knees together, caper or quip.

Flote Then you can't be a Red Nose.

Toulon But I can't not be. I have my orders, eyes front, quick march.

Sonnerie *shakes his body excitedly.*

Flote That's right, sweet Sonn. We can teach you, so Christ can use you, Father Toulon.

Sonnerie *repeatedly hits himself on the head with a rubber hammer whilst* **Flote** *bangs his knees together and hands him a clown's red nose.* **Toulon** *looks at it and shudders.*

Toulon Let us pray for God's help and protection.

Flote I've already done that, Father.

Toulon Not for you, for me!

As they pray intently in the shadows Upstage, there is a cry as **Brodin** *and* **Mistral** *rush in Downstage Left, bristling with swords and dragging a screaming Nun,* **Marguerite Delair,** *and followed by* **Charles Rochfort** *in an old suit of armour, nibbling a roast chicken. They throw* **Marguerite** *down screaming.*

Mistral We divvy up equal 'cept I get to rape this Holy Wagtail first.

Brodin If it's equal why do you get to rape her first?

Mistral 'Cause I'm the leader.

Brodin Why're you the leader?

Mistral 'Cause I get to rape her first. It's logic.

Brodin There's no logic in our breaking world, no leaders either. What we get, we get by force. What we keep, we keep by force. If you can't keep it, you've no right to it.

Mistral Raping nuns is my habit. Stand back, Brodin, I've killed more men than you've had hot dinners.

Rochfort And I know how – you ran 'em to death.

Brodin Defend yourself, crotch-bag. I give you ten seconds to draw a sword. One, two, three, four, five, six, seven, eight, nine, ten.

As **Mistral** *starts to unsheath his sword,* **Brodin** *whips out his dagger and stabs him in the stomach.*

Mistral I'm stained. You was too quick. Foul! Foul!

(**Rochfort** *tosses him a chicken leg.*) Dying over a
nothing . . . one hole for another . . . bones of cuttlefish,
embers of once bright stars . . . when I was young I
blew soap bubbles from a reed . . . (**Rochfort** *mimes
blowing soap bubbles.*) See how they float light . . . (*He
tries stabbing one with his forefinger.*) You've taken all my
days, Brodin. Done for me . . . (*He falls to his knees.*)
My name's Jean Mistral! Jean Mistral! Jean Mistral!

The name comes back in a loud echo.

Echo Jean Mistral! Jean Mistral! Jean Mistral!

Satisfied, he pitches forward dead. **Brodin** *stands over
him and sniffs loudly.*

Brodin I draw up his strength.

Rochfort Do try not to kill without being paid, Brodin.
It lowers the market value of our work.

Brodin The avenging angel circles like the sun and
men and women strike each other down; it's natural. So
without a war it's natural we war against ourselves.

Rochfort Salt. Where's the salt? This bird's not
properly salted. Women never make good cooks, they
aren't generous enough. My father's house had cooks.
Boiled porcupine and wild boar.

Brodin It's your damn Master Pestilence. Remember
we had a good war going – a hundred years, nothing
less. Then this pestilence comes on by and it's over.
Now instead of war and killing we got peace and dying.
Peace?! Peace?!

Rochfort Who won the battle of Crécy, Brodin? I was
there, but nobody told me who won.

Brodin They say the English bowmen won. Arrows
and spears wet with blood, drums toppled, standards
broken, riderless horses lost amongst the dead. We
fertilized the ground with our flesh but I don't rightly
know who won.

Rochfort Chivalry lost, I know. All lost when Robert of Artois fell at Coutroi asking for honourable quarter and a low-born pikeman cut his throat saying, 'Sorry, I don't speak French.'

Brodin *stops sniffing the body and* **Druce** *and* **Scarron** *enter quickly Stage Left and hook* **Mistral**'*s corpse off with them as* **Brodin** *unbuckles his belt.*

Brodin Now for the Holy Wagtail. One thrust made me a dead 'un, another thrust could make me a live 'un. Rut, Sister! Rut!

He grabs **Marguerite** *who starts screaming again causing* **Flote, Sonnerie** *and* **Toulon** *finally to stop praying Upstage and come forward.*

Flote If you attack that Bride of Christ, I'll stand here and make uncouth noises with my mouth. The Church can't stop you sinning but it can stop you enjoying it.

Toulon Remember, the pleasure's transitory, the price excessive, the position ridiculous.

Brodin *picks up* **Mistral**'*s sword and thrusts it into* **Flote**'*s belt.*

Brodin Defend yourself, priest. I give you ten seconds to draw a sword. One, two, three, four, five . . .

Flote *whips out a crayon and parchment and quickly draws on it.* **Brodin** *slowly turns to the audience and looks heavenwards.*

Flote Six, seven, eight, nine, ten. It's done. (*He hands the sketch to* **Brodin**.) Gitto couldn't've drawn a better sword in ten seconds.

Brodin You bacon-faced gullion, I'll . . . (*Looking at the drawing.*) Phswk. Call that a sword? You don't know a sword from a ploughshare. Give me that crayon.

He starts sketching on the other side of the parchment as **Marguerite** *finally scrambles up.*

Marguerite I'm supposed to be raped! What of the raping, spindle-shanks? I was promised marauding prickmen. There'll be atrocities, they said. Rape and ravaging, they said. I want to be first.

Brodin I'm not in the raping mood. Raping means taking a woman by force. You're giving it free.

Rochfort I've never been given anything free by a woman. I always found I had to pay for it one way or another in the end.

Marguerite *snatches the fowl from him.*

Marguerite Salt. Did you say it needed salt? I cooked it, addle-pate. If you don't like it, don't eat it. Five years of prayers and going to bed with a night light and misgivings and I can't even get raped.

Toulon You're pledged to service God not men, Sister.

Marguerite The violation of my body's but another penance, Father. Saint Bartholomew was whipped, I raped.

Brodin *finishes the drawing and shows it to* **Sonnerie**, **Flote** *and* **Toulon**. **Flote** *compares the two drawings.*

Flote Yes.

Rochfort I find it a major work utterly convincing in its palpable use of physical existence . . . (**Sonnerie** *shakes his legs.*) And that too.

Brodin Drawing is in my blood as well as killing. (*He starts another sketch.*) I've got the hands for it.

Marguerite When I was young I had my plum tree shook twice nightly. Now you can't find the men for it. That dead one . . . what was his name? (**Mistral**'s *voice is heard calling* 'Jean Mistral! Jean Mistral!') Yes, Jean Mistral. He was going to try but he fell back into shadow. (*She sits.*) Life is so insulting. I'll never smile again.

Sonnerie *dances in front of her.*

Rochfort I know that song, Master Bells.

He takes out a flute and plays. **Marguerite** *jumps up.*

Marguerite So do I. (*Singing.*) 'With an Oh and Oh, she itching moves her hips. And to and fro she lightly starts and skips. She jerks her legs and sprawleth out her heels. Oh what's this joy, a man and woman feels.'

Flote Christ can use you. And you, gentle fluter. (**Brodin** *shows him his drawing.*) And, yes, you with the lightning hands. (*He takes three coloured balls from a bag and juggles with them.*) God's ordered me to found a new order without orders, bound by no authority except love. We'll work together in singleness of heart, joining hands with Christ to lift fear from Creation. These balls are God, *ally-oop.* (*Without breaking rhythm he passes the balls to* **Marguerite** *who continues juggling.*) Feel Him, *ally-oop ally-oop.*

Marguerite I feel Him!

Still juggling she passes them on to **Sonnerie** *who passes them on to* **Brodin.**

Brodin They're strong and hard, a soldier's balls. We'll take time out from killing and fight Master Pestilence.

Still juggling he passes them on to **Rochfort.**

Rochfort And boredom, which is worse. I fear boredom more than death and repetition more than sin. So long as the balls amuse, I'll follow. What do you want us to be, Father – poor Friars, rich Templars, suffering Saints?

Sonnerie *jumps up shaking his head and ringing his bells in reply.*

Marguerite, Brodin and **Rochfort** Clowns?! You want us to be *clowns*?!

Rochfort *drops the balls in astonishment and* **Toulon**

catches them all first bounce in the bag and snaps it shut.

Toulon Flote, you're preaching vile equality and love again. Look at 'em. One blood-soaked berserker, one renegade chicken-eating aristo and a nun waiting to be raped as a penance. Three fools don't signify and a thousand fools only turn one righteous man into another fool. How do you know God is interested in our laughter and joy? Perhaps He wants our tears and suffering? I *know* He wants our tears and suffering. I stand with one foot in Heaven and the other gloriously in the abyss. Compromise is for the weak, concessions for cowards. I never yield or compromise. I obey. Obedience is the first vow of religion. Our task shouldn't be to make them smile, make them sleep easier in their beds, but to make them tremble. The link between God and man, man and man, is fear. God wants to be feared not loved. Make them bow down and tremble.

Flote If that is life, I don't want it. I'll go through it as a stranger, curl up and die. If that is man, what's the good of saving him? But he is more and God is more. He can be moved by joy as well as tears. Come, friends, first we ask permission of the Goldmerchants' Guild to put on a show of our clowning art in the Goldmerchants' Square, Auxerre, this Eastertide. Then we send out a call for all those Red Nose Zanies waiting in green nooks and dark corners. We'll sing, dance and tell funny tales and all around us people will laugh and up there in Paradise the saints will interrupt their endless hosannas and laugh too. And the angels will forget their nocturnal missions and flutter their wings and chuckle the while. And the Judges of the Last Judgement will have to stop their judging for they will be chortling with glee. And the Supreme Judge himself will turn aside from sad pleas and soul-breaking prayers to hear the unfamiliar sound of joy and, perhaps, He will forget His wrath hearing His people praise Him in laughter, *aaa-ooh-aah.*

*He jerks violently but immediately converts his jerkings
into a soft-shoe shuffle. The others to join in as large, gold-
paper butterflies are lowered from the Flies.*

Scene Two

They stop dancing and **Flote** *is left gazing up entranced
at the golden butterflies as* **Lefranc** *and* **Pellico** *enter
singing Stage Right dressed in long black fur-trimmed
coats and gold chains and pushing a huge mountain of gold
on wheels.*

Lefranc and **Pellico** (*singing*) 'Gold, gold, gold.
Bright and yellow, never cold. Molten, graven,
hammered, rolled. Hard to get and good to hold.
Gold, gold, gold.'

They bow to the gold mountain.

Lefranc Great luminary keystone of the world's arch,
symbol of heaven's highway, incorruptible metal. We
declare this, the twenty-fourth meeting of the Auxerre
Goldmerchants' Guild, now open. Though they lived
by the golden rule – those that have the gold make the
rules – Guildmasters Renard, Frogues, and Dubry have
all met their death day. The burn-boils, the Black
Death buboes!

Pellico We Guildmerchants Pellico and Lefranc are the
only two left living out of four hundred. Suddenly the
world is cold, and we are mortal, despite our gold.

As **Flote** *is still staring up in wonder at the gold
butterflies,* **Toulon** *steps forward to introduce the others.*

Toulon Master Pellico, Master Lefranc, we . . .

Lefranc Father, this is a private meeting of the
Goldmerchants' Guild. As a special dispensation you

can watch but you mustn't interrupt the solemn
proceedings.

Toulon But we've urgent business.

Pellico Later, Father, first can you make sense of it all?
We Merchants are the best. Creators of wealth,
employers of labour, owners of property. Frugal and
sober, we wore modest colours, kept strict ledgers,
bolted our doors early. Money was our stout buttress,
maximum intensity of greed our first principle. Such
goodness worthless against this pestilence.

Lefranc That's why we had to change to stay alive.
Instead of thrift we waste, instead of working, we
debauch like little Neros. Pleasure's the best plague
cure, voluptuousness and excess will prolong our lives,
cu, ca, po, fo.

As they wave **Toulon** *and the others back and throw off
their coats to show they are dressed in brightly coloured
jerkins, striped breeches and golden codpieces,* **Camille**
and **Marie** *enter Stage Right stamping and chanting.*

Camille and **Marie** Cu, ca, po, fo.

Lefranc Oh a good set of dairies and buttocks is better
medicine than all your plague cordials, ointments and
charms.

Pellico Whores, whores, must have me some whores,
wanna kiss the whores. My pego's bigger than a mule's,
stouter than a bull's, so long you just put it in and walk
towards me. Whores, whores, wanna kiss the whores.

Camille We've business to discuss first. (*She hands
each man a list.*) Our new plague rates for whoring as
sanctioned by the Whores' Guild of Auxerre. Fees for
all one hundred and twenty-four ways of threading:
back, front, singles, doubles, triples and the rest.

Pellico (*reading*) 'Twenty-two denari for the missionary
position'? The whoremaster who wrote this must've had

his tongue in his cheek and every other orifice. I just hope I can raise my peg as high as your prices.

Camille Yer getting the *crème de la crème* certified free of all infection. The Whores' Guild still keeps up standards. (*Singing.*) 'Oh Blessed Virgin we believe, that thou without sin didst conceive. Teach us then how thus believing, we can sin without conceiving.'

Marie If yer want *à-la-carte* humping, yer have to pay for it.

Lefranc We'll pay for it with pleasure.

Camille With pleasure it'll cost you more.

Lefranc Here's socket money. (*He opens his codpiece and money falls out.*) There's four hundred for night on night till this long night's ended and the plague worms' blister dead. Kneel, Marie, Queen o' Heaven, Handmaiden of Joy. I clothe thee with the sun.

As **Marie** *kneels,* **Lefranc** *pours gold dust over her.*

Marie I've gone down on the stiffest coral-headed pleasure-tube, squeezed the plumpest jingle-jobs. Money's better. Smooth, hot, hard, my darling gold. Let me kiss thee, roll thee between my apples, slip thee between my thighs, *aarr.*

Pellico Lefranc, Lefranc, I try but I can't forget, that's Guild gold yer spilling. Dead members' fees; years of graft and cheating there.

Marie Cheap at the price for in our arms you'll come like the animals, rut your way to life.

Camille Stags and stallions empty it in one short thunderclap, goats and buck rabbits six times hourly, leeches do it to themselves and elephants can bugger an ant given enough time and patience. Pigs grunt, *grrr grrr,* vultures groan inside dead carcasses, *urrr urrr,* frogs ride twenty days at a time, *huhh huhh. Grrr grrr, urrr urrr, huhh huhh.*

Camille *and* **Marie** *leap on* **Lefranc** *and* **Pellico,** *twining their arms and legs round them. They jerk about grunting loudly.*

Toulon The pestilence has sent 'em mad. See, death thrusts hard.

Brodin 'Taint death thrusting but life.

Toulon Humped-backed crotch-thumpers! I cannot keep silent whilst you wallow in this disease of nature, honeyed poison, body's bane, soul's perdition – lust, mere lust.

Rochfort I've always found mere lust very agreeable – its pleasure is so short. Anything longer would be tedious.

Marguerite I should've been told sooner. This isn't a private meeting, it's a public orgy!

Toulon Stay, Sister Marguerite, remember thy holy calling.

Marguerite Rahab was a harlot, Bethseba leaped into bed with her husband's murderer and from those holy loins sprang the holy line of Jesus. I want to join those divine bawds. Forward with me!

Camille *and* **Marie** *drop off* **Lefranc** *and* **Pellico**.

Camille Not unless you've got a fully paid-up Guild card you can't.

Marguerite I'm coming!

Camille If you come, we don't. This is a professional hump. No scabs allowed 'cept those got in the line of duty. And with all due respect, which ain't much, it'll cost you peepers fifteen denari for the privilege of watching.

Marie *crosses to* **Brodin** *who has been sketching.*

Marie And what've you been doing with your hands?

(*She looks at the drawing.*) I'm broad-minded to the point of obscenity but that's filthy.

Pellico Filthy? I'll take six copies.

Toulon We'll not pay fifteen denari to watch sin, madam.

Marie When I was Brothel Queen in the Vatican Whorehouse, we charged twenty. Of course, you pay for style.

Rochfort I've always looked down on whores, usually through a hole in the ceiling.

Camille Master Bells, you got bells all over? Never had it with bells. (**Sonnerie** *sensuously shakes his body*.) Really . . . ? That sounds different.

Pellico Come, let's get to the humping.

Camille Sorry, Master Bells, I have to work.

Camille *and* **Marie** *are about to jump on* **Lefranc** *and* **Pellico** *again.*

Toulon Father Flote, are you still with this company or are you just going to stand there using up air?

Flote I was looking at the butterflies and thinking we are in Paradise.

Pellico No, this is supposed to be the twenty-fourth meeting of the Goldmerchants' Guild.

Flote Why butterflies?

Lefranc Devices to shift the plague worms from the stagnant air.

He gestures and the paper butterflies flap their wings.

Flote Ah, they enchant, friend.

Toulon We've no time for idle chatter, tongueless talk, there's business to discuss.

Lefranc Not in business. Death's put an end to business.

Flote We're Christ's Clowns and we wish to use Goldmerchants' Square for a public display this Easter Monday.

Toulon Here's ten denari to seal the bond.

Lefranc Money's lost its value, salt its flavour, we're for pleasure.

Flote Ravished by joy, we'll give you pleasure on Easter morning. A show to dazzle and delight.

There is a loud whip crack and **Grez** *and two* **Flagellants** *lurch in Upstage Centre.*

Grez Blood, ravished by blood! My blood, their blood, our blood, God's blood. It's the salvation of blood.

Camille Who's this loon? Somebody must be giving away free tickets.

Marie Whips'll cost you more. (**Grez** *hits himself.*) Would you like me to do that for you? Twenty denari, special offer.

Lefranc Sirs, this is a monthly meeting of the Goldmerchants' Guild. Non-members are simply not allowed. Have you no sense of occasion?

Grez We sought Pope Clement in Avignon, found him a sucking dog-leech selling Christ's cross and flesh for profit. His court is a stinking bank of usury. We say no man need go to Avignon or Hell to find Pope or Devil. Both lodge in his own breast. We shall proclaim it this Easter morn in Goldmerchants' Square, Auxerre.

Flote The square is ours, Master Grez.

Toulon No double bookings!

Pellico I'm an old man, just want to dip my dildo. Just want to lie bell-clapper to belly.

Lefranc Gold we've got, humping we want – debauch! debauch!

Camille *and* **Marie** *leap on* **Lefranc** *and* **Pellico** *again and they jerk around grunting.* **Grez** *stabs his thigh repeatedly with a knife.*

Grez On Easter Monday in the square in Auxerre we'll denounce false world, false Church. We're Christ's red meat, hacked raw. They that sow in tears shall reap in joy. Closest to Him when speared, flayed, racked.

Flote On Easter Monday in the square in Auxerre we'll put on a honey-pellet show that'll set the toes a tap-tap-tapping. Your suffering's nothing to mine. Despised, rejected, laughed at, I'm closer to Him than you. And I've got better legs.

To the encouragement of the other clowns he puts on his red nose and hits himself with a slapstick. **Pellico** *and* **Lefranc** *stop jerking about.*

Pellico *Huhh, huhh,* buttock and twang! Can't do it. Me rhythm's gone.

Lefranc It's these rut-watchers, *huhh huhh.* I've lost the beat too.

Flote *repeatedly hits himself with the slapstick and moves convulsively.*

Grez (*stabbing himself with increasing fury*) Become all fire this Easter, God's purifying flame. Beaten, tortured, saved! (*He slashes his throat by mistake.*) *Uuuuugggg?*

Flote Devour my pride since it's devouring me. Transform me into Christ's substance, give me as food for the afflicted. (**Sonnerie** *slaps a custard pie in his face and he jerks violently.*) *Aa-ooh-aah,* let me be witless since Thou, Lord, art God and I am nothing. Use me, *aaa-ooh-aah.*

Grez (*staggering*) *Uuuuugggg.*

Flote (*jerking*) *Aaa-ooh-aah.*

Lefranc *Aaa-ooh-aah?* Did you say *aaa-ooh-aah?*
That's good.

He imitates **Flote**, *jerking violently up and down.* **Pellico**
copies him.

Pellico *Aaa-ooh-aah,* we've got a good rhythm here.

Lefranc *Aaa-ooh-aah*'s the carnal beat, my bawds.

Pellico *and* **Lefranc** *repeat* **Flote**'s *jerkings exactly with*
Camille *and* **Marie** *clinging desperately to their backs.*

Pellico *Aaa-ooh-aah*'s strong stuff.

Lefranc Our thanks, Father, the square is yours for
Easter!

Pellico *Aaa-ooh-aah.*

The **Flotties** *cheer and one by one pick up* **Lefranc**'s *and*
Pellico's *rhythm. As the two* **Goldmerchants** *exit*
Upstage Centre with **Camille** *and* **Marie** *pushing the*
pile of gold, **Flote, Toulon, Rochfort** *and* **Brodin**
follow on behind in a line. Despite themselves, **Grez** *and*
the **Flagellants** *join in and they all exit in an all-jerking,*
all-spastic version of the Conga.

Scene Three

Marguerite If you can't join in, orgies're about as
interesting as watching cabbages grow. I used to pig it
thrillingly every night with my Jacques, wild peacocks
and rainbow-coloured whales. It was all as easy as
hawks fly and fish leap. Of course I was very young
then and knew what I was doing. When we met I let
him make the first move and he did – filthy beast, the
Lord be praised. I'd often say, 'Get thee behind me,

Satan' and those were the worst words . . . When
Jacques died of the hot sweat, I felt the Church 'tween
my thighs misery-moaning and holding me. I thought
cold chastity would clean my bones, sober my heart.
Mistake. Dead, Jacques was more alive than the living
Christ. Mountains crumble, seasons pass and I grieve
for what is gone, staining the night with tears. How to
cure the sunlit years, Master Bells? Affairs of the heart
– who really knows? Sometimes I forgot to get up or
straighten my hair. My life became full of low ceilings,
walls set at right-angles. But with Father Flote's help
I'll break 'em down and soar. I've so much to give yet I
beat my gums in the wind. I'm a giantess who's hidden
her life. I want to leave my mark. (**Sonnerie** *rings his*
bells.) 'Close your eyes, Marguerite, and change horses.'
So, so . . . there's no rage in you like the rest of us,
Master Bells. You're a gentle gentleman, tell me about
bells? (**Sonnerie** *jumps and gestures, ringing his bells.*)
Yes, Squilla, Nola. Kodon. Krotalan. Cornguincula and
Cymbalum. And the bells you wear? All Tintinnabula
. . . I see. What? Roman Emperors hung bells on their
triumphant chariots to remind them of human misery
and a bell guided Lazarus back into this world from the
dead. Why bells, Master Sonnerie? (**Sonnerie** *takes out*
two handbells and rings them softly. He stops, then rings
them again with more emphasis.) Your children were
dying. You shouted, 'Don't die, I love you all so much'
but they went on dying. So much love and no way of
defeating death. Perhaps the bells'll bring them back
like Lazarus . . . Ah . . . Teach me the language of
bells, Master B. (**Sonnerie** *gives her a handbell; he rings*
his and she replies with increasing confidence.) Straight
ring, back ring, roll, semi-roll, swing. I hear the passage
of time. You're the only sane man in this brain-bald
world, Master B. (*He changes his handbell from one hand*
to the other; she laughs.) And I'm . . . ? What? Tender
as an oriole, matchless as the sea, hidden starlight,
moonglow, enough sunshaft in my hair to burn another
Troy . . . You've the true gift of tongues, Master B. (*He*

rings his bells.) 'Bid me live and I will live . . .' (*She replies by ringing.*) 'A loving heart to thee . . .' (*She rings.*) 'A heart as soft, a heart as kind . . .' (*She rings.*) 'That heart I'll give to thee.'

They dance together accompanied by their bells and the butterflies, which gently beat their wings in time to the song. It ends and the butterflies are taken up.

Scene Four

Brodin *and* **Rochfort** *enter Upstage Centre in monks' habits, pulling a small, half-painted, portable stage. It is large enough for two actors, with steps up either side and a primitive curtain.* **Sonnerie** *assists* **Brodin** *painting the stage and* **Marguerite** *helps* **Rochfort** *with two masks.* **Rochfort** *puts the comic mask in front of his face.*

Rochfort People are dying this year who've never died before. Princess Joan, the daughter of the English Edward's been taken plague-sick on her way to marry Pedro of Castille. I used to have a sneering acquaintance with Pedro.

He gives **Marguerite** *the masks to hang on the side of the stage, then lies back, yawning.*

Marguerite I'll toss a coin, Brother Rochfort. If it lands on its edge you start working.

Rochfort Sister, there're three classes: nobles who do the enjoying, clergy the praying, and the rest the working. I belong to the first class but am forced to travel third. We were rich. My family never wanted for anything. Except Cousin Pierre, who's wanted for arson and murder. But I had no portion in my father's inheritance and no other calling but arms. Bastards are given no caps for their heads when they take to the road. When I left nobody noticed I'd gone. But they'll notice when I return. Oh, there'll be a fine noticing when I return.

Marguerite Anyone can see you were born a gentleman, you're so useless.

Brodin Genoese pikemen are now scouring the plains of Champagne for plunder; found only thorns and brambles, bitter bones, sick ghosts and ruined walls. They sent word for us to join 'em. I said it wasn't worth it till Master Pestilence is seen off and Mars reigns again. (*He slaps on red paint.*) Give us rest and peace the people cry. But rest in peace is for tombstones. Father Flote'll make people laugh again, give 'em back the courage to kill and be killed.

Rochfort Perhaps I shouldn't think of myself so much, though it is an interesting subject. I find it difficult to do the same thing twice, even once. War, women and drink are just a series of amusements to help me escape boredom. I shrug, nothing makes any difference. But Flote's different; perhaps he'll change it.

Marguerite Yes, he's a man who puts on his shoes backwards and walks into himself.

Flote *enters Stage Left, reading a Bible. Looking up he sees the portable stage and, without pausing, tap dances up the steps, across it and down the other side.*

Flote Isaiah – who had one eye higher than the other – chapter 51, verse 11: 'Oh thou afflicted, tossed with tempest and not comforted, behold I will lay these stones with fair colours . . .' So lay on the fair colours, Master Brodin.

Toulon *enters Stage Right.*

Toulon Are you ready, Father? The new recruits are here. Every halfwit and quarterwit left breathing.

Flote The bright-eyed and hopeful?

Toulon The dull-eyed and hopeless. They come for free food and lodging not for love of God.

Flote It's always Ash Wednesday with you, Father, never Easter. If they've skills, we need them in our troupe. The loving can come later.

Toulon Let's judge them then.

Flote Never judge, Brother Toulon. We're here to see if Christ can use them. Who's first?

Toulon (*reading from a list*) First is Jean Le Grue and Charles Bembo.

Shaking slightly with palsy, **Bembo** *enters Upstage Right carrying a canvas bag and a small drum strapped round his waist and accompanied by blind* **Le Grue,** *furiously waving a white stick and hitting* **Toulon** *savagely with it as he passes him.*

Flote Are you Jean le Grue?

Le Grue (*facing the wrong way*) No shafts, flashes, gleamings! Sunrise, sunset, shades of memory. Eyes like dead mussels swimming in gravy *ugh*. Why should you see and not me?

Flote Could you tell us what you can do?

Le Grue Le Grue's the name, the great Le Grue. You've heard of me? Speak up, damn you, can't you see I'm blind? Take out their eyes, Lord, as mine were took.

Flote It would be best if you started.

Le Grue Do? I juggle. I'm the best stone-blind juggler in the French and Norman lands. 'Tis said Father Flote and his God-mad hoddy-doddies will feed us? Time's wasting, best get started, Bembo. (**Bembo** *takes three plates from the bag, stumbles across and shakily hands them to him;* **Le Grue** *gestures confidently and* **Bembo** *plays a drumroll.*) I've got dead peepers, so all's done

with my feather touch – better than live eyes. (*He
throws the plates up one by one: one by one he misses them
and they fall and smash to pieces on the ground, but he
continues to smile confidently and juggle the empty air.*) I
juggle so fast I can't feel 'em. It's one advantage of
being blind, other senses're sharpened, *a-haa.* Watch
the hands! The hands! (*He mimes throwing one plate
higher than the others and passes another between his legs.*)
Good, isn't it? Hi-up, Bembo. (*He throws the imaginary
plates to* **Bembo** *who mimes catching them.*) You've
never seen anything like that, eh? You admire now?
There's more. The woods, Bembo! The woods!

Bembo *hands him three wooden clubs and plays another
drumroll.* **Flote** *and the rest move back instinctively as* **Le
Grue** *throws the clubs into the air and misses them. They
fall on his head and he slumps down with a groan.*
Bembo *picks up the clubs, bows to acknowledge the non-
existent applause and drags off the unconscious* **Le Grue,**
Stage Left. **Sonnerie** *rings his bells, dazed.*

Marguerite Le Grue must be to juggling what Attila
the Hun is to needlework.

Brodin If I'm not back by Wednesday, break down the
door and let me out.

Toulon (*reading*) Pierre Frapper – quick wit and stand-
up jibster, singer of songs and sender of frolics. Pierre
'I-suffered-for-my-art-now-it's-your-turn' Frapper.

Frapper *enters Stage Right.*

Frapper S–s–s–s–sires a f–f–f–funny thing h–h–h–h–
er–er–t–t–t m–m–m on the w–w–w–ay but I c–c–c–can't
r–r–remember w–w–w–'twas. I–I–I–I m–m–m–ay be
slow b–b–but m–m–my act is s–s–sloppy. E–e–e–e– r–r–
r . . .

Brodin *guides him out Stage Left and returns.*

Rochfort Someone should throw a shoe at him and
forget to take out their foot.

Toulon (*reading*) Alain and Jacques Boutros. The Boutros Brothers!

The **Boutros Brothers** *enter Stage Right on crutches to the tune of 'When You're Smiling', thumping down on their one good leg as they tap-dance across the stage and exit Stage Left.*

Brodin Don't panic.

Toulon Did you ever see such Satanic pride? Pull it down, thou art cut worms under the spade. That blind wretch acting as if he could see, the dumb one speak, the one-legged dance. It's God's judgement that the blind, dumb and crippled stay so, till prayer and repentance change it. They're guilty and must accept their punishments, not make light of them in their vaunting pride.

Flote It wasn't pride but hope, hope shining anew despite of every discouragement. Brother Toulon, we just saw the very apotheosis of Christianity: the triumph of hope over experience.

Toulon A definition the Supreme Pontiff will be most interested to hear. (*He hands* **Flote** *a document.*) This just arrived. The Holy Father, Pope Clement VI, commands your attendance at his court in Avignon.

Flote We must go to him immediately, if not before.

Sonnerie *waves his arms.*

Marguerite Yes, my pigeon. Father, what of the Triple Threat – Le Grue, Frapper and the Boutros Brothers?

Flote They join us, of course. Did you not hear the laughter? Failing to be good they succeeded in being completely bad.

Brodin They'd never make soldiers. I've got veins in my nose bigger than their arms. But such spirits raise the spirits. (*Chuckling.*) Remember Blind John of

Bohemia who fought with us at Crécy?

Rochfort He faced the wrong way as well. Killed more of his own men than the enemy. (*Chuckling.*) He was funny too, now I come to think of it.

Marguerite (*laughing*) Those plates, those plates!

Flote (*singing*) 'Let them join us. No weak link. Must keep trying. Else we sink. Join together just us few. Pierre Frapper and blind Le Grue. Charlie Bembo and the other two.'

Toulon (*singing*) 'Join together? Man's too frail. He's divided. It will fail. Join together not that crew. Pierre Frapper and blind Le Grue. Charlie Bembo and the other two.'

Le Grue, Bembo, Frapper *and the* **Boutros Brothers** *enter Stage Left, singing.*

All 'Join together. That's the plan. It's no secret. Man helps man. Work together, make it new. Pierre Frapper and blind Le Grue. Charlie Bembo and the other two. Join together stick like glue. Pierre Frapper and blind Le Grue. Charlie Bembo and the other two.'

Lights out amid laughter and shouts of 'Avignon! To Avignon!'

Scene Five

Darkness. An owl hoots. An unseen animal slithers past. The sound of **Flote** *and the others singing 'Join together' in the distance. A lantern light appears Upstage Left, followed by a line of lights from eight more lanterns behind the first. It is* **Flote** *and his troupe. They slowly make their way across the stage with* **Le Grue** *in the lead.*

Flote Master Le Grue, I have a shrewd suspicion we're lost.

Le Grue Lost? How can we be lost? I'm blind, aren't I? It's night, isn't it? Night is mother's milk to me. I live in it – curse these stone eyes. My senses are sharpened in the dark. Even now I can feel the warm rays of the early morning sun coming up over my left shoulder.

Rochfort That's my lantern, you loon.

Frapper I–I–I–I–I–I . . .

Flote Is everyone still here?

Toulon I'm here but I wish I wasn't.

Sonnerie *rings his bells.*

Bembo Bembo's here.

Flote Where are the Boutros Brothers?

Brodin I'm carrying Boutros One.

Marguerite And I'm carrying Boutros Two.

Boutros Two Careful, Mistress, I've only got one leg – that makes me lop-sided.

Le Grue Save your breath, Master Boutros, there's no sympathy for cripples here.

Frapper I–I–I th–th–th–th–think w–w–w–e–e . . .

The sound of slow wingbeats overhead.

Marguerite What's that?

Rochfort An owl, an auk. Could be an ostrich bird?

Marguerite Ah, something touched my face.

Brodin I only ever killed those I could see. Didn't like doing it in the dark. Something shameful there.

Frapper A–a–a–are . . .

Toulon Yes, Le Grue, where are we?

Le Grue On the road to Avignon. I can smell the lemon trees on my right and the cool wind from the mountains strokes my left cheek.

Toulon You mean you don't know.

Flote You must have faith, Father, in men as well as God.

Le Grue Faith. Tell him, Bembo, we've travelled this road a hundred times, there's firm ground under our feet and I *aaahh.*

There is a loud splash as **Le Grue** *falls into a stream. Shouts from the others.*

Le Grue I'm blind, I can't swim in water!

Flote Pull him out.

Rochfort I have you, Le Grue. Steady.

Rochfort *is heard pulling* **Le Grue** *on to the bank.*

Bembo There shouldn't be a stream there.

Frapper L–l–l–lost.

Toulon Well said, Master Frapper. Short and to the point. Lost. Father Flote, you expect to save this whole decaying world and yet you can't get us from Auxerre to Avignon.

As they come Stage Left they see the ragged figure of **Count Etienne Vasques** *sitting stock still illuminated in half-light.*

Flote Friend, can you direct us?

Vasques Don't move muscle, eyelid, nostril, stay stock still; though ants bite, birds nest in my hair, mongrels piss up against me, I don't move. Move and you die. Plague worms attack anything that moves. I eat, drink, move my bowels only at night so they don't see me

move. When I was scholar and arse-licker at the Papal
Court I shot up the greasy pole, bowed, sneezed,
carried out orders. Now the afflictions of the hour make
the greatest sit on the ground and I'm tired of thinking.
It's why I live like a rock, think like a tree, abandon my
mind, observe the thought forms fading and the gaps
between the thought forms and I know nothing not
even whether I know or do not know, only knowing I
don't move for if I move Death will see I move and I'll
move no more.

Vasques *shuts his eyes and goes rigid as his light fades
out.*

Frapper W–w–w–w–h–h . . . ?

Brodin I agree, Master Frapper.

Rochfort Have you noticed how you meet a different
class of people at night?

Le Grue Onward, onward! Up and under!

*As they move across the dark stage another half-light
comes up ahead of them to show* **Bigod**, *a burly man in a
woman's dress and wig, wiggling his hips provocatively.
His face is thickly painted and his long black beard tied
with ribbons.*

Bigod Hello, sailors, I'm gorgeous, aren't I? Gorgeous,
untamed and immortal. It's the feminine principle,
female gender that survives. We women spin and weave,
all day, every day, spinning and weaving the tapestry of
life and death, threads appearing and disappearing;
everything that is, comes from us. (*Putting his hands on
his hips.*) Do you like my dress? Dazzling, isn't it? And
the colours won't run, at least not unless they see you.
Women endure war, famine, drought, pestilence,
childbirth, childdeath; clearing the cesspool of the ages
we develop muscles. I saw it when I was Chief
Magistrate of Auxerre. Had adultresses stoned and
witches burnt and they were stronger than me. Men

break, we women endure. It's proven twice as many men are plague-dying than women. This dress doubles my chances. If Death comes I'll give him the soft eye. You men are all alike, the earth shakes but I'm as steady as a three-legged pot. The Virgin Mary looks after us girls, she does, and Death will pass me by.

He rushes away into the darkness and his light quickly fades out as **Sonnerie** *shakes his arms.*

Toulon You're right, Master Bells, their hearts tremble, the terrors of death have come upon them.

Marguerite A man must really be frightened if he wants to live like a woman.

There is the sound of **Black Ravens** *harshly caw-caw-cawing, high above them in the dark. Their lanterns tremble.*

Boutros One Time we moved on.

Boutros Two Which way?

Bembo Any way, so long as it's forward.

Le Grue Watch me. Stay close. I always move forward despite my affliction.

Lanterns and brazier glow Downstage Right.

Flote Lights. See, see there are warm, comforting lights down there.

Le Grue I can't see 'em.

Brodin Of course you can't, you're blind.

Le Grue Oh yes . . . well, you don't have to keep reminding me.

Flote They'll know how far we are from Avignon.

Rochfort 'Twill be safer if we take the long way down.

Le Grue No, no, I know a short cut.

Toulon Ignore him.

Flote A song to overcome night fears, friends.

Frapper L–l–let's h–h–h–a–a 'S–s–sit a–a–amongst the L–l–l–l . . .'

They move off singing.

Floties 'Sit amongst the lilies. Play your silver spoons. Kidney beans and privies. Spindle on your looms . . .'

The line of the lanterns disappears Upstage Left and a spot comes up Downstage Right on a small cart overflowing with dummy corpses. **Sabine Patris** *is on top of it, stripping the corpses and throwing down the clothes to her husband* **Henri Patris** *and mother,* **Mother Metz.**

Sabine Eight of my sons buboed gone. The youngest first. Death plays no favourites. Burn boils in his groin and armpits, his body shaking under fever winds, drowning in his sweat. I prayed to God, 'Save my child, Lord' but it's hard labour making God human. Oh, my pretty fig boy. He came so still like dew in April falling on the grass. He'd've grown into a fine thief and cut-throat. Make his parents proud had he lived. My mother lives – you wormy dogmeat. (**Mother Metz** *cackles.*) The hairless stay upright, the young fall.

Patris If our boys had lived, we wouldn't be working now nights as well as day. Everybody left breathing prospers 'cept us. Too poor even to live off the dead we live off the men who live off the dead – the Black Ravens *caw-caw* who tell us to spit on the dead fat-bellies. Spit.

They ritually spit on the corpses.

Sabine We spit but we still have to pay 'em for the privilege of pillaging what's left of their corpses. We didn't draw no prizes in the lucky bag of life, Henri. (*She suddenly points at* **Mother Metz.**) Thieving mould-warp! I saw her, she stole something from us.

(**Patris** *punches* **Mother Metz** *and snatches a silver buckle from her.*) Knock out her teeth, it'll mean more food for us. Die, snot-dribbler, die!

Mother Metz I'd rather kill myself than die. I'll die the day after you die. You won't know it burning in Hell. Oh, there's no hatred like a mother's hatred for her daughter – she keeps giving me mirrors. You try to kill me, axe, rope, mortal poisons, but I survive beaver-bright, my will is stronger, chitty-head.

Sabine *is about to scramble down after* **Mother Metz** *when* **Flote** *and his troupe enter with lanterns Downstage Left, singing.*

Floties 'Sit amongst the lilies. Play your silver spoons. Kidney beans and privies. Spindle on your looms.'

Sabine They sing idiot, there's no sense to it. It's Lucifer, Prince of Nonsense and his demons!

Flote No, it's Father Flote, Father Toulon and friends.

Toulon They're no friends of mine.

Marguerite *sinks exhausted with* **Boutros Two**, *whilst* **Brodin** *dumps* **Boutros One** *beside him.*

Brodin Where are we?

Patris The Municipal Burial Yard.

Le Grue You see, journey's end thanks to me. The Municipal Burial Yard, Avignon.

Mother Metz The Municipal Burial Yard, Auxerre. This is Auxerre, laddie.

Rochfort But that's where we started from!

Le Grue Absolutely, so we're not lost, are we?

Toulon You eyeless oaf.

Flote Le Grue, Le Grue.

Le Grue I warned you. It's a madness expecting me to show you the way to Avignon. I'm blind.

Patris Avignon or Auxerre, death turns both places into the same no-place. But a blind man leading, there's something wrong here. I'm no fool.

Flote But I am. Flote the Fool.

Patris I've heard of you and your zanies. I've got some good bird impressions – I eat worms.

Toulon Not tonight. Could you just put us on the right road to Avignon?

Mother Metz You take the left fork out of Auxerre.

Le Grue I knew it!

Patris We never help nobody. It doesn't pay. But we're corpse-collecting that way tonight. You can follow us.

As **Sabine** *and* **Patris** *begin dragging the cart off, they start to sing the* Dies Irae.

Marguerite 'Day of Wrath'? That's a tune that sets spirits sinking fast.

Sabine It's our favourite.

Toulon Mine too.

Flote It's the way it's being sung. Sing out with a joyful heart and oh the difference . . . (*Singing lightly.*) 'Day of Wrath, O day of mourning, see fulfilled the prophet's warning . . .'

The others take up the new upbeat version of the Dies Irae *as they disappear into the darkness, Stage Right, their lanterns bobbing jauntily in time with the singing.*

Scene Six

A choir singing the Exultant Caelum Laudibus *drowns out the* Dies Irae. *Lights blaze in the ante-chamber of Pope Clement VI in the Palace of Popes, Avignon. There is a doorway Upstage Centre covered with a rich purple curtain of velvet emblazoned with the coat of arms of Clement VI. Papal banners hang either side. A loud fanfare of trumpets and* **Flote** *and his followers are led in by a* **Papal Herald** *Downstage Left.*

Herald Bow heads, bow knees for you are in Avignon in the Palace of Popes, the beating heart of Mother Church. Bow heads, bow knees in obedience.

Flote *and the others kneel Downstage Right.*

Flote Is this all you do, Master Herald?

Herald Yes, but I do it well, don't you think? Bow heads, bow knees for St Peter's Successor, Keeper of his Keys, Visible Head of the Universal Church, the Ultimate Earthly Judge of what is lawful and unlawful, Christ's Vicar on Earth, Summus Pontifex, Pontifex Maximus, His Holiness, Pope Clement VI.

A great fanfare and the purple curtain opens Upstage Centre. Behind it is a large magnifying mirror set at an angle to show the adjoining room where the white-robed **Clement VI** *sits between two burning braziers. He holds up his hand. The* **Floties** *approach and kiss the ring on his forefinger in the mirror.* **Le Grue** *misjudges the distance and cracks his forehead on the glass. He collapses with a groan.*

Clement VI Eighty thousand florins I've just paid that thieving bitch Queen Joanna of Naples for Avignon. Eighty thousand florins for this pest hole. Fifteen hundred died here last week. That's flosey Avignon.

Brodin But it's easily defended, Holy Father.

Clement VI I'm glad to hear you say that, Master
Brodin. You view it with a soldier's cold eye. Besides I
need a permanent home in France, Rome isn't safe.
(**Sonnerie** *shakes his left leg.*) Who would want to kill
me you ask, Master Bells? Who wouldn't?
Unfortunately few are graced with your grace.
(**Sonnerie** *shakes his arms.*) Too true, Master Bells,
without power it is easier to be graceful.

Flote Why do you lock yourself behind a mirror, Holy
Father?

Clement VI I fear contagion so I sit till the pestilence
passes.

Flote And the fires, Holy Father?

Toulon As a reminder of the fires to come, are they
not, Holy Father?

Clement VI No, my physician de Chaulic said they
would singe the wingy plague worms . . . I tried to
obtain credit from your father last month, Master
Rochfort. Too many Jews are being killed. I've no one
left to borrow money from so I'm forced to depend on
local lords – without success.

Rochfort My father is so mean he never breathes out.
He believes charity begins at home and should stay
there.

Clement VI Sister Marguerite, they say all the Sisters
of Mercy fled the convent but were caught dead; God's
fine hand there. Only you survived. You must be a
woman of singular virtue.

Marguerite I am, Your Holiness. A strict penitent
mumbler. Long fasts on short bread, that's how I've
kept my figure. I drink spring water and sleep on
nettles. It does wonders for the skin.

Clement VI And you are Pierre Frapper?

Frapper Y–y–y–o–u–u–H–h–h . . .

Clement VI You must tell me a joke, when I have a week to spare. The Boutros Brothers – blessings on you. And Master Bembo and Le Grue.

Le Grue *has recovered.*

Le Grue The Great Le Grue. There's only one, Your Holiness. Give him the teeth, Bembo, and the whole personality.

As **Bembo** *and* **Le Grue** *smile toothily,* **Clement VI** *gestures for them to step back.*

Clement VI Now I wish to speak with Fathers Toulon and Flote.

The others move away Stage Left and kneel.

Toulon Your Holiness?

Clement VI These are hard times, my sons. The Church lies gutted. I've no healthy clerics left for the important work of collecting taxes and drafting new laws. Meanwhile kings grow more powerful daily and nation states rise up to challenge the Universal Church and I'm giving up hope for Lent.

Flote The Church is corrupted from within, Your Holiness. The Shepherds of Christ fleece their flocks, buying livings cheap and selling indulgences dear. There's no goodness any more.

Toulon I try to tell him, Holy Father, the corruption of the Church is final proof of the strength of our faith. If the Church were perfect there'd be no merit in obeying its dictates. Make it more corrupt, Holy Father, more lustful, usurious. The greater the Church's corruption, the greater the test of our obedience. Christ lies in his grave but will sprout up green above those clouds.

Clement VI No mysticism, Father Toulon, this isn't the place for anything spiritual. Men've been corrupt since the Fall, the wax drips into eyes and ears. Goodness is the real danger, not corruption. Guard against the corruption of goodness, Fathers. Who knows what will result from one wild act of goodness. Charity makes destitution permanent. To give everything you possess to a beggar is to kill a consumer and put a hundred men out of work. A soft heart is a millstone. Remember St Augustine's prayer, 'Make me a good man, Lord, but not yet.' Don't be good, Fathers, be right! And we can only be right with and by the Church, for history has provided no other way of being right.

Flote But where is God?

Clement VI Go ask a theologian. I'm only a Pope, elected by French Cardinals, supported by a French King. And I'm too busy trying to hold this world together as it breaks to pieces. It's why I must have men about me who're better than good, men who know when to fight and when to run, when to make promises and when to break 'em. No action too vile, no task too bloody. Give me wolves. Sheep I can find. But where are the wolves who'll serve? (*He howls like a wolf.*) *Arrwaaa.* Where are the wolves? *Arrwaaa.*

Flote But wolves don't see the hurt man or hear the starving child, the lark's summer song.

Clement VI It's a small price to pay to remove the terrible necessity of free choice from mankind. The people want bread and certainty. But that's not for you, Father Flote. Do you truly believe you can lighten the suffering of those who aren't lucky, rich or clever enough with your red noses, orange wigs and Easter Festivals? Are you and your Holy Rollers of use to the Church?

Flote When St Francis came before Innocent III, His Holiness told him to caper in the dirt with pigs. St Francis did so and God opened the Holy Father's eyes and Pope Innocent blessed and sanctioned St Francis and his Franciscan Order.

Clement VI I'd've sent St Francis away with a flea in his ear, which he no doubt would've blessed – Brother Flea, Sister Louse. Since the Franciscans have elected an anti-Pope and have been burnt at the stake for heresy, they're not a good example to follow, Father.

Toulon Flotism would encourage worse rebellion, Your Holiness. Laughter produces freedom. It's against all authority, ripping off the public mask to show the idiot face beneath. When we're lifted to joy, we're taken out of the world and glimpse the world as it could be. Only God can be trusted to give us those delights.

Flote I'm God's blind instrument, His obedient servant, chosen to bring the salvation of joy to the fearful and pain-racked.

Clement VI You talk of obedience. Will you disband your Red-Nosed Brotherhood if I ask?

Flote Holy Father, Holy Father, when I was born my father said, 'Put him back, things are terrible enough as it is.' My mother cried so much the ale ran out of her eyes. Don't make me put out the light, spit on the spirit. God calls me to open Hell's gate.

Clement VI And if I call you to forsake mirth, will you obey?

Flote Holy Father, I twist in the wind, seared and shrivelled over five eternities.

Clement VI Will you believe I am His true voice on earth, Christ's voice, and obey?

Flote Flesh breaks! I obey, *aaa-ooh-aah*. (*He jerks violently.*) Noses go down. I renounce mirth and joy. (*He falls on his knees.*)

Clement VI You don't have to, Father. I summoned you to Avignon to bless your Red Noses. You are to be encouraged and financed by the Papacy. In time, draw up a Rule so the Floties can be recognized as a

Religious Order. Now I order you up, Father, up.

Flote *staggers to his feet as* **Toulon** *sinks.*

Toulon No 'tis a mistake, Holy Father.

Clement VI And you're it. Living behind a mirror, I
look out and see there's liberation in the plague air as
well as worms. The restraints, customs and laws of
centuries buckle, the old moulds crack – happen they
should crack – but the green force that liberates the
poet and thinker also frees the maniac with a butcher's
knife. The way's rough; no level roads left. I see you as
a useful lubricant, Father; holy oil.

Toulon No. He's grit in the wheel. This man sins,
Holy Father. What would you call a priest found
consorting with a lusting, wanton nun?

Clement VI Lucky. No more tit-knackeries, Father T.
The Church is endangered. My liver turns hard as rock
and I'm snared in the web of the world. New enemies
call for new methods to combat 'em. Go out, Father F,
give 'em joy this Easter. Dazzle 'em and take what's left
of their minds off the harsh facts of existence. Ripple
and spread!

Toulon Bright dew turns to frost; lies run down the
walls. I cannot look on your face, Holy Father.

Clement VI Go out in the name of the Lord. Ripple
and spread, Floties!

Flote Ripple·and spread!

Flote *and* **Toulon** *join the others who leap up and throw
confetti over themselves in delight.* **Clement VI** *makes the
sign of the cross over them and they are all ushered out by
the* **Herald,** *Downstage Left, as lights go down to a spot
on* **Clement VI.**

Clement VI I'll pray. Lord, protect those who're still
heroic and loving, not seeing the futility of being heroic
and loving. Protect Father Flote; let him remain a blind

instrument. Don't open his eyes as mine were opened. When I was young, I was a holy vaulter too. I had wings and a full head of hair. Every year I competed with the spring. But there's been a drying out. Heart's not the same. I've used up all my bright gold. A life which can't answer the question, 'Why live?', isn't one. (*A distant choir sings the plainsong* Te lucis ante terminum.) Despair without bottom, distrust so deep you distrust your distrust. Misery without meaning. Soul's hinges rust. (*Singing.*) 'And that's just fine. I mean, it's fine that all things fade. And when they write about these times. A hundred years of war and plague will get one line. And that will do. If they recall these days of death. They'll be asking Clement who? They won't care or even try to guess what men went through. And that's fine too. Because I've work to do . . .' And stop that pestilential howling. You call it singing, I call it neuralgia. Curtain!

The curtain falls across the mirror. Spot out. The plainsong fades.

Scene Seven

Easter bells ring out joyfully as lights up on bare main square of Auxerre. **Brodin** *and* **Frapper** *drag in the freshly completed small portable stage Upstage Centre, followed by* **Flote** *and* **Toulon** *rehearsing their parts in the coming playlet. The portable stage is placed Downstage Left. As* **Toulon** *gestures grandly and* **Flote** *corrects him,* **Marguerite** *enters Stage Right helping* **Sonnerie** *put on a bonnet and bib.* **Rochfort** *enters Downstage Right with* **Le Grue** *and* **Bembo**.

Rochfort Father Flote, surely my part in this Easter play of yours is too small, considering I'm one of the few here who can read?

Flote Later, Brother Rochfort, later.

He exits hurriedly Stage Left with **Frapper**.

Frapper M–m–my p–p–part is v–v–v–very v–v–v–very l–l–long.

Rochfort You're lucky. I've only some five lines to say.

Frapper I–I–I've only g–g–g–g–got one.

Le Grue What're you complaining about, Rochfort? I've got no lines at all. I stay dumb.

Toulon That will be the day, oh Lord.

He exits Stage Left.

Le Grue And Bembo, Bembo doesn't say anything either.

Bembo I rarely do. I've no chance.

He guides **Le Grue** *off Downstage Left as* **Sonnerie** *shakes his body.*

Marguerite Yes, I feel nervous too, lamb, like I did the first time I lost my virginity – I was always leaving it around though I've still got the box it came in. This is our first public performance. Will we be a success?

Rochfort Never fear, sweet chuck, I'm sure you'll get a warm hand on your opening.

Brodin But what of the parts we've been given in this Easter play? Father Toulon playing God?

Rochfort To call him wooden is an insult to trees.

Marguerite I love his voice though except for two things – my ears. And what of Master Frapper?

Rochfort He doesn't stop a show, just slows it down a lot.

Brodin And Father Flote playing Death? It's obvious I should be playing Death. I know about death. I'm not your everyday Everyman.

Sonnerie *jumps and shakes his legs.*

Rochfort You're right, Bells. It's up to us four to make this entertainment a success. But I confess to beads of sweat I haven't felt since I was at Court and the King actually spoke to me.

Marguerite What did he say?

Rochfort 'Move over, crow-bait, you're standing in my sunlight!'

Brodin Sweat! I can tell you about sweat. Before a battle I used to sweat buckets. Ah, but afterwards.

Marguerite Why, what did you do after a battle?

Brodin Bleed.

Church bells ring again.

Marguerite It's time, red-nosey time. The audience is coming!

Marguerite, Brodin, Rochfort *and* **Sonnerie** *hurry off Downstage Left. A bright banner with the words:* Christ's clowns present the play – everyman *unfurls Upstage as* **Peasants** *and* **Artisans** *enter Upstage Right and* **Sabine** *and* **Patris** *pull on their small cart Upstage Left with* **Mother Metz** *on top of it.*

Sabine Putrid prune! Smell-feast!

Mother Metz Flaggy dustworm! Stinking mard!

Sabine You're no mother of mine, funge-bucket. Don't just stand there, Henri – throttle her. Why is she still living?

Mother Metz Because I sleep with my eyes open, scrat-face. If you relax just once death slips in. I never relax. So I breathe, *pa pa pa.*

Druce *and* **Scarron** *enter Upstage Left, cawing.*

Scarron You sneaked away, Master Patris. The army
of the oppressed grows. Even the dead march with us.
For they know at least what it is to be poor, lying in
cold dirt and shadows, living out their deaths, as they
lived out their lives. The Emperor of Eternity who puts
the damp in walls and the white in old men's hair will
be leading us, the Dark Angel who tempted Eve out of
that puerile garden and said, no, to the status quo.

Patris But all we did is come to see if there's any
laughter in the poor-house air.

Scarron There isn't and you don't need it. Stay hard,
learn to touch the very bottom, then the only way is up.

Mother Metz *throws back a corner of the sacking on the
cart to show the corpses underneath.*

Mother Metz They don't know how, Master Scarron.
They're too soft to spit. But I spit. See, here's Dr
Antrechau and there's a forgotten Prince who once had
cap and knees of all men – now just things left behind.

She spits on them as **Scarron** *leaps up beside her.*

Scarron My thanks, Mother. Remember the oppressed
are legion. And when all the holes in their belts are
used up, we'll destroy the soft hands, fat bellies and
take their fine places.

Mother Metz Then will I have furs enough to cover
the moon? Wine enough to drown Jerusalem? Alps of
powdered sugar, stewed prunes and mutton for dinner?
Silk, worsted and fine yarn stockings, pockets in my
goodly robes so I can say, 'Give me the money 'cause
I'm the only one with pockets'? Will I have six
petticoats and lace ruffs? Will I be rich?

Scarron You'll be better than rich, you'll be of value.
The poor come truly rich when they give themselves
value. Spit!

He and **Mother Metz** *start to spit on the corpses as*

Marie, Camille, Pellico and **Lefranc** *enter Upstage Centre and cross Upstage Right.* **Druce** *hastily covers the corpses on the cart.*

Druce Scarron, you're making an exhibition of yourself. I'm embarrassed, there are ladies present. We're in enough bad odour as it is.

Mother Metz That's the corpses. They can stink something awful. No one listens to freedom's call, Master Scarron. I tell 'em the bread's crucified, the onion weeps, the paper's ground to dust and they don't listen.

Sabine Your brains are wet straw. Die, damn you, die!

As **Mother Metz** *cackles,* **Le Grue** *bustles in Upstage Centre waving the people into their places with his stick whilst* **Bembo** *adjusts the small drum strapped to his waist.*

Le Grue Spread out, you clodpoles. This way, follow me. You go there. No, you . . . dummy. This is the best position to see everything. (*He has his back to the small stage.*) If you *ahh* . . . Bembo! (*He bumps into* **Camille** *and feels her body with his hands, lingering over her bosom.*) Charles? Charles Bembo? (*He feels her face and kisses her.*) You're not Charlie Bembo! You can't fool me. (*He staggers away.*) Anyone who's plague-stricken during the performance, have the decency to die somewhere else. Don't spoil it for others.

A loud whip-crack and **Grez** *and two* **Flagellants** *enter Upstage Centre.*

Grez Whip-scarred, Cain-marked, my brother came to me in tears, dying. I appealed to God who pronounced His most terrible sentence – life! He was given a life sentence. So my wretched brother lives. That's just one of the stories you would have heard if the Flagellants had been given the square this Easter. Stories to purge you with the terror and the pity of it. But in dark times people want creamy bon-bons not solid fare, hard tack. So you'll be entertained, *ugg*.

Le Grue Try not spattering blood all over the place, Master Grez. Somebody has to clean it up. *Shhh*, the show, the show begins!

A trumpet sounds and **Bembo** *beats his drums and* **Frapper** *enters Upstage Centre with a proclamation. The* **Audience** *facing the portable stage, Downstage Left, settle down in anticipation.*

Frapper (*reading*) O–o–o–o–o–o . . .

Bembo *gently takes the proclamation from him and reads.*

Bembo Oyez, oyez. Give audience to our play. 'Tis called *Everyman* and fair or foul, it will include one short interval. Mirth's our purpose, so smile. And if you like it, clap your hands the while. See the first scene's in Heaven, where God dwells. We thought you'd had too much of Hell.

The small stage curtain rises to show **Toulon** *in a white robe, seated on a wooden throne against a blue backdrop. He puts on a paper crown and a white wig. All the performers have on their red noses.*

Toulon I'm God.

Grez It's a lie. I know that voice. He's not God. It's Father Toulon.

Bembo *shoos him to silence.*

Toulon I'm God! But all my creatures now live without dread of me. Blind to my power, forgetful I sent my son down, felt his thorns and split side. Who now gives thanks for my mercies? (**Brodin** *enters in a smock Upstage Left and falls on his knees in front of the small stage.*) Ahh, my sweet favourite – it's Everyman. He has not forsaken me . . . (**Brodin** *rolls a pair of dice.*) Ingrate, drowning in sin! You'll come to feel my anger. I summon Death.

Gasps from the **Audience** *as* **Flote** *with a whitened face enters Upstage Right and goes on to the small stage.*

Scarron Death? Another lie. That's your red-nosed sallow-pate, Flote. We Ravens know about death.

Druce Where're the women, Scarron? I came here for the women.

On the small stage, **Toulon** *beckons* **Flote** *to him.*

Toulon Death, see how they live without fear. Go visit Everyman in my name and take him on his last journey. No, wait, he prays.

Brodin (*kneeling*) Lord God, only hear my prayer. I can never get a fire started. Could you make me a burning bush in my backyard?

Toulon Oaf imperfect! Go Death, bring him to his reckoning.

Flote Lord, I cut down the fairest flower at your command. But I must be suitably attired first.

Toulon Put the fear of God back into him. Drag him off to judgement. Go down, Death!

Flote *bows, the curtain on the small stage falls and* **Marguerite** *enters Upstage Right with pot and dishes and crosses to* **Brodin**, *followed by* **Sonnerie**, *dressed as a baby with a bonnet and bib, and holding a rattle.* **Marguerite** *puts down the pot and the others gather round as she ladles out porridge.*

Marguerite Did you pray for riches, Everyman? You promised me riches and everything that goes with it and all I got was everything that goes with it.

Brodin You can be very outspoken, my dear – but not by anybody I know. You make a happy man very old.

Marguerite Remember how it rained at our wedding. Even nature wept.

Brodin Why don't you go for a walk in the woods and trample on the flowers? You'd like that. (**Sonnerie** *gurgles and flicks porridge at him.*) That's not my son. I've seen better specimens in glass jars. When you said you wanted to hear the patter of tiny feet, I told you to rent some mice. Oh misery, when the warm weather comes I'm going to drown myself. It can't get worse.

The curtain rises on the small stage behind them to show the white-faced **Flote** *dressed in a long black cloak and gloves and carrying a scythe. The* **Audience** *gasps:* 'It's Death. Death's amongst us!' **Flote** *moves menacingly down the small stage steps, becomes entangled in his cloak and falls headlong with a cry.* **Brodin** *and the others look round as* **Flote** *scrambles up.*

Flote Sorry, I was trying to make a good entrance. I like to sneak up on people . . . I used to think I was indecisive, but now I'm not so sure. You're wondering who I am? Guess . . . White face . . . black cloak . . . scythe . . . No? Prepare thyself, Everyman. I'm Death.

Sonnerie *throws a spoonful of porridge in his face.*

Marguerite It's some stark pimp, a straw-in-the-hair moon-loon. And stop annoying my little boy.

Brodin You don't believe anybody. If he says he's Death, he's Death. He looks like Death. A face like that must've worn out at least two coffins. But I thought you'd be thinner.

Flote (*wiping his face*) Thinner? Me? There's not a spare gram of flesh on me. Thinner! Lookee, Everyman, God has sent me down to take you on a last journey. In His infinite wisdom He feels you've had it too easy. You aren't suffering enough so He sent me.

Grez *starts hitting himself in the audience.*

Grez No one suffers enough, it's why we're plague-cursed! Only feel pain, the redemption of pain.

Brodin You'll feel the pain of my fist if you don't stop airing your gums.

Flote No one disturbs your public whippings, so give our show a chance.

Shouts of agreement from the **Audience**.

Marie Let 'em play.

Druce There's a lewd woman.

Camille Who's closed for the day, Master Wagtail. Padlocked.

Pellico And paid for.

Brodin To return to Everyman and Death. Thank you . . . I'm Everyman now . . . What do yer mean, God doesn't think I'm suffering enough? I'm married, aren't I? My wife's got a tongue that can clip a hedge. In the beginning she took to me like a duck to green peas. Now it's so quiet in bed I can hear ice melting.

Flote I can't stay listening to you, Everyman. I'm a very important person.

Brodin You look terrible but you don't look important.

Flote Depressing, isn't it? I didn't even enjoy getting to look like this. Everyman, prepare for the journey, *aah*.

Sonnerie *repeatedly hits him with his rattle.*

Marguerite You'd like to go, wouldn't you, Everyman? Anything to escape your responsibility. You'd up and leave me without a word. All you think of is your own enjoyment.

Brodin I'm not going because I want to, woman. I've no choice, have I, Death?

Flote None.

Marguerite Oh, you men always stick together.

Brodin Death, if I go, can I take a friend with me?

Flote If you can find someone stupid enough. The more the merrier, *aah*. That child is a monster, Madam.

Marguerite It's true, we have to take him everywhere twice – once to apologize – but don't forget you're a guest in this house.

Brodin I'll ask Good Fellowship to come with me.

Rochfort *enters Upstage Left, followed by* **Bembo, Le Grue** *and the* **Boutros Brothers,** *all colourfully dressed.*

Rochfort Start the applause, Good Fellowship is here. That's me. Full of good fellowship and good sense. Like – 'A man who laughs when things go wrong has just that moment thought who he can blame it all on.'

Brodin Fellowship, Fellowship . . . (*He forgets his lines. Low:*) Prompt . . . prompt.

Frapper F–F–Fellowship, F–F–Fellowship, I–I–I g–g–go o–o–on a h–h–hard journey, w–w–will you c–c–come w–w–with m–m–me?

Brodin Fellowship, Fellowship, I go on a hard journey, will you come with me?

Rochfort I'll never forsake you, Everyman. We'll all come and lighten your steps thus.

Brodin Gramercy, Fellowship. Our journey's to the Last Judgement. This is Death. He's taking us.

Rochfort Death? Did you say Death? *This* is Death . . . ? I thought you'd be thinner. Are you the Death that makes dead worlds and field mice stop breathing?

Flote And I can throw a wet blanket the entire length of a room.

Rochfort That changes the picture quite, Everyman. I recall pressing business elsewhere. Exit fast, lads. It's Death. D-E-A-T-H.

Rochfort *and the others exit Upstage Right.*

Marguerite Tavern loafers! If they were a hobby they'd be collector's items.

Flote Everyman, I want us gone. I've got others to attend to. Birds, trees, stones, distant stars are dying. I must be there. Say thy farewells, Everyman.

Sonnerie *starts shaking his bells and* **Marguerite** *comforts him.* **Brodin** *takes out his pair of dice.*

Brodin A last game. Do you play dice, Death?

Flote Does a cock crow? Is the Seine a river? Do I play? You've heard of dicing with death?

Brodin If I win give me an extra day of life. If I lose I come smiling.

Flote I don't know if I should. I'd be taking an unfair advantage. You're obviously a simpleton. Tell me what is three plus three?

Brodin Nine.

Flote Nearly. Only two out. Right, we'll play, Everyman. (*They kneel and* **Flote** *shakes the dice.*) Tut-and-whistle-show-some-gristle. (*He throws.*) Two fives.

Brodin (*rolling the dice*) Two sixes. (*The* **Audience** *laughs.*) Shall we make it truly interesting and play for money as well, Death?

Flote Two sixes . . . ? I don't carry money when I'm working.

Brodin You've accoutrements.

Marguerite *feels* **Flote**'s *cloak.*

Marguerite Poor stuff, look at the width of this hem.

Flote This is insanity. You can never win, friend Everyman.

Brodin Well, my wife already thinks I'm mad because I like pancakes.

Flote Nonsense. I like pancakes.

Brodin Oh good, would you like to see my collection? I've got hundreds.

Flote All right. Throw the dice.

As they start to play again a sharp high-pitched sound stops them. They and the **Audience** *turn to see* **Mother Metz** *shaking with laughter.*

Mother Metz Hundreds of pancakes . . . hundreds of pancakes . . . I see hundreds of pancakes . . . (*As her laughter grows louder she suddenly slumps down.*) I'm Mother Metz and earth is in my ears. I relaxed and dusty death's slipped in through the cracks . . . Pancakes . . . I'm dying . . . *Heee-heee* . . . I mustn't laugh . . . If I stop laughing . . . *Heee-heee* . . . I'll live.

She dies.

Sabine She's dead.

The **Audience** *shrinks back.*

Patris (*laughing*) Now that is funny. Here lies Mother Metz, who when her glass was spent, kicked up her heels and went.

Sabine (*laughing*) Poems and epitaphs are but stuff. She laughed and died . . .

Druce That's enough! Let's get rid of her quick. I want to see what happens next in the play.

Using his pole, he quickly hooks the body off Upstage Right.

Camille The play! The play!

The playlet continues and **Flote** *resumes rattling the dice amid laughter.*

Flote Tut-and-whistle-show-some-gristle . . . (*He throws.*) Curses. Four and three.

Brodin (*throwing dice*) Two fives.

Flote Your dice are as hollow as my head. Cheat, cheat!

Brodin It's a lie. I've nothing up my sleeve.

Marguerite And very little down your pants. Your clothes, Master Death.

Flote I've fallen into a nest of thieving daws, *ahh*!

Amid howls of laughter from the **Audience**, **Sonnerie** *dumps a bowl of porridge on his head as* **Brodin** *and* **Marguerite** *rip off his breeches.*

Even the **Players** *laugh.*

Flote (*whispers to them urgently*) No 'corpsing' please.

Brodin What are those hairy things you're wearing?

Flote Hairpants. They're more uncomfortable than the traditional hairshirt. Hands off me, Madam!

Marguerite Cloak and jerkin.

Brodin Debt of honour, Death.

Flote Save me!

As **Marguerite** *tears off his cloak and jerkin,* **Toulon** *appears as God on the small stage behind them.*

Toulon I'm the Alpha and Omega, the Life, the Way, the Truth, and I can't boil an egg or get my commands carried out. Death!

Flote *stands shivering in his hairpants.*

Flote Lord, why are you always watching? Don't you trust me? I'll win it back. It isn't my fault. I was doing my best.

Toulon Your best? I told you I didn't want failure! What race have I bred up who can send back Death a bare-arsed beggar? You are reprieved, Everyman, for the days you won back. But Death will come again.

Brodin We'll not fear him, Lord. For he's proved a cogging cheat. Death doesn't count, and probably doesn't read or write either. When he comes again we'll play it to the very end. Whether dying in a privy or marble halls, green field or white bed, the hand pointing to zero, the smell in your throat, don't do Death's job for him. Don't start dying before you die, already half dead. Don't go easy, make him work for you, let the calendar tear its own leaves, fight dirty.

Flote Ah, but after life's drudgery, when you are weary . . . ?

Brodin That's the time to be merry.

Bembo *plays the drum,* **Sonnerie** *rings his bells, as* **Rochfort,** *the* **Boutros Brothers, Le Grue** *and* **Frapper,** *enter Upstage Right and Left. They jump, cartwheel and tumble, wave coloured ribbons, throw streamers and join* **Flote** *and the others as they come forward singing.*

All (*singing*) 'No one complaining. No one disdaining. Their loss or gaining. Your heart retaining. And goodness remaining. And laughingly to agree. A chip and a cherry. A dill and a derry. A trill on the berry. Whatever the devil that may be. But lovingly to agree. Sleep well every night. In living delight. And lovingly to agree. A chip and a cherry. A dill and a derry. A trill on the berry. Whatever the devil that may be. But lovingly, lovingly, lovingly to agree . . .'

Flote *and* **Company** *bow amid tremendous applause and shouts of approval from the* **Audience,** *which disperses Stage Left and Right, leaving* **Flote** *and the others laughing and congratulating each other on their triumph.*

Flote The Holy Father said ripple and spread. We'll ripple and spread to every town and hamlet, village and dingly dell. Spin, Brothers, spin. Spin and lose all sense of direction, let God guide you. Round, round, round!

Flote, Marguerite, Rochfort, Frapper, Bembo, Sonnerie, Le Grue *and the* **Boutros Brothers** *all spin.*

Marguerite We spin! And fall!

They stagger and fall.

Flote Now whichever way you are facing that's the way God wants you to go to carry His glorious words of joy and bring down the walls with laughter. Up, Brothers, up and exit smiling!

They get up and exit fast whichever way they happen to be facing. There are peals of laughter and applause Offstage at the various points they exited as the lights go down to the cries of Floties! Floties! Floties!

Act Two

Scene One

Lights up on the main square of Auxerre. A tired **Flote,**
Rochfort, Toulon, Brodin *and* **Marguerite** *enter at*
various points Stage Left and Right.

Flote We've rippled and spread, Brothers and Sister,
these long days. My body aches but my heart sings
songs of morning. We've given light to the dawn, stars
to the night and joyful motion to the dancing company
that encircles the Universe. Standing on tip-toe we
struck our tents amid stricken villages, roamed the
unreaped cornfields and showed them God and life
triumphant.

Marguerite (*singing*) 'Everyday smiles we had. Though
the plague be sore and bad. No use crying, how sad,
how sad. We come to banish sorrow, banish fear. Smile,
my dear, my dear, my dear . . .' Six pregnant nuns
bearing out their bellies before 'em, joined me in
singing that sweet song. It was wondrous.

Rochfort Unbeatable, unmissable, the highlight of the
year, they called my fluting in Chablis.

Toulon In Vency, they said I was ludicrous. Ludicrous.

Flote 'Beautifully' ludicrous, Father. There's a world of
difference there. It means they liked you. Our fame
grows. Now people come to us for comfort.

Brodin After every campaign, even the successful ones, it's custom to tot up the butcher's bill – casualty check front and centre! Bembo and Le Grue I saw an hour past.

Rochfort The Boutros boys are safe.

Toulon And I spied Frapper on the road earlier, telling a joke to some villagers. He'd been at it four hours already so he should be joining us later today.

There is the sound of bells.

Flote And that's Master Bells, so all are accounted for, God have mercy.

Marguerite No, those are bitter bells, not our own sweet Bells.

Instead of **Sonnerie,** *three* **Lepers** *shamble in Upstage Centre. Their faces and hands are completely wrapped in dirty bandages and leper bells hang round their necks.*

First Leper Lepers, lepers, unclean, unclean. Flesh, bone, speech, rot. The black pestilence shunssss ussss like the plague. There's no quick bursting burn boils for lepers. Men pay us to haunt houses. Our bodies rusty knives and sickles. Unclean, unclean. Make us laugh, Fathers, bring us joy. They accusssssse us and the Jews of starting the plague by poisoning the wellsss. We're dragged to fire-pitssss pushed through eternity's doorss. Kingsss decree all leperssss be banished, Princesss of Provence set mobs to massacre ussss.

Rochfort Scapegoats are needed. The poor are always destroyed, not because they're poor but because they're weak.

Brodin Hunting wouldn't be such fun for lords if the rabbits had swords. Cuirassiers, Brother Leper! Cuirassiers!

First Leper *Sister* Leper. I'm Sister Leper! Fathers, clothe our sick bones with flesh, show us skies without blemish, clear mountains, ponds of silver, a sudden glimpse of Paradise.

Flote It was easy for Christ, he only had to heal the sick, raise the dead, cleanse the leper. He didn't have to make them laugh, make them feel superior to someone worse off than themselves.

Toulon Let me try, Father Flote.

Flote The stage is yours, Brother T.

Toulon William Raimbaut had a new sash. Fell into the fire and burnt to ash. Now the room is chilly. We haven't the heart to poke poor Willy.

Flote Well told indeed, Brother Toulon.

As **Flote, Brodin, Rochfort** *and* **Marguerite** *enthusiastically applaud* **Toulon** *they turn and see there has been absolutely no reaction from the* **Lepers**.

First Leper Despair deeper than that.

Second Leper We drown in the river of our tears.

Third Leper We walk into our deaths and leave only our silence behind us.

Flote *takes off his false nose, kisses the* **First Leper** *on the mouth and bows formally.*

Flote Madam, may I have this dance?

He grasps the **First Leper** *and they dance.* **Toulon** *and* **Brodin** *take a* **Leper** *each as a partner and dance too, whilst* **Rochfort** *plays his flute and* **Marguerite** *hums 'Red Roses for a Blue Lady'.*

First Leper Balloons rise in us. For a moment I am daughter of the sun, glimpse mimosa trees, rainbow bridges, star flights.

The dance ends. The **Lepers** *clap their hands in muffled applause.*

Second Leper Now know what we're missing. We
must take our share of such delightssss, come out of the
shadowssss. Show the world who we are.

*She unwraps the bandages round her face to reveal nothing
underneath except a rusty metal frame in the shape of a
face. Suddenly there is the sound of a* **Crowd** *off,
shouting,* Lepers! Lepers! Kill! Kill! *and a motley
collection of* **Men** *and* **Women,** *carrying crossbows and
black streamers on poles, surges in Upstage Centre. Before
anyone can react they raise their crossbows at the huddled
group of* **Lepers.** *There is the sound of arrows in flight.
The* **Lepers** *are hit, stagger and fall dead. All is suddenly
quiet, except for the distant 'cawing' of the approaching*
Black Ravens.

Toulon Polluted sons of Balaam, this is private
property! You're trespassing, spawn of Sodom.

Flote You've shed innocent blood, friends, and birds
have no trees to nest in.

Flote, Toulon *and* **Marguerite** *hold up their crucifixes,
whilst* **Brodin** *and* **Rochfort** *pull back their habits to
show their swords. But the* **Crowd** *remains menacingly.
As the two sides confront each other,* **Le Grue** *enters with*
Bembo *Stage Left, holding a fistful of knives. All his
fingers are bandaged.*

Le Grue Where are you grubbers?! (*He stumbles against
a dead* **Leper.**) Asleep? Whilst you've been dormicing,
Bembo and me've been out working and practising. Yes,
practising. Though I'm the best I'm never satisfied.
That's the mark of a true artist. I've worked out this
new bit of juggling. With knives. Yes, knives. Watch.
(*But the sight of* **Le Grue** *preparing to throw the knives is
enough for the* **Crowd.** *They quickly head for the exit
Upstage Centre.*) Creeping away on tippy-toe, eh? I can
hear your big feet, I've got ears. No eyes but ears.
Crump-backed thumpers. You don't know what you're
missing. An artist like me isn't content with the old

routines. This is all new stuff. New and brilliant. Le Grue does it again. Wait! Wait! (*He stumbles after them Upstage Centre.*)

Flote Brothers, keep an eye on him, as his eyes are blinded. (**Brodin, Rochfort** *and* **Bembo** *hurry after* **Le Grue** *as* **Flote** *looks down at the corpses.*) So I considered again all the oppressions that're done under the sun. And beheld the tears of such as were oppressed and they had no comfort.

Marguerite *and* **Toulon** *exit sadly Upstage Right,* **Flote** *kneels and prays as* **Scarron** *and* **Druce** *enter Stage Left, 'cawing' and singing.*

Scarron and **Druce** (*singing*) 'We are two ravens sat on a tree. Down a down, hay down, hay down. We are two ravens sat on a tree. We are as black as we can be.'

Druce I knew there'd be garbage to collect. Butchered for poisoning the wells, eh?

He hooks the corpses off Stage Right with his long pole.

Scarron If the wells were poisoned, we did it – the Black Ravens. They know but they're too frightened to move against us. Did you try to save 'em, Father? I could've saved 'em. My *caw-caw* would've sent the butchers running. What did you do, but make 'em laugh.

Druce Are they still laughing as they rot in eternity, Father?

Scarron Don't pray to your God of joy and laughter, He's shut up shop long since. Pray to the Butcher God who did this fine work.

Druce Pray, Father, pray.

Flote As a boy my father put me on a ledge and told me to jump and he'd catch me. I jumped, he moved and I fell on my head and he shouted, 'That'll teach you never to trust anyone, not even your father.' But I trust, trusting You, Lord, even when you took my wife Marie and my three little ones. My home was blasted for a purpose. Ordained, I followed and trusted Your light, Lord. I'll not let it flicker now. For still it is a joy to come in skipping, leaping and dancing like a mad fool and plucking folk's hair and making them swear by God. Exit dancing Flote.

He dances off Upstage Centre as **Grez** *and the* **Flagellants** *enter Stage Right, chanting,* 'Pain, pain, pain' *and collapse.*

Grez In Rheims, Troyes, Bruges our flayed brethren march in chanting and the streets are lined ten deep. They attract multitudes of men, we can't attract flies. Our sacrifices go for nothing though our Brother here broke his leg for them.

Scarron How did he do that?

Grez Easy, I took a hammer and went bang. No one was interested. We need new ways to hold the public's interest and fetch 'em to salvation.

Scarron The people suffer enough, they've no need to watch your suffering. They want no more bloodstained martyrs for Christ.

Grez Stinkards, you travel through your lives in the bowels of the world like Jonah in that stenchy fish. Cleanse yourself of hate and pride.

Scarron Penance-dribbler!

Grez Toad-eater! . . . Ah, converts.

Patris *and* **Sabine** *have entered Stage Left.*

Patris Gentles, could you help us?

Grez Ave Maria, we return to Christ's passion, *ahhhhh.* (*He stabs himself.*) They that sow in tears shall reap in joy. (*He clubs the other* **Flagellants**.) No mortification too great, no penance too hard. Ask anything of us. Ask!

Patris Do you know where Flote and his big Red Noses are performing?

Sabine We're off to see the funnies.

Grez *stops clubbing.*

Grez The Devil is now let loose to end the world and you want to see that flyblown sot, Flote. Decadent strumpet!

Patris We've had too much of misery.

Scarron That's the world they've made for you. Change it. Spit, grease and change it, *caw-caw.*

Grez No, repent; repent and change it. Time stops, the book closes. (*A trumpet note is heard off Upstage Centre.*) The Last Trumpet sounds for Last Judgement!

But the trumpet note turns to a merry 'toot-toot', followed by a drumroll and laughter of a crowd.

Sabine It's the Floties! The Floties!

Grez *clubs the* **Flagellants**.

Grez Stay! Stay for the salvation of blood! See me smash his other leg.

Patris Old stuff. Laughter's the new thing. Suffering and revolution is too hard. We want dolphins and dancing mice.

Druce I think I'll join you.

Laughing in anticipation, **Sabine**, **Patris** *and* **Druce** *exit Upstage Centre.* **Grez** *stops clubbing, leaving the injured* **Flagellants** *groaning on the ground.*

Grez I could have sat at home by warm fires, drinking wine in bowls. I was tutor to King Philip and slept on silk. I forsook all that, to help people like that, yet I couldn't hold them. The fault is in me. I've been too gentle. (*The* **Flagellants** *groan.*) We've not been suffering enough, Brothers.

Scarron No, only here in France is your Brotherhood of the Cross rejected and we Black Ravens are left without support. It's Flote.

Grez Yes, he's a clever fool. I once asked him which was more important, the sun or the moon? And he said, 'The moon because it shines at night when we really need it but who needs the sun when it's already broad daylight?' I confess, I've always had a soft spot for Father Flote.

Scarron A peat bog in the northern Ardennes. I say we grease the Noses dead.

Grez We're pledged to commit no violence. I must try and persuade him to join our Brotherhood of Whip and Cudgel.

Scarron The way he flogs old jokes it should be easy.

Grez But if he doesn't see the light?

Scarron We snuff it out.

Grez Well, so it goes. So it goes. We who come to cleanse the world of foulness are befouled by you cawing swine-scratchers.

Scarron Dog-leeches, you befoul life by taking away man's liberty and giving it to Heaven. But I don't care who we join forces with – integrity's for failures. Death to the Noses!

Grez Death to the Noses! Brothers, you look slovenly. Straighten up there, don't slouch. (*Chanting.*) 'Pain, pain, pain. Our journey's done in holy name . . .'

He exits Stage Right, with **Scarron**. *The* **Flagellants** *drag themselves out after them, feebly chanting,* 'Pain, pain, pain'.

Scene Two

Flote *enters Upstage Centre, carrying a large wooden Cross, followed by* **Marguerite** *with a pile of washing in a basket. As he places the Cross upright, Upstage Centre,* **Brodin** *and* **Frapper** *enter Stage Left with a long trestle table and two benches, followed by* **Rochfort** *playing his flute. The table is placed diagonally Stage Left and the benches either side.* **Brodin** *sits and carves the wooden face of a puppet, whilst* **Frapper** *watches intently.* **Flote** *exits and re-enters with* **Sonnerie**, *Upstage Centre, with bowls and plates for the table as* **Marguerite** *hangs up the newly-washed clothes on the Cross to dry.*

Marguerite When you're young the summers never end, later you can't hold a day. I'm losing time washing the crut from your holy underbreeches. I keep asking myself, is monastic life separating me from God?

Rochfort 'He pressed me, I stumbled. He pushed me, I tumbled. He kissed me, I grumbled. But still we kissed on.' I wrote it for you, Sister Marguerite, to go with the air you love so well.

Marguerite 'He pressed me, I stumbled . . .' How shall I sing it?

Rochfort Under an assumed name. Didn't we meet before somewhere?

Marguerite It's possible, I've been somewhere. 'He pushed me, I stumbled.' My thanks, Brother R. I'll make you some wine, I've got very big feet.

Frapper I–I–I w–w–wish I–I–I could s–s–sing. But I–I–I've g–g–got n–n–n–no sense of p–p–p–pitch.

Flote *and* **Sonnerie** *start bringing in various dishes of food Stage Left.*

Rochfort Brodin, you should've seen Sister Marguerite and me in Chablis. All were dead in the manor house except for one goose-girl in her mistress's gown, dancing in those long forsaken halls. I calmed her with playing my flute.

Marguerite He proved a very perfect gentle knight.

Rochfort My brother was dubbed a true one, invested in the robes, arms and the spurs of knighthood.

Brodin Hypocrites all. The horses've more breeding than the knights who ride 'em. Give me a fearful man-at-arms who knows when to run, not your glory-bound knight. (*He finishes carving.*) These hands have stabbed, slashed and clubbed fair flesh into two groats' worth of dead meat. Yet these hands are delicate enough to carve a doll's head and carry a fart to a privy. (*He gives the puppet to* **Frapper**.) Here, it's yours, Brother.

Frapper M–m–m–much th–th–thanks, B–B–B–Brother B–B–B–Brodin.

There is a horrified cry as **Toulon***, who has just entered Upstage Centre, looks up at the washing on the Cross.*

Toulon Knickers? Fouled knickers and lace-edged underpants on the sacred sign of Christ's Passion! Christ's triumphant Cross bedecked with pogy undergarments.

Flote These pogy undergarments are but symbols of our devotion, Brother. Newly cleansed of body's corruption, they are offered up like our cleansed souls to God.

Toulon Your tongue's boneless, excusing every lace sacrilege. I don't see my hairshirt. Where's my hairshirt?

Marguerite Burnt. It was rotted with lice and dead blood.

Toulon I was attached to that hairshirt, Sister Marguerite. I had it with me man and boy.

Marguerite We'll buy you a new one for Christmas, stuffed with holly. I thought we'd eat out here, Father Flote, as it's the last day of summer.

Le Grue *lurches in with* **Bembo** *Stage Right.*

Le Grue Snouts in the trough, trotters in the swill. Hog-hog-hogging without us, eh? I told you I smelt roast pork and neat's tongues, Bembo. No eyes but I've got a nose.

Bembo You've got that.

Flote What've you been doing, Brother G?

Le Grue Practising, what else? It takes practice to reach the standard I've set myself. I'm the Great Le Grue after all. They expect something special when I'm out there juggling. Where's the food?

Flote Yes, let's pray and eat. We won't wait for the Boutros Brothers. They've gone to see their wives in Volgre.

Rochfort Actually they live in St-Cyr but they look better from Volgre.

All rise.

Flote Lord, as this bread upon the table was in separate grains and being gathered together became one good thing, so let all men and women be gathered together from the ends of the earth into one family. In the name of the Father, Son and Holy Ghost. Amen.

He makes the sign of the cross. They sit and, with **Flote** *at the head of the table, immediately attack the food, laughing and talking loudly.* **Frapper** *tries to manipulate the puppet.*

Le Grue (*piling food on his plate*) Sot-faces, which of you's snaffled my lace-edged underpants? That's stealing from a blind man!

Marguerite Can't you see I've washed 'em for you?

Do you like Brother Rochfort's special basted pike with crayfish sauce?

Brodin I'm for deep pots, wide pans, not mimsy portions served in separate dishes.

Toulon Ah, what food these morsels be. But we should only care for the spirit, not meat and drink – pass the truffled capon *à la moelle*.

Marguerite Don't eat so fast, Le Grue. It's the first time I've seen anyone get sparks from a spoon.

Flote Pity there's no white wine. White wine's the most suitable for poultry, if you can get 'em to drink it that is.

Toulon The people of Vency gave Father Flote three chickens gratis for being such a selfless benefactor of old jokes like that, which had nowhere else to go.

Rochfort Look, this chicken's got one leg shorter than the other.

Toulon Are you going to eat it or dance with it?

Rochfort Time was I used to dine on godwits and pheasants, snipes in osmagone sauce, boars' heads, rabbit fritters and iced eggs.

Marguerite The night before he died, my father sat up eating rabbit fritters.

Brodin Mine was badly murdered robbing a church.

Toulon I was adopted, which is almost as good as being real. Jesu, there's a black thing with legs swimming in my soup.

Flote What did you expect him to do, Father, lay there and drown? Come, let's help him out or at least stop him making waves.

Le Grue (*blindly taking food from* **Bembo**'s *plate*) Neats' tongues! Why aren't there neats' tongues? (*He stabs at*

Bembo *as he tries to take the food back.*) Hog off. That's a blind man's food you're stealing.

Flote How went the day, Brothers and Sister? Master Bells, you always have a good tale to tell.

Sonnerie *rings his right and left arm and then shakes his body, and his right leg. All lean forward listening intently whilst still eating. Reaching the climax of his story,* **Sonnerie** *leaps up shaking arms and legs simultaneously. The others bang the table in approval.*

Brodin Marvellously well told.

Toulon It will be hard to better that.

Flote Father Toulon and me visited the plaguey houses of Vency.

Toulon I told the dying there they should wrap themselves in their shrouds and walk to the cemetery. But *very* slowly so's not to start a panic.

Flote He told it well, believe me.

Toulon Yes, I think it had a certain style. Pass the pepper sauce.

Marguerite Brother Rochfort and me knocked them stiff in Chablis – stiffer than they already were that is. Sometimes the soul lays hold of a voice and makes it sing what the soul has experienced and the voice doesn't know what it does. It happened to me in Chablis. I sang melodies I'd never heard before and I didn't know what I sang or how.

Brodin Then I joined them and we had a great success in Cheyenne. We was lucky. Their tax gatherer, old Gentile Bardi – the one with the money-bags under his eyes – hung himself just before we arrived. It got us off to a swinging start.

Rochfort Trying to get money from him was like trying to get dawn past a rooster.

Toulon Money flowed out of him like drops of blood.

Brodin Is this wild rice?

Marguerite No, tame, but you can mix it around if you like and make it mad.

Le Grue Applause. I'm deafish but I can always hear applause. It washed over us like the great sea. Not enough of course. It never is enough. Not for what we was giving 'em. We was brilliant. (*Leaning over* **Bembo**.) Wasn't we brilliant, Bembo?

Bembo (*protecting his plate*) Passable.

Flote What do you say, Brother Frapper?

Frapper (*finally manipulating the puppet's head and mouth*) The seething sea ceaseth seething . . . (*They all stop talking.*) Is there a pleasant peasant present? That's a three-twisted twist. Oh, list, list. Poor stuttering Pierre here prevented me before; always talking with his mouth like he'd swallowed a set of spoons but I'm in fine spoon fettle now. I tolerated him because he's an example of my kind of stupidity. I've words now, a whole world of words. In the beginning was the word and the end too. Words raise a wordy man above brute beast. Oh, my dame hath a lame crane. Pray gentle Jane, let my dame's lame crane home again. Come, stuttering Pierre, we'll share a single cedar shingle and certainly let my dame's lame crane home again.

All get up and crowd round **Frapper** *with applause and congratulations.*

Le Grue I've got ears. That's a new voice.

Frapper An old voice, new found. Oh Brothers, oh Sisters, it's always easy to find fine friends to feel sorry for you but it's rare to find ones who will be happy because you're happy. My heart explodes in star-born whorls. The serpent spoke to Eve, cats and dogs to witches and warlocks, even echoes, without mouths, articulate and return the voices of men in concave caves and hollow places. But I couldn't speak. Now my once broken words are the soaring wings of my soul, lifting me up to joy so I cease to grieve, to rage unspoken. I've whole words now so let the loud earth be at peace, let the upper air, hurricanes and tumults be still and the onslaughts of curling waves, mouths of mighty rivers and outswelling springs fade down, so my brightly blessed words, words, words can burst, burst, burst above you.

Le Grue No, that's not Brother Frapper.

Frapper But I know behind the words are other words inaudible, and behind those words, there is silence. We don't fear it, thanks to you, Father Flote. You've made this another garden in Eden, opened Heaven so we can hear the angels sing, see the light that never darkens, made the mountains dance like rams and the hills leap like kids, blown away the miseries of the world as the wind does chaff and stubble so the sky is serene and fair again and the lands as rich as they ever were. In a word, Father, amongst so many words, you've made our hearts beat faster.

Le Grue No, that's not you. You can't fool Le Grue. I'm blind but I've got second sight. I spy strangers.

Scarron Too true, Le Grue!

Grez You do!

They turn and see **Scarron** *and* **Druce** *and* **Grez** *and his* **Flagellants** *have entered silently Stage Right.*

Flote Welcome, Brothers, there's food left.

Scarron Flote, you can't see the writing on the wall because your back's up against it. I'm greasing you!

Before anyone can stop him, he steps forward and breathes straight into **Flote**'*s face.* **Druce** *'caws' in triumph but* **Flote** *just stands there.*

Druce But they always fall when you breathe hard on 'em, Scarron.

Puzzled, **Scarron** *puts his hand in front of his mouth and breathes hard to test his own breath; he staggers back, shuddering.*

Flote I've kissed the leper, sucked in the wormy air of a hundred plaguey houses. Your breath's too weak to grease me out, Brother Scarron.

Grez Brethren of the Cross, it's time to inflict pain on others. Club down this grinning Anti-Christ. If you've a best foot left, put it forward!

As the **Flagellants** *start to move,* **Brodin** *and* **Rochfort** *pull back their habits to reveal their swords. The* **Flagellants** *stop.*

Brodin Move anything and we lop it off.

Grez Defending yourselves, eh? I might've guessed you'd be up to such low tricks. Father Toulon, join us and suffer.

Toulon Suffer? You don't know the meaning of true suffering till you've made a red-nosed idiot of yourself daily.

Grez You're not of this company, Toulon, join us.

Toulon No, you're too selfish for me.

Grez Selfish? How can we be selfish? We have nothing.

Toulon Then why do you act as if you have something?

Grez What, what, what?

Toulon Your bodies. You punish your bodies as if they're yours. They're not; bodies belong to God.

Marguerite Are you twiddle-poops eating with us or just standing around like a row of knackered Jack Puddings?

Scarron *stops testing his breath.*

Scarron Chaos and death! Black Ravens, *caw-caw-caw.*

Flote Sheath your swords. It's no time for killing,
Master Pestilence needs no help from us. We'll judge
who wins, who loses, who stays, who goes, by signs not
swords. We'll appeal to Heaven. Let Heaven decide.

They all look up.

Scarron *Caw-caw-caw.* You up there, hear me, I sing
the tender song of homicide. There's no Heaven or Hell
but if a man has good fortune and lives well, that's
Heaven, and if he lives poor and miserable that's Hell
and he dies like a dog. Poor dogs are right in
whatsoever they do to break out of ignorance and want.
Hear me, hear me.

Grez *Ahh-ahh-ahh.* Hear me, Lord, I sing pain's song
for Adam cast out of Paradise and the blood of Cain's
brother crying to us out of the earth. Christ foresaw our
falls, paid he not the price? War, strife, drunkenness,
murder, we fall sore, we suffer sore. By suffering and
obeying the God in their hearts men find their true
strength and His favour the very seal and sign of an
election in Christ before the beginning of the world.
Hear me, hear me.

Flote *Aa-ooh-aah.* Lord, hear me, I sing joy's song,
green sunsets, purple mornings and crested coots. They
asked, 'Why do you laugh while I am crying?' I
answered, 'Because you are crying while I am laughing.'
Life is given to us to be lived. God thunders, 'Marcel,
you are still a fool.' I didn't see. Oh but now I see God
shining, shining in glory. And I must tell you for a start
– She's Black . . . Before our jibes lacked salt. But every
jest should be a small revolution. We come to ding
down dignity and make a new world, opening the gates
of Paradise above and here below. Hear me, hear me.
Only give us a sign, Lord.

Silence. Then a faint rapping sound. It grows louder and more frenzied as finally the **Boutros Brothers** *hop in frantically, Upstage Centre, rapping their crutches on the ground to attract attention.*

Boutros One The plague! The plague is over!

Toulon Over? Over where?

Boutros Two Everywhere! The cities of Paris, Villiers and Melun are clean.

Le Grue Why wasn't I told?

Boutros One Rejoice. The Black Death ends and we live.

Stunned silence.

Marguerite Live?

Brodin Live.

Frapper Live!

Suddenly shouting and dancing, the **Floties, Flagellants** *and* **Black Ravens** *find themselves hugging each other in a spontaneous explosion of joy.*

Flote It's the sign! God's sign we asked for. Explode the heart; air melt with joy. Deck yourselves with banners and with flags. It's time to cast off old ways, old thoughts. The old brown leaves are falling. Confronting death daily made us defiant, not humble, joyful not sad, sunflowers crazy with the sun. Blow trumpets for a new age, new world, light, birth. Master Scarron, Master Grez, we three are in the Millennium business and it's a waste to fight amongst ourselves. All forms of rebellion must come together. (*Singing.*) 'Join together, that's the plan. It's the secret. Man helps man. Join together, that's the stuff. Black Jack Scarron in you we trust. Battered Grez and the rest of us.'

Grez (*singing*) 'Join together, purge all guilt. Live life fully. To the hilt. Red-nosed Flotie in you we trust.

Black Jack Scarron and the rest of us.'

Scarron (*singing*) 'Join together. Go, go, go. Change conditions here below. Red-nosed Flotie in you we trust. Battered Grez and the rest of us.'

All (*singing*) 'Join together. Make it new. Who's invited? All of you! Grez and Flotie in you we trust. Black Jack Scarron and the rest of us.'

Marguerite Bells!

All look at **Sonnerie** *who has been dancing on the table. He is shivering violently. Trying to get down, he collapses and falls.* **Brodin** *catches him and lowers him to the ground. They all gather round.*

Flote What is it, Master Bells?

Toulon The plague cough and burn boils on his neck.

Grez He shivers in pain.

Frapper And spits black bug's blood.

Flote Is it the pestilence, Master Bells?

Marguerite It can't be. Didn't you hear, sweet Bells? It's over.

Rochfort The war's over but there's always one last arrow fired, one last gallant to fall though he shouldn't.

Druce They go like this on the instant; cough, shiver, bleed, die.

Scarron Even the best.

Brodin Never cry quarter, Bells – fight!

Sonnerie *shakes his right arm.*

Toulon Rest, Master Bells, save your strength.

Frapper And you surely shall see the sun shine soon.

But **Sonnerie** *continues to shake his arm.*

Flote I can't hear you, Bells . . . Quiet please, let
Brother Bells speak . . . Yes . . . you have a vision . . .
you hear the music of the spheres . . . see lakes and
towers and bells . . . their fragrance . . . one hundred
thousand bells . . . and beyond them a hundred
thousand times a hundred thousand ringing in the blue
. . . Oh Bells . . . I can't hear you, Bells . . .

Sonnerie's *arm drops. He dies.* **Marguerite** *sobs.*

Brodin Ashes to ashes, dust to dust is a beggar poor
bargain but it's the only one we're given.

Toulon His foot was as light as a four-year-old's. All
those who saw his holy dancing were changed, for in
their hearts he worked both weeping and rapture in one.

Toulon *and* **Flote** *make the sign of the cross over*
Sonnerie. **Brodin** *and* **Rochfort** *pick up the dead man
and hoist him on to their shoulders. Heads bowed, the other
men line up behind them with small handbells with their
clappers muffled, which they ring softly on each step they
take. The light begins to fade as the funeral cortège slowly
crosses the stage to exit Upstage Left.*

Marguerite When a good man dies, letters still come
for him. I want to pray but can only pray to my light,
my dove, my dear, dead Bells. It was over so quick, he
was dead before God got the news. Now you're gone
what's Hell to me? I'm punished sure. If there is life
after death, why do we have to die? My thoughts race
round and round, going somewhere to come back from
nowhere. Bells, you've left me a poor dizzard. Why
didn't you spit in Death's face and tell Heaven to wait?
I needed you more, you gap-toothed gloak. Oh but
stars, suns, moons, flowers, honeys could not express
my Bells. He was so sweet, so fair. A sad wind blows.
Black flags fly over Auxerre, Graverie and beyond. I am
already heart-sore for thee my heavenly Bells.

Rochfort *enters Downstage Right.*

Rochfort Save me, Marguerite.

Marguerite Save you?

Rochfort I'm no longer amused.

Marguerite Be serious.

Rochfort I am. When amusement ends, my only defence against boredom is hatred. The world's turning back again; perfectly organized and perfectly dead like poor dead Bells. And like Flote and the rest will be if they don't submit. The holiday is over.

Marguerite Was that what it was, Brother, days of sun, days of freedom?

Rochfort Summer warmth for plants and trees. Wind and rain for fish and dragons. Just another dream. It's time to unsheath my sword and flash it. I've told Brodin, I'm booting it free again. Leave with me, Marguerite. I'm a wrong-side nobleman but handsome – lofty brow, legs majestic. I know I'm conceited but what's my opinion against the mirror's?

Marguerite You've a pretty wit and I've always preferred fake politeness to sincere boorishness.

Rochfort Come close and save me, Marguerite, be my spur and purpose. I'll reinvent war, carve out an empire, tilt the world for you. Only come closer.

Marguerite If I come any closer, I'll be behind you. I'm a woman who always lets her body go to her head. Oh, but your body's velvet soft. I feel the movement of your loins – my chuck, my chuck.

Rochfort Save me and I'll pull down the pillars of the earth, eat your tongue, leave my teethmarks black upon your lips.

Marguerite You'll be my Altar, my Vespers, my Mass!

Rochfort Come with me! Live happy ever dafter!

Marguerite Oh my mallard, I'll live dafter! . . . No, it wouldn't be right to come now. We owe Father Flote that loyalty.

Rochfort 'Loyalty' – there's a fine word.

Marguerite For loving friendship's sake we must stay for the Nativity he's set his heart on. When it's over we'll eat the world together. Just wait a little and I'll come.

She exits smiling Stage Right.

Rochfort When you wish to see your enemy's face, look into a mirror. I wanted to reach the shore of the sea that has no shore and she talks of loyalty and friendship. Fine words, fine words. I never heard them in my father's house. (*He gets up and takes off his monk's habit to show he is wearing his armour and sword underneath.*) Marguerite, none but the brave desert the fair. I can't wait for any woman to come.

Brodin *enters Upstage Centre putting the finishing touches to a banner, which he shows to* **Rochfort**.

Brodin Do you like it?

Rochfort I like it but I begin to smell the Crécy stink of defeat. We've swords to sell again, Brodin.

Brodin *lays out the banner on the ground to dry.*

Brodin I've lost the taste for blood. Laughter's turned me soft. I've no more pride in the manly arts of war, sword thrust, axe blow. Like Antony, my god's abandoned me.

Rochfort Never. You're Brodin. Whose name made whole populations flee? – Brodin. Whose voice was thunder? – Brodin. Remember how we fought south of the walls, died north of the ramparts and the morning light shining on bright armour? Man, man, there's work for us. It takes force to re-enforce order. Archbishop Monselet and the Civil Authorities will pay good money for our swords.

Brodin I'm corrupted. Before I could hire out to whatever side paid most – English, French, Swiss, no matter, I fought loyally for 'em all, sometimes in the same battle. Now I can only fight for right. (*There is the faint sound of a trumpet and a horse galloping away into the distance.*) There, hear it! I told you, it's the god Mars fartsing off, leaving me . . . He hasn't left you yet, Rochfort. You're still in his service. But you won't find it easy changing sides. Monselet and the rest won't just take an honest soldier's word he's turned turncoat.

Rochfort No, they'll want proof. (*He takes out his red nose.*) Give it back to Father Flote. Tell him I'm taking up my old trade again. I have to be true to myself.

As **Brodin** *takes the red nose,* **Rochfort** *grasps his wrist and pulls him violently forward.* **Brodin** *grunts with pain, a dagger in his stomach;* **Rochfort** *has stabbed him.*

Brodin Rochfort?

Rochfort A dagger in the gut-sack, Brodin? Tut, you'd never have fallen for that old trick in the old days. Your death is all the proof they'll need I've truly turned turncoat. At least I've spared you dying in bed, white hair, wet legs, beating toothless gums. Go die like a soldier, Brodin, whilst I live like a lord.

He exits Stage Left, playing his flute, as others are heard approaching Stage Right. **Brodin** *drapes the banner around him to hide the dagger.* **Flote, Toulon, Marguerite, Le Grue, Bembo, Frapper** *and the* **Boutros Brothers** *enter Stage Right.*

Toulon Father Flote, for those of us gazing up from the lower slopes there's a simple choice of tactics – submission or defiance. There's a pike under the reeds and its name is Monselet. Do nothing to disturb the water.

Brodin *tosses Rochfort's red nose to* **Flote**.

Brodin Brother Rochfort's farewell. He's signed off, gone back to killing.

Marguerite So, so, he couldn't wait for me to come. I thought he deserved me, but what man deserves any woman?

Frapper He wasn't a pleasant peasant but he had a presence.

Le Grue Some people I can't see 'cause they're never there. But that velvet-hosened gent I could always see.

Flote He had a wit and a way. We'll miss him. But he'll return. Meanwhile, we must practise our Nativity play: *The Birth of the Son of Light*. Brother Brodin, let's hear your piece.

Brodin *puts on the crown and his red nose.*

Brodin In this Nativity I play Herod.

Others (*singing*) 'Herod! He's Herod. The very devil of a Herod! Some think him God. Others just a sod. He's Herod! He's Herod!'

As they sing, **Brodin** *thumps up and down in a furious dance.*

Brodin The Romans made me King of Galilee. What makes me a born leader is my desire to organize other people's lives and make them worse. My father was Herod . . .

Others (*singing*) 'Herod! He's Herod. The very devil of a Herod! Some call him God. Others just a sod. He's Herod! He's Herod!'

Brodin *finds himself dancing madly again.*

Brodin . . . the Great. I've trodden in the footsteps of the master. (*He smells his foot.*) Well, I've trodden in something. The family motto was 'Do unto others – then run'. I'm a man of peace. A piece of this and a piece of that. But my father, Herod . . .

Others (*singing*) 'Herod! He's Herod, the very devil of a Herod! Some call him God. Others just a sod. He's Herod! He's Herod!'

Brodin, *looking furiously at them, dances, but less energetically now.*

Brodin He once led Judah into war. We fought for gold! Gold! Gold! Well, you think we should've fought for zinc? Though I'm the son of Herod . . .

Brodin *dances even before they start singing.*

Others (*singing*) 'Herod! He's Herod! . . . Etc., etc., etc.'

Brodin (*sinking exhausted*) I believe in free speech. When I make a speech I never charge admission. We Herods . . .

He twitches his legs in the air in a token dance. The **Others** *laugh.*

Flote I like it, Brother B, but the final collapse should be more final. Comedy is funniest when it's most true. (*He mimes* **Brodin***'s dance.*) Make it more real, realler than real. Otherwise you'll die the death.

Brodin (*laughing*) But I am, Brother, I am.

As he attempts to get up, the banner draped around him falls open to show the dagger and the wound. The **Others** *gasp.*

Toulon What is it, Brother Brodin?

Brodin A parting gift from my friend, Rochfort. Sent with love.

Marguerite I had his love too, it kills.

Brodin No reproaches, Sister Marguerite, for our murdering friend. He's turned slaughterer again, so he slaughters. And no tears for me, I've slaughtered too, in my time. Cuirassiers at the ready!

Flote Forgive me, Brother, I didn't know.

Brodin But I go out in joy, friend. I expected to die alone screaming on some forgotten battlefield. Instead

I'm dying amongst friends, in the midst of life. There's no loneliness or death in this dying. Only you'll have to play Herod, Father Flote, the very devil of a Herod.

Boutros One What's happening?

Boutros Two I don't understand.

Le Grue Don't be blind. Death hangs in the air.

Bembo We lose another friend.

Frapper Amid mist and coldest frost, Brother Brodin is singing his last sad song.

Toulon No one will be as good as you, Brother. You were touched with such grace.

Brodin I had class. Lookee who's here. Death's come. Not enough time left to confess me, Fathers. I've lived like a man, that says it all. Lift me up, I want to face him. (**Toulon** *and* **Flote** *lift him to his feet.*) My regrets, Sister Marguerite, I never did rape you.

Marguerite Another time perhaps. Would you like your sword in your hand?

Brodin No, a jest would be more fitting. This is a good one. Once when I was captured, the enemy commander asked, 'How many men in your army?' 'I'll never tell,' I said. 'Prepare the boiling oil,' he roared. 'Do your worst, sirrah,' I yelled back, 'I'd rather be boiled in oil than betray 34,635 men!' (*The* **Others** *laugh.*) Oh it's good to take smiles with us into that last darkness; they light the way. (*The lights go down.*) Halbardiers advance! The show, the show! I can see it. The bright lights and the bright banners. Then the trumpet toot-toot-toot and drums up, up, up my heart and we're on . . . What's that you say? Crécy? We *did* lose at Crécy. Ah, now I know.

He falls dead in the darkness.

Scene Three

There is a tremendous crash and shattering of glass in the
darkness. Lights up on the antechamber of Clement VI.
The magnifying mirror set at an angle Upstage Centre is
smashed. **Clement VI** *steps out of the adjoining room into*
the antechamber.

Clement VI Behold I come forth in iniquity, back into
the world of dust, dirt, dung, carrion and fools. Who
keeps holy day for Judas? Cold days, sharp days, long
nights come apace. Save me, Lord. No, I'll not appeal
to the Lord. It's madness to put on gloves when one is
stark naked. If there's butcher-work to do let's not be
coy about it. Bring on the wolves, *arrrwaaaa. (He howls*
like a wolf. **Archbishop Monselet** *enters, Stage Left,*
with documents, and **Attendants***, who strip* **Clement***.)*
Now the plague has passed, we must immediately limit,
tame, subordinate, rule. Submission and belief, the twin
poles of the world must be restored. And quick, else
they acquire a taste for the other way. When I heard
you'd crept back, my dear Monselet, I knew the danger
was over. The last time I saw you, your knees were
beating each other to death.

Monselet Holy Father, only he who survives is right.

Clement VI Don't just stand there, be of use. We've
work to do. Christ's work. First, increase the taxes on
the clergy and loan Philip fifty thousand gold florins for
his war against the English. We'll support his coming
campaign to crush the Black Ravens by proclaiming
them anathema. In return, Philip will support us against
the Flagellants.

Monselet Many of your Cardinals are disposed to think

well of them as a new penitential discipline.

Clement VI Don't they see the danger to the Church of allowing independent manifestation of zeal? More important, what's to become of the most profitable function of the Holy Office – selling salvation – if men can cleanse themselves? If they're getting it free from the Flagellants we'll be forced out of the salvation business. Issue a Papal Bull condemning all Flagellants. You look graveyard grave, Monselet. Is there a thought growing in the brain that must lie behind that face?

Monselet Noses! Noses, Noses everywhere. Streets, squares, barns and halls filled with crazed Noses, thundering herds of Red Noses roaming the land like bison. Flote's Noses, Your Holiness.

Clement VI I appointed you Archbishop because you're free of the slavery of talent. Christianity is a system designed by geniuses for execution by idiots. Its continued existence proves almost anything can be made to work. Don't you remember, you sanctioned Father Flote's Red-Nosed Fools and I ratified the decision. A good decision. He's helped keep unrest down to a minimum; made men more readily accept their miserable lot. Flote's proved useful. A revolution never returns.

Monselet It's certain we gave him his chance. But you've often said, 'Give a man enough rope and he'll hang you.' Flote's joining with the Flagellants and Black Ravens.

The **Attendants** *dress* **Clement VI**.

Clement VI I smell the sour smell of sour grapes. Whilst you sat on some fat mountain, Flote and his Red Ones stayed below fighting death to a decision.

Monselet Holy Father, you taught me only the weak are unselfish. As Archbishop I couldn't afford to be

seen dead. I'm glad Flote stayed on my orders. It was
proof I had not deserted my flock. But consider the
man's power. I set Father Toulon as a Red Nose to spy
for me and I've had nothing from him but insults.
Father Toulon was a zealot's zealot on obedience, yet
he's been turned in his turn.

Clement VI Because Flote loves with a full heart. He
has all the makings of a saint. In other words – trouble.
I take note of your warning note. Eye to keyhole,
Archbishop. Report to me of Flote's activities. (*He puts
on jewels.*) The centre must glitter once more. We mark
plague's end with displays, tourneys, masquerades to
celebrate the defeat of chaos and a return to normality,
order and symmetry.
The plague left them trembling but free
But man is too wicked to be free.
It is the nature of the viper to crawl and spit venom
And the nature of man to obey.
Submission and belief are the twin levers which raise
     me high.
Now I summon back the great engines of authority,
Rack, stake and gallows, palaces, courts and counting
     houses.
You strong leaders must leave your bed of worms,
You kings, high dukes, lords, judges and the rest
Adjust your gowns and crowns, sharpen your swords.
Charles of Bohemia, Casimer the Great, John of France,
Amadeus, Green Count of Savoy, Dandolo, Doge of
     Venice,
Cantcuzene the Ottoman, Yussef of Granada, Pedro the
     Cruel and Charles the Bad,
Rulers of earth and sky, dissent is a sin.
Crush it and reimpose the three-fold chains of State,
     Church and Marriage
And quick, else they learn to like another way.
The remedy of disorder is terror;
Go break the spine of the world.
The plague was a time of tearful innocence,

Now a greater darkness falls
For we return to normal.

They exit Stage Right to wolflike howling.

Scene Four

*The howling changes to wedding bells ringing joyfully in
the main square of Auxerre, whilst gallows are pushed in
Upstage Left and three wooden stakes Upstage Right by*
Guards *in black armour. They exit Upstage Left and
Right as* **Pellico** *and* **Lefranc** *enter Downstage Right.*

Pellico Marriage is a desperate thing, Lefranc. My
bride-to-be can't even cook. I'll let a woman ruin my
life but not my stomach.

Lefranc Thousands of men are married and even
happy. The plague's gone. Our duty's plain. The
Church insists we set an example. We remarry for
money and heirs. Our new wives are rich – and
breathing. We can't ask for more. As newly appointed
Magistrates of Auxerre, we must restore our morality
and fortunes.

Pellico But you have to like women inordinately to
actually live in the same house with them. There're
other things to life besides money. But then you need
money to enjoy 'em. 'Gold, gold, gold . . .'

Lefranc and **Pellico** (*chanting*) 'Molten, graven,
hammered, rolled. Chains of gold are chains that hold.'

Solemnly chanting, they cross Downstage Centre to meet
Camille *and* **Marie**, *entering Downstage Left as brides
with veils and small bouquets, and* **Monselet**, *in surplice
and white stole. The couples kneel in front of* **Monselet** *as
the bells ring out again and he conducts a wedding service,*

though the words cannot be heard. **Pellico** *and* **Lefranc** *put rings on their brides' fingers and* **Monselet** *makes the sign of the cross over them.* **Pellico, Lefranc, Camille** *and* **Marie** *rise and the bells stop ringing.*

Pellico It's tradition for bride and groom to smack a big wet one, kiss-kiss.

Marie Kisses cost money.

Camille No. Now all lip work comes free.

Marie Free?!

Camille We've lost our professional status, Marie, no longer honest whores, we've shrivelled to wives. Careers blasted on a 'love, honour and obey . . .' I could've been the greatest whore-mistress in Avignon, if I'd kept my mind on my body and my body under a man. Fame and fortune thrown away and for what?

Lefranc Respectability. They'll never look down on you again from a hole in the ceiling. They'll look up, Madam.

Marie And for respectability's sake we lose our self-respect. Men like you've always preyed on women like us. Before I had a business.

Lefranc Calm yourself, Madam. You've entered marriage, that's a business too. We're only interested in using your money, not your private parts. As husbands, we prefer the simulated enthusiasm of a whore to the dignified acquiescence of a wife.

Pellico Speak for yourself, Lefranc. I'll copulate till dry. I plan to spend the equivalent of two hundred florins a night on forbidden dainties.

Monselet Leave the higher-tariff items till later, Master Pellico. Content yourself with a quick kiss on the lips as is the custom . . . (*Drumbeats as* **Scarron** *and* **Druce** *with two* **Guards** *enter Upstage Left and are escorted on to the gallows in chains.*) My Right Worshipful Magistrates, it's time to do your duty.

Pellico Duty? Since the plague left us, all that's left us is duty.

Nooses are placed round **Druce***'s and* **Scarron***'s necks.* **Lefranc** *and* **Pellico** *put on black hats. The drumming ends.*

Lefranc The accused, known as the Black Ravens, come before this seat of Justice for greasing. That is, spreading plague pus to stimulate the pestilence which was a time of luxury for them. They did also cut the throats of the rich and entered their houses to rob them. We, the Magistrates of the High Council of Auxerre, do hereby solemnly pass sentence.

Pellico, Lefranc *and their* **Wives** *fall under a fusillade of old shoes, thrown by* **Flote, Marguerite** *and* **Frapper***, as they enter Downstage Right.*

Flote Are we late for the ceremony? We mean to drink the happiness of the brides and grooms and sing naughty songs outside the bedroom windows.

Monselet You missed the wedding but you're in time for the funeral.

Marguerite Archbishop Monselet, you're back, the danger must be over.

Frapper You're lucky, Sister Marguerite, he'd never accept that from a smaller woman.

Lefranc We're hanging these men. They've confessed to being greasers.

Flote *and the others turn and see* **Druce** *and* **Scarron** *on the gallows.*

Druce Ladies, I've serviced you, do me a service now. Don't let 'em shovel cold dirt into my mouth. I've claimed so many with my sugar-scented breath. Oh, my fancy never died. I've been a rampant face-maker, fathered more into this world than I've ever taken out. Weighed in the balance, I come down on the side of life.

Marguerite Ladies, he blows great horns of joy, the love-look is on him. Show him mercy.

Camille What's mercy's colour, size, shape, weight? What price mercy? We can't afford it. Respectability's cleaned us out. Hang him. Let him dangle.

Druce I've never let it dangle, not ever, ladies.

Marie Take heart, hanged men have the mightiest erections. When you go limp, you go hard. Hang 'em.

Flote Before you can hang 'em there must be a trial, lawyers, Inns-of-Court men, arguing pro and contra. (*He puts on a lawyer's gown.*) No case too small, no fee too large. You prisoners are the victims of the grossest injustice and judicial corruption. Have no fear, your case is irrefutable. Just one question – what are you accused of?

Marguerite (*putting on a lawyer's gown*) Your Worships, *de minimus no curat lex* – the law does not concern itself with trifles.

Frapper (*producing his dummy in a little lawyer's gown*) *De similibus idem est judicium* – in similar cases the verdict is the selfsame.

Marguerite It's hard being a lawyer, lying awake nights worrying about your clients, imagining what they'll do to you if they ever get out of prison.

Flote Your Worships, must we wheel out the bloody engines of Justice again, stocks for vagrants, whips for harlots, ropes, weights and brands for felons, knife and gibbet for murderers? God's put away His weeding knife and scythe, so should we. The power of forgiveness spreads like a garden; unused it recedes from us. Sun and sky plead for these men. The West Wind too. But speech is blasphemous, silence a lie; beyond the speech and silence, blasphemy and lie is another way. (*He calls softly.*) *Chick-chick-chick, sweer-sweer, toe-toe, cee-tu, cee-tu, tirruffi, tirruffi.*

Monselet *C–c–c–r–r–r–k–k*. The God of Mercy said,
'Thine eye shall not spare the murderer.' Hang 'em.

Frapper Before your Worships do, I wish to bring
vital new evidence to your attention. Your Worships,
the accused have money.

Pellico Money? You show great skill, Brother Frapper.
A Paris Inns-of-Court lawyer couldn't've put it better.

Lefranc Some lawyers know law, others know judges.
There are few legal problems money can't solve. Father
Flote, you should've mentioned this vital new evidence.
We impose a harsher sentence now. A fine of five
hundred gold florins will bite deeper than hemp rope.
No protests, Archbishop, this is Juro Civil no Canno
Juro.

Monselet Five hundred gold ones can purge rape and
murder in a civil court but not vile sedition. These men
preached equality!

Flote No, they merely advocated forming a moderate
Party of Slow, Lawful, Orthodox Progress – S.L.O.P.,
SLOP.

Pellico On the rumoured charge of preaching equality,
we shall give you a suspended sentence – a week
hanging by your thumbs.

All *offer congratulations to* **Druce** *and* **Scarron**.

Scarron Rabbit-suckers, rather the Milky Way round
my throat, eternity in my ears, than SLOP. I killed the
Fats with the ferocity of an avenging angel.

Druce Not me, not me, I was always a loving flounder,
quick to love, slow to die.

Scarron I loved too when I was greasing 'em dead.
The poor are like trees in winter, nothing green about
'em. To make that part of mankind happy, I'd happily
slaughter the rest.

Flote Your Worships, torture's loosened his wits.
Gentles, never confess anything till you feel rigor mortis
setting in.

Scarron No, it's time to hang me out. I'm one who
missed his chance. I failed. I broke the eggs but I didn't
know how to make the omelette. I dreamed, dream-
wide of a different ordered world, no will yielding to a
superior will, no blocks, knives, axes, swords. But I've
seen the rich fall, the priests run, the mighty tremble
and that's something better than Christ's palmy
triumph on an ass entering Jerusalem!

A **Guard** *pulls the lever at a signal from* **Lefranc,** *and*
Druce *and* **Scarron** *fall through a trapdoor, then are*
jerked up high. As **Flote** *and the* **Floties** *bow their heads,*
Pellico, Lefranc, Camille *and* **Marie** *look up intently*
at **Druce.**

Flote Sky dark as mud, God no longer tickles me *ooh-*
aah-ooh. The warm milk turns to vinegar in my mouth.
The plague's past but there's no light only a dark that
sucks out the light and my voice is a shout in a dream.
Lord save me from the hooded angel, the four-breasted
bird, the shrieking flower. Lord save me from the
heaviness which is the end to mirth.

Drumbeats. **Grez** *and two* **Flagellants** *enter Upstage*
Right, chained and gagged and escorted by two **Guards** *in*
black armour. **Toulon** *walks with them. The* **Flagellants**
are tied to the stakes Upstage Right by the **Guards.** *The*
drumming stops.

Monselet Pertinacious heretics, you continue to
disobey the Holy Father's edict. The stake is the only
remedy for such disobedience.

Lefranc But it comes expensive when the authorities
have to bear the whole cost of wood, rope and straw.

Flote *crosses and removes* **Grez**'s *gag.*

Monselet Now they'll talk so much, their tonsils'll get

frostbite. Where's your obedience, Father Flote? I speak
for the Universal Church. Father Toulon knows.

Toulon I know the sooner I never see you again the
better it'll be for both of us when we meet, Archbishop.

He removes the **First Flagellant***'s, and* **Frapper**, *the*
Second Flagellant*'s gags.*

Flote Master Grez, I fear our friend Master Scarron
has fallen through a trapdoor. He'd've hurt himself if he
hadn't had a rope round his neck at the time.

Grez And we'll fry; fricassee'ed Flagellants. Father Flote,
put away your Nose$. There's nothing for laughter here.
The divine evaporates. The brutal alone remains.

Flote Never, we'll fight it down. Come, let's give 'em
the play and save them – and the darkening world.
Bembo! Le Grue! The play, the play!

Monselet First the Flagellants.

Pellico First the play. The frying can come later.

Beating his drum loudly, **Bembo** *enters Stage Right with*
Le Grue *pulling the small portable stage Stage Left.*
Flote, Frapper, Marguerite *and* **Toulon** *hurriedly*
exit Downstage Left.

Bembo Oyez! Oyez! Christ's Clowns present a brand
new activity. It is our version of the Nativity. The
Christ child is born into a world much like this one.
Will you laugh or weep when you see what's said and
done? . . . (*The* **Audience**, *including* **Patris, Sabine,**
Artisans *and* **Peasants**, *enter shivering Upstage Centre*
between the gallows and stakes and join **Pellico,**
Lefranc, Camille, Marie *and* **Monselet**.) Oyez! Oyez!
Our new play is called *Christ and Kings*. And shows
Herod, Balthazar and the rest. Who were there at the
birth of sweet Jesus. Our first scene is at Herod's Court.
He is a king, he seems to loom. But he couldn't find his
way out of an empty room.

There is a fanfare as **Toulon,** *in robes and a red nose, enters Downstage Left as the High Priest Noncios and places a throne opposite the portable stage whilst* **Bembo** *exits behind it, Stage Left.*

Toulon I am the High Priest Noncios and I command you all keep silence for one of the rulers of the earth – Jude et Rex Israel – King Herod!

Another fanfare. There is a scuffling behind the portable stage curtain, muffled curses and finally **Flote,** *as Herod, crawls from under it, crown and robes askew and red nose gleaming. As the* **Audience** *laughs,* **Flote** *comes down off the stage and crosses to the throne.*

Flote I'm a king, so why can't I make a good entrance, Noncios? Kill whoever's responsible. Why do people take an instant dislike to me, Noncios?

Toulon It saves time, Sire.

Flote Now hear, all you serfs, vassals and slaves, I, King Herod, decree the word 'wicked' shall be replaced by the word 'noble'.

Toulon A far-sighted decision, noble Herod.

Flote Kill him!

Le Grue *stumbles in Stage Left.*

Le Grue I want to make my home in your kingdom of Judah.

Flote This man is an idiot!

Le Grue I'm also blind.

Flote A blind idiot – that's different. What do you do?

Le Grue Nothing. I'm a nobleman.

Flote Noncios, make him a government minister with the rest of the nobility. (*His crown falls over his head.*) Plagues of Egypt, I'm blind!

Le Grue You're blind? I'm the one who's blind. You wouldn't last a day blind. It takes character!

He exits Stage Right. **Flote** *recovers.* **Toulon** *gives him a sceptre.*

Flote Who else comes to my door this morning, Noncios?

Toulon Well, Sire, there's a Tinman, a Strawman and a Lion outside looking for a little girl with ruby-coloured slippers.

Flote Who isn't, Noncios, who isn't?

Toulon Yes indeed, Sire. There are also three Kings from the East.

Flote Kings are my sort of people. Open the gates and let 'em in.

Toulon *claps his hands and the richly gowned figures of* **Bembo** *and the* **Boutros Brothers,** *complete with golden crutches, enter, bowing, Stage Left.*

Bembo Most noble Herod. (**Flote** *hits* **Toulon** *with his sceptre.*) I'm Balthazar, this is King Jasper of Taurus and this Melchior, King of Aginar. Twelve days ago a bright star appeared in our heavens. We followed it here to Jerusalem, for our prophets foretold it would lead us to a newborn babe who will be the Saviour of Mankind, a King of Kings.

Flote Why wasn't I informed, Noncios? I spend a fortune on informers and all I get is information. A King of Kings you say?

Boutros One It's why we came bearing gifts in hope he'll remember us in his coming days of power.

Boutros Two It never hurts to be on the winning side. And all the signs confirm this babe's a winner.

Flote On your way back, tell us who the lucky little bas– fellow is. So I can pay him homage.

Bembo A noble thought, noble Herod.

Flote *hits* **Toulon** *again as* **Bembo** *and the* **Boutros Brothers** *exit Stage Right, bowing.* **Flote** *chuckles.*

Flote Idiots. They're all idiots. When they return, kill them. But only after they've told us where this kingly babe is hiding. I promise you his reign's going to be very short. One king in Judah's more than enough. Why is it me who always has this trouble? Messiahs, Saviours, one-legged kings. Did you see, Noncios, those two only had one leg apiece? Odd. First thing I noticed.

As **Flote** *and* **Toulon** *exit Stage Left behind the portable stage, its curtains open to show a traditional Nativity scene in the Bethlehem stable with* **Frapper** *as Joseph,* **Marguerite** *as Mary and a doll as the infant Jesus in the manger.*

Monselet Anathema! You mock God. For the authority of kings, yea even Herod's, comes from God, and in mocking them you mock Him.

Pellico Mirth and jollity's not enough for them now. They want to make us think.

Camille That's not fair.

Marie We didn't come here to think.

Lefranc See, they pour their black pitch on the Holy Family. That stuttering simikin's not Joseph and that licentious nun's never been a mother or a virgin.

Sabine My mother was a saint in her own lifetime.

Patris We worship the ground she's buried under.

Frapper *and* **Marguerite** *continue the Nativity.*

Frapper I–I–I'm J–J–Joseph. (*He picks up the Jesus doll and loses his stammer.*) I shiver. Is it dread of Herod or of the cold?

Marguerite I'm Mary – yes, I *have* been a virgin and a

mother. Not both at once, of course. That only happened to the Virgin Mary – that's me. Stop complaining, Joseph. It's all your fault. I leave you to make the travel arrangements and look where we spend the night. And stop shivering. Our blessed laughing babe will soon warm us. He brings us light and love and hope. He's a token of God's tender care for mankind, coochie-coochie.

Monselet I've heard enough! This is a nest of pertinacious heretics all. In defiance of the Papal Bull October 20th, 1349, the cursed Brethren of the Cross, the Flagellants, remain unrelaxed heretics, and are hereby handed over to the secular arm for punishment. Burn 'em.

Lefranc Burn 'em.

As **Flote** *and the other* **Clowns** *rush in Downstage Left and Right, still in their Nativity costumes, light plays over the* **Flagellants**.

Flote I'm bent double.

Marguerite It's only clowns like us that speak of love, laughter and the life everlasting.

Toulon God is strictly neutral.

Grez Stand easy, friends, it's much easier to die well than to live well. Fiercer fires than these scald my soul. We've been tricked, sold dogmeat for mutton. We embraced pain when we should've tried to eliminate it. You were right, friend Flote. God's a joker gleeful at the sight of men staggering under the axe blows of life. He doesn't want our suffering.

First Flagellant Now he tells us!

Second Flagellant What's it matter? This is my last chance. No more cries, *ahhh-ahhh*. I've got a thousand last words I've never used. 'Miasma.' That's one, and 'harmony' and 'sunset'. Last words are important.

Makes a man's name remembered after. 'Sunrise' –
there's another . . . 'star-stretched' . . . 'pear-shaped'
. . . 'Zion' . . . *ahhh-ahhh.*

*The light flickers fiercely over them as they burn, writhe
and die to loud drumming as* **Clement VI** *enters in
dazzling white, Upstage Centre between the burning*
Flagellants *and hanged* **Black Ravens**. *He is
accompanied by four* **Guards**, *the* **Herald** *and a
bejewelled* **Rochfort**. *The* **Audience** *and* **Floties** *kneel.
The flickering lights on the* **Flagellants** *die down as*
Monselet *quickly crosses and kisses the ring on* **Clement
VI**'*s finger.*

Monselet Now spoil, rack, pierce these Noses with
your cold iron, Holy Father.

Clement VI Archbishop, your power yields to one
greater. Dwindle to your normal size. My new
secretary, Count de Rochfort, has told me all I need to
know about the Floties.

Monselet Your Holiness, why do you have a cynic like
this Rochfort as your secretary?

Clement VI Because all my secretaries become cynics
in the end. I thought this time, why wait? Fathers
Flote, Toulon, Sister Marguerite, come.

Marguerite, **Flote** *and* **Toulon** *stand before* **Clement
VI**.

Monselet But Your Holiness, 'Count' Rochfort used to
be of their company, a Red-Nosed Flotie.

Marguerite Now he's joined the new generation of
Judas that walk the earth. You had the chance to
transcend yourself and be my very perfect knight. And
you gave it up – for what?

Rochfort Everything. I entered my father's house
another Joseph and it was all mine. How my family
embraced me when I returned and how they wept when

I kicked them out. No man forgets where he buried the hatchet. Thanks to His Holiness, I've estates, position, power. And I gave up nothing except a little love. No, I still love.

Flote Talking of love isn't love; it's the acting of love that's love.

Marguerite Go spill your guts out in a field for not waiting for love.

Rochfort Love I can buy on any corner, market-day.

Clement VI I've found me a fine ravaging wolf, eh? I feel safe with his treachery and greed. It's honest, God-driven men like you, Father Flote, I can't trust. You live by no rules except what's in your heart. Without rules and laws, every man becomes a law unto himself. So I must give your company strict rules and orders.

Toulon What need we of rules and orders? There's no buying or selling here as at Avignon, saw-teeth and hook-claws. We hold all things in common. No man is wronged where no man is a possessor.

Clement VI So, Father Toulon, you've changed horses in midstream?

Toulon Yes, the old one drowned, Holy Father.

Clement VI Unless you submit, Father Flote, I'll grind your Noses into dust along with the Flagellants and Ravens.

Flote What must I do, Your Holiness?

Clement VI Please the populace with passing shows; relax them with culinary delights – meringues, jellies and whipped cream. But give them no meat to chew on.

Flote But the Lord is my consuming fire. He lights my soul; eyes and tongue aflame. I'm still combustible.

Clement VI *takes a water bottle from* **Rochfort** *and pours the contents over* **Flote**.

Clement VI Obey or die.

Flote I'll not hang or burn up my friends, Holy Father. The dream fades, the rain's colder, the stone's in my throat. The Floties will submit.

Clement VI Then continue with your show. Make us smile and forget it. (*He crosses himself.*) Pray for me.

Toulon Why do you cross yourself, Holy Father?

Clement VI I've crossed everyone else. Rise, my children, and see the birth of the Christ child.

The kneeling **Audience** *rises.* **Marguerite** *rejoins* **Frapper** *on the portable stage and* **Flote** *and* **Toulon** *disappear behind it as* **Bembo** *enters Upstage Right, banging his drum.*

Bembo Oyez, oyez. In a stable the infant Jesus chose to lie. Amongst the poor who never die. They've never lived so how can they die? But now, Joseph and Mary once more take their bow.

He exits Upstage Left whilst **Marguerite** *takes the baby from the crib.*

Marguerite Lookee, look how my sweeting laughs. Oh he's a prince divine.

Frapper (*taking the baby*) All mothers say that about their sons. He's comely, full of Godhead. But why call him Jesus? It should've been Ezekiel. That's an easy name to forget. (*A star is dropped from the Flies and hangs in front of the small stage.*) Strange. I've just seen a bright start, and it's still morning.

Marguerite You've been drinking again.

Bembo *and the* **Boutros Brothers,** *as the three Kings, enter Upstage Right bearing gifts. They kneel in front of the portable stage.*

Boutros One Hail Lord, I bring this cup of gold in token you are without equal.

Boutros Two Hail Lord, I bring this cup of incense in token we bow down and worship thee.

Bembo Hail Lord, I bring this cup of myrrh in token you'll restore mankind to life. (*They put the three cups on the small stage.*) Only remember in Thy coming years of triumph, kings paid you tribute. We bend knee to you so your followers will bend knee to us after. (*The baby gurgles agreement; they rise.*) We promised to see Herod again. If that royal clodpoll had more sense, he'd be a halfwit. When he's said 'hello', he's told you all he knows. Just take up your child and flee to Egypt and you'll be safe.

The **Three Kings** *exit laughing, Upstage Right, whilst* **Frapper** *and* **Marguerite** *frantically scoop up the gifts, baby, crib and straw and follow them. The small stage curtain falls as* **Flote,** *as Herod, rushes on from behind the portable stage with* **Toulon** *as Noncios.*

Flote Out, out, out! Bring me my cleavers, chisels, meat hooks. Not one king returned as promised – there's friendship, there's gratitude. Where do I find this miraculous babe, this future king of Judah? Where? Everywhere! Ah, you have to get up pretty early in the morning to catch Herod.

Toulon About twelve noon. You must be careful, Sire. Even the shepherds are beginning to talk.

Flote Influential shepherds?

Toulon Jewish shepherds.

Flote Intellectuals! Let 'em talk. Wheel in my knights! (**Le Grue** *and* **Bembo** *enter Upstage Right dressed like the Guards, only their 'armour' is made of paper.*) Sir Knights, there's a traitor risen in Judah who usurps my authority. Go seek out and kill all the newborn males in Zion.

Marguerite *enters from behind the portable stage as a*

poor woman in a tattered shawl, cradling two dolls in swaddling clothes.

Bembo We're men of noble blood, Herod, not butchers.

Toulon 'Happy shall he be that taketh and dasheth thy little ones against the stones.' Psalm 137.

Flote 'The little ones die or you die.' Herod 138, 139, 140.

Le Grue If it's a choice between them and us, it quickly dwindles down to us. I see the necessity of it.

Bembo Another plague has entered the world. It's wrong but we are under orders.

The **Boutros Brothers** *enter Upstage Right as Guards in paper armour, carrying a large wicker basket filled with dolls in swaddling clothes which they tip on to the floor.*

Marguerite Don't take them from me! They are my babes, my joys, my lovely days.

But **Bembo** *and* **Le Grue** *take her dolls and throw them with the others. As the parody* **Guards** *move towards them, they make the sounds of babies crying and screaming.* **Marguerite** *joins in the babies' terrified howls whilst the* **Audience** *shouts.*

Sabine Stop! Are you men?

Patris Spit on your orders!

Monselet We were promised soothing syrup.

Lefranc But see what they give us.

Pellico Where are the jollies?

Marguerite Don't cry, my little lambs, my lambkins. If you had lived you would have learned to love your rulers for the way their softest whisper is obeyed like a shouted command. But you only lived long enough to feel their sharp swords. (*She slowly kneels.*) Lamikins,

lamikins, go down, go down. All go down. Babylon go down, Ninevah go down, go down with me.

The cries of the 'babies' finally stop.

Clement VI It isn't funny!

Flote No, it isn't funny. In the days of pestilence we could be funny but now we're back to normal, life is too serious to be funny. God's a joker but His jests fall flat. (*He takes off his red nose.*) It isn't funny when they feed us lies, crush the light, sweep the stars from the heavens. Isn't funny now inequality's in, naming rich and poor, mine and thine. Isn't funny when power rules and men manifest all their deeds in oppression. Isn't funny till we throw out the old rubbish and gold and silver rust. Then it'll be funny. (*He tosses the red nose on to the ground.*) Holy Father, I can't submit. I tried to lift Creation from bondage with mirth. Wrong. Our humour was a way of evading truth, avoiding responsibility. Our mirth was used to divert attention whilst the strong ones slunk back to their thrones and palaces where they stand now in their saggy breeches and paper crowns, absurd like me.

Clement VI Stand aside from that man. He is anathema!

All *shrink back instinctively from* **Flote** *who takes off his paper crown and throws it to* **Rochfort**.

Flote It's hard to die. Only the young talk of that easy leap into death. I tell you, when Death comes a-knock-knock-knocking the best course is to run. But just sometimes you have to stand your ground and dance!

Flote *slowly moves forward, arms stretched wide, feet rhythmically stamping as he begins dancing the Greek Kolo.*

Clement VI Stand aside from that man. He is marked for death.

Toulon Flote, you're a great fool. But now's the time for final choosing. On the one side, the Holy Fathers, Archbishops, Goldmerchants, Herods and Kings. On the other, the Fools, male and female, Father F, Sister M, Bembo, Le Grue and the rest. Reason can't help me choose. So I choose without any reason other than my taste for good company and my aversion to bad. (*He takes off his red nose and throws it on the ground beside Flote's.*) Once I was hot for obedience and scorched the earth with fire. Father Flote showed me how to illuminate it with kindness and mirth. You're a mad zad, Father Flote, and I never learnt to play a tune on my head or rub my knees together, like the 'Human Grasshopper', but I'd rather rot, lose my life than your friendship. Though I'm no dancer, I'm dancing with you.

Stamping his feet rhythmically, he takes his place on the right of **Flote**. *Arms on each other's shoulders they dance as* **Marguerite** *takes off her red nose and puts it with the others.*

Marguerite Pig-gelders, you'll never be the men your mothers were. I could've built cities, pleasured a thousand strong men. And shall I die with this undone? But you can't saw sawdust. It's over. We lived the vision, rolled back the stony heart a little and the glory is measureless. Nothing to lament, let's pierce the circumference of Hell and dance!

She takes her place on the left of **Flote**. *They put their arms on each other's shoulders and, with* **Toulon** *on the other side, dance, as* **Le Grue** *comes forward and throws his false nose with the others.*

Le Grue I'd like to stay with you but I'm blind. I'm a blind coward, you see. Lived in this darkness, frightened to face that darkness. You understand. Must love you and leave you. Feet, do your stuff. Run. Feet! Feet! (*He starts to dance.*) No, run feet, run. Feet?! Feet?! Look, Ma, I'm dancing!

Despite himself he links up with the line of dancers as
Frapper *puts his false nose with the others.*

Frapper I just thought a thought but the thought I
thought wasn't the thought I thought I thought.
Thanks to Father Flote I'm no longer a shy fly in a flue.
I can say 'boo' to all of you.

He links up with the dancers as **Bembo** *throws his nose
on the pile.*

Bembo Why wait till my hair turns white? I choose my
death. Three days in a hot oven and perhaps I'll rise
again.

He links arms with the line of dancers whilst the **Boutros
Brothers** *throw their noses on the pile.*

Boutros One Don't leave us out.

Boutros Two We're the professional dancers.

*They throw away their crutches and join up on either end
of the line of dancers. Arms linked, they circle the stage,
stamping rhythmically, whilst the* **Audience** *clap their
hands in time to the dance. At the climax the* **Floties**
come Downstage, shouting and laughing. **Clement VI**
raises his hand.

Clement VI Let them taste it!

The **Guards** *raise their crossbows and fire. There is the
magnified sound of dozens of arrows in flight. The*
Dancers *are hit. Some cry out, others gasp as they spin,
stagger, fall and finally lie still. Only* **Flote** *remains
miraculously unharmed. He looks down at the bodies all
around, then steps forward smiling.*

Flote This reminds me of the condemned man who was
being taken up the steps of the gallows and suddenly
burst out laughing. 'You mustn't do that,' said the
executioner, shocked. 'This is a solemn occasion.'
'Sorry,' said the prisoner. 'But I just can't help it. You
see you're hanging the wrong man . . .' How long is it

good for a man to live? Only as long as he does not prefer death to life. I've seen men die sitting, lying, dropping on their knees like bulls, but never upside down, standing on their heads. One must have sport even with death.

He kneels and slowly levers himself up till he is standing on his head. **Clement VI** *raises his hand again.*

First Guard Your Holiness, we can shoot a man in the back, but not standing on his head. It isn't natural.

Rochfort *takes the crossbow from the* **First Guard**, *aims it at* **Flote** *and fires. There is the magnified sound of a single arrow in flight, followed by a thud as it hits its mark.* **Flote** *topples over, dead.* **Rochfort** *plays a funeral air on his flute and the* **Audience** *silently disperses Upstage Centre.*

Clement VI Build them no monuments; no funeral urns, no civil rites must mark their termination. We have no further use for them. Let the Floties sleep forgotten, their light, ashes. They have never been. Sand out their names. Yet to be nameless and have lived, showing how men should live, is a true remembrance. The Canaanite woman helping Jesus lives more happily without a name than Salome with one. Better the nameless good Samaritan than Herod, these poor clowns than Pope Clement VI. Father Flote thought he'd failed. No man fails completely who shows us glory. I live, rule, drink blood. Say a good word for me, Father to Father. Wind blow the poppy seeds over them and us, *aaaaawwh.* (*He howls softly as the lights fade down to a spot on the pile of noses.*)
Heaven is dark and the earth a secret.
The cold snaps our bones, we shiver.
And dogs sniff round us, licking their paws.
Monsters eat our soul.
There is no way back.
Until God calls us to shadow.
So we rage at the wall and howl.

Go down, she said, go down with me.
World go down, dark go down,
Universe and infinity go down,
Go down with me, *aaaaaaawwh.*

Epilogue

White mist and a single Spot on the pile of false red noses Downstage Left. The ghostly voices of **Flote** *and the others are heard in snatches of conversation and sounds from the past.*

Flote's Voice Lord, as this bread upon the table was in separate grains and being gathered together became one good thing, so let all men and women be gathered together into one family . . .

Sounds of eating.

Brodin's Voice I'm for deep pots, wide pans . . .

Toulon's Voice Ah, what food these morsels be . . .

Marguerite's Voice Don't eat so fast, Le Grue. It's the first time I've seen anyone get sparks from a spoon . . .

Le Grue's Voice Neat's tongue! Why aren't there neat's tongues . . .?

Frapper's Voice The seething sea ceaseth seething . . .

Bembo's Voice Passable . . .

There is the sound of **Sonnerie***'s bells.*

Brodin's Voice Marvellously well told, Master Bells . . .

Scarron's Voice There's no Heaven or Hell but if a man has good fortune and lives well that's Heaven, *caw-caw* . . .

Grez's Voice By suffering, men find their true strength *ahhhh* . . .

Flote's Voice Every jest should be a small revolution . . .

Boutros One Don't leave us out . . .

Boutros Two We're professional dancers . . .

All (*singing*) 'Join together that's the plan. It's the secret. Man helps man . . .'

Flote's Voice It isn't funny. God's a joker but his jests fall flat . . . (*The magnified sounds of arrows being fired.*) No, it isn't funny. It's serious . . . Oh, but, oh, a world ruled by seriousness alone is an old world, a grave, graveyard world. Mirth makes the green sap rise and the wildebeest run mad. Not the mirth born of anxiety and fear but the mirth of children and sages, the laughter of compassion and joy.

Toulon's Voice Father Flote, this was to be a résumé of what we said when we were alive. You never said that.

Flote's Voice I should have done.

Toulon's Voice Father, we're about to be ushered into the Creator's presence. No old jests. If He asks how we got up here, please don't sneeze and say, 'Flu.' We've other matters to discuss.

Marguerite's Voice I want to find out how He came to make such a botch job of everything.

Frapper's Voice I'm going to ask Him if He meant giraffes and camels to look like that or was it an accident?

Bembo's Voice God's up for judgement.

A single clear trumpet note in the distance and tinkling bells.

Toulon's Voice That's us, Brothers.

Le Grue's Voice I can see a light.

Brodin's Voice Father, we were famous but do you think we'll live?

Ghostly laughter.

All (*singing*) 'Join together. No weak link. Must keep trying. Else we sink. Join together all of you. Pierre Frapper and blind Le Grue. Charlie Bembo and the other two . . .'

Flote's Voice God, count us in.

The sound of their voices grows faint as the Spot on the pile of noses fades out.

The Spirit of Man

I am, like all the others, trying to define the indefinable, fathom the unfathomable and screw the inscrutable.

I wanted *The Spirit of Man* to be about faith and language. Only language irrigates an event with a value that extends beyond the fact it merely exists; only language outlasts the dying it describes.

As for faith, *The Spirit of Man* is like the story of the rabidly anti-Christian Jew who asked for a Catholic Priest on his deathbed. The Priest received the old man into the Church and gave him the last rites. Afterwards, the old man's son asked him angrily, 'Why did you do it? You're a Jew who's always hated Christ. Now you're a Christian.' With his last breath the old man snarled, 'That's right, another one of the bastards less!'

Which reminds me of the story of Rabbi Zusia who, before he died, said, 'When I face the celestial tribunal I shall not be asked why I was not Abraham, Jacob or Moses, but why I was not Rabbi Zusia.'

Peter Barnes
1990

I

A HAND WITCH OF THE SECOND STAGE

A Hand Witch of the Second Stage was first broadcast by BBC TV as the first part of the trio *The Spirit of Man* on 23 August 1989 with the following cast:

Father Nerval	Peter Bayliss
Marie Blin	Dilys Laye
Claude Delmas	Clive Merrison
Henri Mondor	John Turner

Directed by Peter Barnes
Produced by Richard Langridge
Music by Stephen Deutsch

Darkness. A choir sings the majestic Dies Irae.

Quick fade up on a large prison, 1437 with a crucifix on one wall.
Marie Blin *is spreadeagled on a raised rack in the centre. The
Executioner,* **Henri Mondor**, *in a leather apron, stands to her right
with a brazier with hot irons in it and a large bucket beside him.* **Father
Nerval** *is seated on a podium to the left whilst the chief witness,*
Claude Delmas, *stands opposite, swaying backwards and forwards.*

Delmas Besom – besom – besom. Oh Yamma, Amma, Ahrsman,
she had a magical amulet marked with the seal of Solomon –
big – and the pentagram stamped on her forehead here, here,
here; hot needles riven up through brain parts, wrinkled warts
on the soul and all the time live toads lie hidden in the bread!
Raphael couldn't touch them, never, she was the Queen of
Egypt dancing backward to Jerusalem or wherever, the puki,
pooka and mashim, the seven signs of the Zodiac and men
cocking up their legs and women naked as the moon: bellies
floating off into the night, next week it'll be knees and elbows!
Oh, incubi and succubi, oh ki tu la puh SKILAR . . .

Mondor *throws water from the bucket over him.*

Nerval Master Delmas, this is a preliminary investigation into
the charge of witchcraft brought against Marie Blin and if it is
to end with the guilty verdict we all desire and passed on to
higher authority, you must deliver your testimony *soberly*. We
appreciate you've had a hard soul-jarring, seen down into the
Pit. But facts, give me facts, facts condemn the guilty. Give me
strict account and I'll give her strict justice. Where, when, how?
Dates, times, places.

Mondor Let me suck it out, rack, screws, hot irons.

Nerval Silence when you interrupt me, Master Mondor. Your
hour comes later. Dates, times, places, Master Delmas.

Delmas Date, October 31st, 1437. Time, midnight. Place, Lyon
Cemetery. I was on my way home from 'The Swan' tavern,
Father. I need that warm company of an evening since my wife
and children were pierced by plague worms, my crops blasted by
whirlwinds, my house consumed by Firebrands. God's Will be
done, though why He has to do it so completely to me is a
mystery. It's someone else, someone else, else, else is the cause!

They look at **Marie.**

Nerval It's my opinion that wherever evil is going on, women are at the bottom of it. Continue.

Delmas There was a mist that night, clouds across the moon but I saw what I saw – the accursed Marie Blin dancing over the graves. There were others but cloaked, masked, creeping round a cauldron, throwing in dead lizards, rat's tails and rock arsenic, besom – besom – besom. Oh Yamma, Amma, Ahrsman, puki pooka and mashim, SKILAR . . . (**Mondor** *throws more water over him.*) I was dragged over and saw Marie Blin anoint our hands and a pile of broomsticks with the cauldron's foul stuff. We put the broomsticks between our legs. Soul's doom, the brooms reared up, up and up, and we were night-flying across the face of the moon. She was leading. Down, down below was Lyon and the dark fields. Ahhh, I clung hard . . .

Mondor If God had wanted man to fly, he'd've given us wings.

Delmas An owl flew past me and perched on the end of Marie Blin's broom and they talked owl-talk. I heard them 'too-wit-too-wooing'. We circled Monterray Wood and started coming down . . . *eeee . . . eee . . ee . . ahh.*

Nerval What happened?

Delmas I hit a tree. When I picked myself up I saw we were in a clearing. There were some 30 men and women there, I couldn't see their faces but they were at a long table full of quarters of mutton, haunches of venison, sauce bowls of broth, plates of custard dainties and great bowls of wines. Some of the women were washing their feet in them.

Nerval In the wine? Horrible. Horrible. The Devil and Woman entered the world at the same time. Continue.

Delmas Yes, he was there. At the top of the table, between two naked girls was this huge black dog, baying at the moon.

Nerval What sort of dog?

Delmas Great Dane . . . or a German Shepherd . . . or it could've been a St Bernard.

Nerval No matter, it was *black.*

Delmas Black; absolutely black; blacker than black. Marie Blin rushed over to it and kissed its muzzle and the dog bit one of the girls on the right breast and left the mark of the pentagon on it and I saw it wasn't really a black dog baying at the moon but a green monkey.

Mondor A green monkey – that's a new one. But green's the Devil's colour.

Delmas It was preaching a Sabbat sermon. Nobody could hear what it said for it spoke a monkey growl but they all bowed to it and Marie Blin and the other Sorcerers rushed over and dragged me down to pay homage. And as they chanted the Liturgy of Hell, I saw a long crucifix on the ground which they made me walk on, whilst vice-haunted wantons cavorted and did spit on it – *spit – spit – spit*! I cried out for Christ's protection. Sweet Jesus, Sweet Jesus, save me in the name of the Father . . . As I was dragged nearer the green monkey, I saw it'd turned into a steaming goat with a devil's head. I was forced down, pressed down, 'gainst that hairy bottom *ugh – ugh – ugh*. My mouth burnt red-hot, my nostrils filled with sulphur-stench, tu puzzi, tu puzzi and Marie Blin spitting and the great goat King of Hell and Death, steaming and stinking. O Yamma, Amma, Ahrsman, puki pooka oh hi tu la puh SKILAR . . . (**Mondor** *throws more water over him.*) After that kiss, I swooned, cock-crowed and I was back in the empty graveyard, my throat aflame and in my head two hundred and thirty-four fire demons pounded iron anvils. I staggered up, glorying in God's infinite mercy and determined to expose this Archdeaconess of Hell, this leader of Sabbats, this witch, this Marie Blin.

Nerval Mother Church in her compassion grants the accuser and judge the right to the confiscated property of those condemned for sorcery. It will be but poor compensation for your night of tribulation, Master Delmas. However, you've done your duty and given us the hard facts we need to judge this woman guilty of witchcraft. Now, 'tis Master

Mondor's turn to do his duty, for she'll deny your facts and so must face immersion in water, boiling oil and purging fires.

Mondor Oh, the guilty deny their guilt always, Father. My instruments root out all such. Screws, saws, pincers, hot irons are tools of truth, God's tools for every turning rack-notch brings the sinner nearer to repentance, nearer to Paradise through pain. Pain, pain, there's only forgiveness on pain, blood and pain, pain and pain! SKILAR . . .

He empties the remains of the bucket of water over himself.

Nerval There's no escape for you, Marie Blin. No man or Devil can help you now. You hang alone against the power of the Church and State, which is set to crush you as a malignant growth. All that you say will be used against you. Marie Blin, you are accused of witchcraft, that you did worship the Devil. Do you deny the charge?

Marie No.

Nerval You were right, Master Mondor, the guilty always deny their guilt, 'tis what proves them guilty. Their Prince is the Prince of Liars, so they lie, lie and lie. Heat the irons, prepare the oil, I ask again, Marie Blin, in the Name of the Father, Son and Holy Ghost, do you practise the Black Arts? Are you a witch?

Marie Yes.

Nerval Mondor, the irons burn the truth out. (**Mondor** *selects an iron from the brazier.*) Marie Blin, you are to be delivered to the secular arm to be . . . What did you say?

Marie Yes.

Nerval Yes?

Marie Yes.

Nerval No, you didn't understand the question. I put it to you that you are an accursed witch.

Marie Yes.

Nerval You mean . . . yes . . . you are?

Marie Yes.

The men stare. **Mondor** *drops the sharp iron onto his foot in surprise, reacts and suppresses a great cry of pain.*

Mondor No . . . that answer comes later . . . (*He pulls the iron out of his foot and sways.*) After I've used the irons on you.

Marie I'll save you the trouble.

Mondor It's no trouble, I enjoy it.

Delmas (*gasping*) Then it was all real? . . . All true? . . .

Marie All real. All true.

He whips a bottle from his pocket and drinks furiously.

Nerval Ah, but as your Prince is still the Prince of Liars, how can I be sure you're telling the truth?

Marie You must take my word for it, there's no-one else who knows the truth.

Nerval No, there isn't.

Delmas What of me, Father? I know . . . time, dates, places. I was *there*.

Nerval You were also at 'The Swan' tavern, stone drunk . . . Marie Blin, are you confirming this man's midnight story?

Marie Yes.

Nerval Do you mean to hang there and tell me you flew on a broomstick . . . through the air . . . at night?

Delmas 'Too-wit-too-woo, too-wit-too-woo', don't forget the owl and the owl-talk.

Nerval So you talked to a passing owl, paid homage to a black St Bernard who turned into a green monkey and then a goat?

Marie Those are but commonplace at a Sabbat which we hold to exchange new curses, spells and incantations; they are ever changing. There's a fashion in evil as in all things and a sorcerer must be fashionable.

Delmas I flew . . . I flew . . .

Nerval If you were old and toothless, Mistress Blin, I'd say you were brain-blocked, moon-touched and babbling. However, you seem whole-brained and un-mooned.

Mondor This is no way to conduct a preliminary witch-trial, Father.

Nerval This is France, not Spain or Bohemia long gone in cruelty and witch-fever. We are here to seek the truth only.

Mondor To be the truth, it can only be hard earned, nicked from bone, torn from the mouth and metres of gut. Truth's never given free. 'Tis why Courts of Law are based on terror; truth is only heard when you hear the water on their knees splashing. 'Tis why my job is to rack and burn till the truth comes out from under. Let me do my job, break, rip, tear, gouge, brand and burn, burn, burn, *ahhhh.*

In his excitement he accidentally slaps a hot iron against his thigh.

Nerval You will please learn to bear your disappointment with Christian fortitude, Mondor.

Mondor Accomplices!

Nerval Cretinous oaf, shut and stump!

Mondor Father, she must have accomplices in evil. Names – we need their names. Pincers're best for name-getting.

Marie I'll give 'em to you without the need of pincers.

Mondor Have you no pride, woman? Put up some resistance. Where's your backbone? Show it to me and I'll break it.

Marie Cut me down and I'll tell you everything.

Nerval Master Mondor!

Mondor (*cutting her down*). It's a disgrace. Nobody's left this rack whole-bodied before – or at least ten centimetres taller. You're not even bleeding.

Marie *comes down from the rack.*

Delmas Now, she'll prove every word I said 'gainst her was true. I'm a poor man but honest, Father.

Nerval Marie Blin, you know the consequences of your confession of witchcraft? You'll be passed to Higher Authority, sentenced, staked, burnt, consigned to Hell.

Marie (*rubbing her wrists and hands*) It's where I've been all my life being a woman, it holds no terrors for me. Evil is eternal; a necessary evil. Without the Devil, there would be no God, without Judas what would've become of Jesus, who owes his crucifixion, resurrection and undying fame to that ginger-headed man. This is a darklin' world and the Prince of Darkness is its lawful Prince. Darkness is a force needed to make things grow. Plants would die exposed to perpetual sunlight. They need the darkness too. A woman, alone, twice widowed, I need protectors and the forces of the night are mine. Look around and see the power that rules men. I abandon myself to Lucifer. Damned, I felt the horned thing moving inside me, now violently, now silkily creeping. Oh, he glides a shiny serpent in my bosom, a toad dancing on my belly, a bat's pointed beak stealing kisses from my lips and in return by incantations, spells, conjurations, I slay infants yet in their mothers' wombs, blast the produce of the earth, grapevines and fruit trees, orchards and pastureland: men, women and beasts I deliver up to pain without pity. Sorceress of the Blackened Heath, Queen of the Dead, I have the key to Hell and I turn it. Oh, I turn it.

The three men make the sign of the cross.

Delmas 'Tis worse than I dreamed of.

Mondor Worse than I've taken out of tortured flesh.

Nerval Names. Give us the names of the others who followed you in foulness.

Delmas I was there but I couldn't see, a mist masked their faces, shadowed my opticals.

Marie We put the mist there for that very purpose.

Delmas Ah!

Marie But I know who was at the Sabbat. I sent out the invitations. Mark down their names.

Nerval No need. I can remember whole libraries. I was taught the Art of Memory by, er . . . Guiseppi Dun.

Marie Here follows the names of the witches and warlocks of the Lyon Sabbat in the Year of Our Lucifer 1437 . . . Jeanne d'Auvergne, Signoret Camnery, Edwige d'Bell, Françoise Amais . . .

Nerval But they are one and all high-born ladies, princesses of the blood, and Françoise Amais is even the mistress of the Prince of Lyon . . .

Marie Pierre Paternotre, Huguet Le Fevre, Georges Belotte, Leon Cahun and sons, Paul Daudet, Jules Breal.

Nerval But Maitre Breal is a magistrate and the others rich merchants, staunch pillars . . .

Marie Alfred Renard, Theophile Banville, Pierre Leautaud, Eugene Claudel.

Mondor But Eugene Claudel held the post of Chief Torturer and Executioner afore me. I was his apprentice eleven years. He taught me all I know today about the Art of Persuasion. Master of the hot and cold irons and what he could do with sharp pincers – pure magic! I rate him higher than Hammerhead Jacques, the Butcher of Arras. Claudel was solid rock all through. Never thought he'd turn to sin in darkness but then the best fall.

Marie They do . . . Bishops Chaville and Caynes, Abbi Verne, Father Arnaud, Archbishop Courteline of Nantes, Prince Ville of Tuscany, Duke Pascal of the Ardennes, the Duke of Burgundy and his Duchess, Blanche de Beaufort.

Nerval I'll hear no more!

Delmas I confirm it all! The mist clears and I see their long pale chinless faces, aristos down to their bejewelled boots, corrupt to their lace cuffs and spindles. You'll be coming into your own now, Master Mondor, spilling blue blood s'well as red.

Mondor And to think I'll have my old teacher in the tight clamps. He never truly appreciated just what I could do. Now he'll feel for himself. I'll map out a classic programme of torture to do him justice.

Nerval But the Duke of Burgundy . . . Bloody Burgundy himself.

Delmas Evil infects rich blood s'well as poor. Spill it, Mondor! Spill it!

Mondor I will. Till now I've only tackled the poor, sick and brain-gone. They were all broken before I broke 'em. Now I'll be breaking people worth breaking; the able-bodied, not scrawny wind-blown tassies. I'll cut masterpieces in their milk-pampered flesh, ripping silk, slashing furs, tearing delicate lace.

Delmas Rich pickings for us. The lands and possessions of those fine folk'll drop to us for denouncing. At best, I thought I'd grab half of Mistress Blin's holdings but now it's beyond the dreams of avarice.

Nerval No, this has dimensions. I cannot see Bloody Burgundy letting go or the Duke of Ardennes and certainly not the Archbishop. They won't let us pull 'em down, strip 'em bare.

Mondor They've been named, Father. Others being named are picked clean and thrown into the fire in the name of sweet Jesus.

Nerval They're above being named. They'll turn and name us for naming them. They have the power.

Delmas It's your duty to root out Lucifer, Father, wherever, whatever.

Nerval The price is too high. This confessed Mistress of Lies must be silenced. Rip out her tongue.

Marie Higher Authority will want to hear my confession, from my own lips. When I open 'em tongueless and I say 'uggh . . . ahhrrrr . . . ugghgghh . . .' they'll ask questions. 'Whose fault is it?' 'Did your knife slip, Master Mondor?' 'Is it a dark scheme to stop me talking?' You might silence me, Father Nerval, but what of Masters Delmas and Mondor? They know and though you force 'em to silence, what of that? Master Delmas in his cups, Mastor Mondor in the heat of his irons, may let slip the truth, that I named names and you suppressed 'em, perhaps because you, too, are a follower of Lucifer.

Nerval You devil!

Marie Thank you, professional compliments are always appreciated.

Nerval I'll confound your lies and prove no sane man would believe that list of names.

Delmas But I saw 'em. I believe.

Mondor And I! The top is touched with pitch and stinkin'. No one's innocent.

Nerval Who'll heed a tavern-drunk sonkie and muscled dolt whose brains melted in the fires long since?! I'll confound and confound your lies, Mistress Blin. Aside from their love of Christ, fear of damnation, why should the Dukes of Burgundy and the Ardennes and the Archbishop of Nantes and the rest crawl to foul Lucifer? Where's the gain? They have it all.

Marie All is not enough. How greedy men are. A thousand worlds are too few for them. They'd have them all at once and more too. Those proud princes wish to rule over the living and dead, the night and the stars, brute nature. Black magic gives it 'em, blacker than the black heart of Lucifer. So they gave their alliance to him in their blood, knowing Satan demands the bond be signed thus, for Christians are cunning cheats who make all sorts of promises, then leave him in the lurch.

Mondor They'd do that and more.

Delmas Nothing's too foul for the rich foul-smellers. They saddle the poor with Christ the Humble, whilst they stand fat and proud in jewels and furs, committing daily acts against God and man.

Marie When I saw the impotency of God, I, like them, renounced the Faith which was mine by the Sacrament of Baptism and now at the instigation of the Horned One, the Beloved of Mankind, Lucifer, we commit such deeds as he commands. In return he opens the secret gates to power that keeps the planets on their courses. Nothing is voiceless. The Devil hears his echo and his praise in all living and dead things. Unseen demons hurry up and down over the whole world when by the power of our art, we sorcerers command them, for they are our knotted and congealed vices which spring not from the stagnant air, but from our own enclosed flesh. Demons are our – your – weaknesses given Life, turned solid devil-flesh. The stronger our weaknesses, the more vital are our demons. We share the same demons, sorcerers and God-fearers alike. Father Nerval, you and I have a cluster of pride-demons named Sheytans; Master Delmas has his liquor-demons – little Mashims and Master Mondor, your demons are demons of cruelty and obedience called Devs and Tchorts. We of the Sabbat, Black Sorcerers all, control them and send them about to do our bidding. There are three classes of witches, three stages of progression in the Black Arts. The first and lowest stage is witch by incantation; those who invoke spells and incantations. Second stage witches are hand-witches, whose magic is performed by gestures of the hands, flexed fingers and subtle wrist. The third and highest stage, the supreme exponents of sorcery art, are the witches of pure thought, who need no words or gestures, but by their will alone move high mountains, pierce the heavens, turn the sky blood-red at noon. I myself am a hand witch of the second stage.

She makes a scooping gesture with her right hand and a large key appears in it. She holds it up. The **Others** *gasp.* **Mondor** *feels round his belt.*

Mondor It's the key to the cells!

Marie *throws it back to him.*

Marie I had my familiar, my pride-demon, Sheyton bring it to me when I beckoned. Lucifer's faithful have these other powers, outer and inner. They lift up their heads and waves of death come, towns lie ravaged, pestilence rages, Hell gapes. I'm but a witch of the second stage but I can still strip each of you bone-bare, see inside your fleshy worm-casing. My inner optic eye scans tripes, livers and beating hearts, burning like an arrow of pure light. It sees yours, Master Delmas.

Delmas You . . . see my . . . heart?

Marie 'Tisn't wax, but black and hard, bloody and cheating . . . I see it, and will hold it. I ask my Sheyton to bring your heart to me.

Delmas (*gasping*) No, it's mine . . . mine . . .

Marie Don't concern yourself, Master Delmas, your heart will be in good hands. Here he comes . . . watch . . . watch . . . careful, Sheyton . . . careful . . . don't let it slip. . . .

Delmas Nooooo . . .

Marie Ahh, I have it . . . hard . . . it's pin-size and hard but beating . . . See, I hold your beating heart . . . in the hollow of my hand . . .

Delmas (*gasping*) Father Nerval . . . Mondor . . . do something . . .

Mondor *and* **Nerval** *whip out their crucifixes and hold them up.*

Marie That will only help them a little, not you.

Delmas (*gasping*) Help me . . . me . . . me . . .

Marie I'll make you past helping . . . See the power of his name, L-u-c-i-f-e-r! I close my hand . . . slowly . . . round your beating heart . . .

Delmas (*gasping*) Feel . . . cold . . . fingers snatch at . . . my . . .

Marie I squeeze . . . squeeze . . . squeeze . . .

Gasping for breath, **Delmas** *clutches his chest and slides to the floor, whilst* **Nerval** *and* **Mondor** *frantically cross themselves.*

Nerval ⎱ In-the-name-of-the-Father-and-of-the-Son-and-of
Mondor ⎰ the-Holy . . .

As **Delmas** *gasps and croaks,* **Marie** *suddenly opens her right hand and makes a quick gesture as though throwing something at* **Delmas**.

Marie Here, take back your heart whilst it's still whole, uncracked. Breathe easy, Brother Delmas, it beats, it beats . . . (**Delmas** *stops gasping.*) 'Tis a bloody business squeezing hearts.

She holds up her right hand to show them the palm is covered with blood. **Nerval** *and* **Mondor** *shudder.* **Delmas** *staggers to his feet.*

Delmas Sonkers! . . . You gave me no protection!

Marie There is none 'gainst the fear inside. Lucifer Star-Maker, Star-Breaker, would break them.

Mindor Not me, not me, I have irons!

He rushes at **Marie** *waving an iron bar.* **Marie** *jerks up her hand and snaps her fingers.*

Marie Lucifer! . . . (**Mondor** *stops dead still.*) Your irons are feeble against the unseen irons wielded by my Lord Lucifer.

Nerval *holds his crucifix up higher.*

Nerval You've forgotten Christ, the power of Christ.

Marie A possible protection if you're strong enough and you remember him waking and sleeping. But time comes when you no longer stand guard, you sink into soul-dreams and sin. So weakness and wickedness come apace and I pounce when resistance is lowest, 2 a.m. death time. Then my little Sheyton slips inside and peels the skin back from your soul and lays it waste leaving you soulless at the throat of Hell, wandering across the marble deserts of Time, through Eternities without God. In Hell there's only everlasting Time and no cable of hope for Christ to draw you back up to him, no forgiveness, no redemption. I know, I've tasted it.

Delmas Ah-ah-ah what can we do?

Nerval Our duty.

Mondor The price is too high. You said so yourself, Father.

Nerval It's your damned cukish greed, Delmas, for this woman's goods!

Delmas It's not my fault I was right!

Mondor It's the cry I hear daily, 'It's not my fault.' It's always somebody's fault.

Nerval Condemn her and she'll blast our bodies, tear our living souls apart, God protect us. If He does and we survive, she'll name names and we'll face the wrath of Princes. The rich and powerful are less forgiving than Satan's Hell hordes.

Mondor Oh, calamity!

Delmas Oh ki – tu, SKILAR!

Marie Stop gibbering. It's 'gainst the articles of the Dark
Sisterhood to show a trace of mercy – cover those traces, cover
'em, cover 'em! But just this once I'll unhook you from your
doom, though the deed will weigh heavy 'gainst me should it be
revealed. Lucifer would not be pleased. So swear by your pale
God to stay silent.

Mondor
Nerval } We so swear!
Delmas

Marie You'll declare me innocent and I shall leave Lyon. Lyon
is too petty for me.

Nerval Petty? It is petty . . . But how do I explain your
innocence?

Marie Your sole witness was drunk. It was all the liquored
dream of this walking sot-bucket.

Mondor That's true. Better than true, it's believable.

Marie In releasing me, you save yourself and gain the
reputation of an impartial Judge. This will be seen as no
blood-spattered Spanish witch-trial but a true French one,
where reason prevailed and truth stood naked.

Delmas And me branded as a lying sot.

Mondor But you are.

Nerval Marie Blin, you are herewith declared innocent of
witchcraft. The evidence brought by the witness, Claude
Delmas, was but the swelling dreams of an ale-sodden brain.
Thus truth prevails, Justice done, in the name of Jesus Christ,
our Lord, amen. Go thy ways, Marie Blin.

He starts to make the sign of the cross over her but stops himself.

Marie Draw a moral from this, my masters – it's always safer
to accuse innocent old crones, the poor, sick and defenceless, of
Satanism and sorcery. Do not disturb true believers hidden like

scorpions beneath the rocks. I am a backslider. Saving you
shows I still have tatters of pity left but your true witches are
truly vicious. Even death cannot stop their hate. They leave
their teeth for pickaxes, their ribs for knives, their girdles for
nooses and wholesale murder for a religion. Cross them and
their hatred is everlasting to everlasting . . . Take this advice on
pain of soul's doom, do not meddle with the Prince, the Demon
of Death; do not hook Leviathan, the Beast, the Foul Dragon;
run from the Angel of the Bottomless Pit; avoid, avoid the God
of this World, the Tormentor, the Serpent, the Real Thing!

Marie *raises her fist but before she can bring it down,* **Mondor,**
Nerval *and* **Delmas,** *rush out, knocking each other over in their terror.*

Marie *stares after them, then slowly opens her fist. She crosses herself*
and kneels.

Marie In the Name of the Father, Son and Holy Ghost, I give
thanks for this deliverance. You didn't help, Lord, but then you
rarely do. But, at least, you gave me the wit to help myself. For
that giving, I give thanks and these prayers. My only weapon
'gainst 'em was their belief in the Devil. I told them what they
wanted to hear. If I'd denied being a witch, I'd've been
sentenced and crisped in a day. The facts would've proved I
was innocent but the facts are the least important part of a trial.
So to survive I confirmed their prejudices, fear of the unknown,
unseen; fear of the dark and the Satan in them. The fear that
accused me, tried me, condemned me without hope of reprieve
was the fear that freed me. So I say: to defeat Authority, use
Authority's weapons.

> Do not deny their fear, increase it,
> Their fear, not your fear.
> Use it, it's there to be used.
> A cheap conjurer's trick with a stolen
>   key made them fearful.
> I cut my hand with it, showed them
>   my palm
> Covered with my blood, not heart's
>   blood, my blood.
> So they trembled at Satan's power.
> And when I squeezed my accuser's heart

I knew he already had trouble breathing
                    easy
Without my phantom squeezing.
Crude tricks, useless without words.
Words kill, create prisons
And the keys to unlock them.
Learn the use of words
And the abuse of words
And my hard words of advice
Dug out from a bone-hard life,
The only advice worth giving and getting.
For those about to be broken under
                    the wheel
Wit, cunning and endurance are more
                        important than heroism
Though heroism, in small doses, helps
                    too.

She laughs as we quickly fade out.

II

FROM SLEEP AND SHADOW

From Sleep and Shadow was first broadcast by BBC TV as the second part of the trio *The Spirit of Man* on 23 August 1989 with the following cast:

Abegail	Eleanor David
Reverend Jonathan Guerdon	Nigel Hawthorne
Israel Yates	Alan Rickman

Directed by Peter Barnes
Produced by Richard Langridge
Choreography by Ben Benison
Music by Stephen Deutsch

Wedding bells ring out joyfully in the darkness.

Lights up on a bare room where the body of a young woman, **Abegail,** *lies on a funeral bier in a wedding dress and veil. There is a wreath at her feet and black candles on each corner of the bier.*

The **Reverend Jonathan Guerdon** *stands beside it, praying.*

Guerdon Soul-thorned, congealed with grief, a weed against the wall, naught can reconcile me to her loss, not God, fate, the interests of virtue or the hope of heaven, naught can ease my heart-torn sorrows weeping forth this prayer on this my wedding day, the Year of Our Lord 1656 . . . 'Rev Jonathan Guerdon, doest thou take Abegail for thy wife? . . .' Eyes die first seeing the foul deformity of death. I have lost my shield, my health, saviour, pilot, bride. Why did He pluck thee from me? Did I not keep your word, Lord, preach the Everlasting Gospel? I fought on the side of right, brother against brother in the Army of the Saints against the Royalist Anti-Christ, King Charles and his pestilential minions, shouting the Lord's name in the morning mists at Naseby, the place of dragons. Many good men died there but we cleansed out the menstrual rags of Rome with our blood and renewed England's Covenant with God to bring order out of chaos. Yet I am punished for it: Abegail is dead. And after the glorious victory, drum muted, trumpet silent, the good Oliver, Lord Protector, plain Master Cromwell to his friends, asked me to stay on his side for the Commonwealth's sake. But the motion of the spirit made me turn aside from this great honour. Men hanker after power but I was not tempted by this world's baubles. I'd cast out pride along with covetousness and the rest. Yet I am punished for it: Abegail is dead. I became a simple pastor here in Southwark who proclaimed the word truly, administered the Sacraments nightly, maintained discipline strictly. Yet I am punished for it: Abegail is dead. Lord, you struck your cold, pruning-knife into that warm breast and her shining rays, so full of love, were snuffed out. All else is base even the brightest love. She was so fair, oh but, rotting black now, even as I weep. This is God's revenge for some unknown sin. I ask forgiveness, Lord, and wait and wait and wait again for the motion of the spirit. But nothing moves in me.

The doors burst open and amid a blaze of piercing sunlight, **Israel Yates,** *with long hair and black coat, enters cracking nuts and throwing the shells on the floor.*

Yates You sent for me and I'm here! Israel-of-the-Ten-Tribes-No-Less-Yates . . . (*He bangs the door shut.*) Thy word called me away from preaching God's word, running up and down, staring at folk, gnashing my teeth and proclaiming the day of the Lord throughout London. Strange acts, friend Guerdon, confuting, plagueing, tormenting, skipping, leaping, dancing like a base fool, naked before women, *ah*! But God was in my mouth burning like an oven in me, setting my tongue aflame. God then fell into my pocket making me throw all my gold and silver onto the ground like these empty shells for love of Him.

Guerdon Brother Yates, I need thee. Abegail is dead.

Yates Now you are hot for me, before you were hot against me and other holy Ranters, simple men who only proclaim God's word, day and night as the spirit moves them, in the streets and market-places. Yet you persecute us up and down, up and down. You had me whipped out of Southwark, Brother Guerdon, called me a mad, bad blasphemer.

Guerdon And still do when you use profane language, are lax in conduct, enjoy bawdy, mixed dancing, singing extempore songs, wearing your hair shaggy, think Moses a mere conjuror and worse, say that God has told you that hats should be worn during prayers!

Yates They should! They should! If Christ would not take off his hat to his earthly father, Joseph, why should we to our Father in Heaven?

Guerdon Hats in prayer are blasphemy!

Yates But I'll wear 'em and still do all those things you speak of though less sprightly now as my bones winter. What day did I grow old, Brother Guerdon? No matter, I'm still able to rant with the best that God made all men from one mould, and this land, once lost to the rich and lordly, belongs to the poor and forgotten, forever and forever.

Guerdon We are of one mind there, Brother Yates. We fought side by side at Naseby against the King for that.

Yates And by that victory England is made a free Commonwealth.

Guerdon We swept away all vestige of kingly authority. And rightly. But you, Ranter, would sweep away all order, so things would fall into disorder like yourselves.

Yates Yes, everyone their own master, answering to no authority except the God in their hearts.

Guerdon Like the rest of your kind you are still a notorious ranting, Lord of Chaos, Israel Yates!

Yates Of-The-Ten-Tribes-No-Less-Yates. So why call on me, Brother Guerdon?

Guerdon It's a measure of my despair. In normal times I wouldn't have you in the house. But once we were comrades-in-arms in the glorious Army of the Saints.

Yates I've no time to talk of battles past when there are so many new ones to fight. We've seen Englishmen at last throw off the chains of slavish fear. But for how long? At heart they are a servile crew. They long to fawn and scrape and kiss the hands that keep 'em low. They fear freedom more than any chains and ache to bow down once more to lords and kings.

Guerdon Help me, Brother Yates! You are a sinner but you have the power to heal the sick.

Yates If I'm a sinner perhaps my power comes from the Devil?

Guerdon No matter God or Devil, heal my bride, Brother Yates. Heal her!

Yates Indeed there is no Heaven but women and no Hell but marriage.

Guerdon I am on the rack. Bring her back to me and you can have my soul!

Yates Keep it, it is too small.

Guerdon Bring her back to salavation, Israel.

Yates I've seen the bright lights in Buckinghamshire and Leicester but I've never seen a miracle.

Guerdon You've seen a King fall, a Commonwealth rise, and Englishmen standing upright and free.

Yates Yes, that is a miracle.

Guerdon Then heal my bride, Brother Yates. Israel-of-the-Ten-Tribes-No-Less.

Yates I cannot.

Guerdon I beg you.

Yates The dead are dead.

Guerdon *Aeeeeee.*

Yates Cry long, cry loud. Only Lazarus returned, the first and the last. And I don't believe he was truly dead. You need her, the Lord of Life claims her. She's Christ's bride now. No remission. Finis.

Guerdon *Aeeeeee.*

Yates You gather thorns not vines. Wide is the gate and broad the way that leadeth to destruction and the good always seem to go through it first. I've had five children – three boys, two girls and they died. Five pretty babes in a row . . . five . . . all five . . . five different mothers but it did not stop the Lord of Mercy taking them through destruction's gate!

Guerdon Did you cry?

Yates Whole seas. I told myself death is only a short-lived lie but it was no help. So I prayed. Have you prayed?

Guerdon Hard and long.

Yates Pray harder, longer. Do you believe that Christ lived and died and rose again?

Guerdon Yes.

Yates If you can believe that you can believe anything.

Guerdon Not this.

Yates Have the courage to pray again that she might live again!

They kneel.

Guerdon Lord God Almighty give us the word of life.

Yates In the name of Jesus who overthrew the grave, give us comfort. Let Abegail live.

Guerdon Let her live.

Yates Live!

Guerdon She does not move.

Yates You were right. All things are possible, but not this.

Guerdon *Aeeeeee.*

Yates Not even the faith that feeds us can raise the dead, if they are truly dead.

He gets up, takes a handful of feathers from his pocket and drops them on **Abegail***'s face.*

Guerdon (*rising*) If they are truly dead? Is there hope in that 'if'?

Yates Perhaps she sleeps?

Guerdon You torment me with 'if' and 'perhaps'.

Yates In hard winters I've often encased myself in a sack of feathers to keep warm but they can be dangerous, they make you sneeze. How many larks and kingfishers have I missed because I sneezed?

Guerdon You lie, she lies still as death.

Yates Not her, the feathers, man. The feathers about her face. The rest are motionless, but those . . . See the faintest whisp of breath . . . one moves . . . there . . . there . . .

Guerdon A trick of the light . . . no . . . it rises . . . and falls . . . breath . . . it must be breath . . . her breath moves it. Lord of Life it is a miracle!

Yates Or bad eyesight.

Guerdon A single feather moves and I am knee deep in June. See, see, she lives and breathes!

Yates Breathes? – just. Lives? – that's a harder question . . . (*He removes the feathers from her face.*) Half-dead, in half-shadow. Catalepsy, Brother Guerdon. She's fallen into deep sleep.

Guerdon Sleep is a kind of death too. I've never trusted it. I say my goodbye to the sun nightly and tremble.

Yates I dreamed last night the prophet Elijah stopped me and claimed the world was coming to an end. When I objected he tried to sell me a box of figs. Of course we might have it all wrong. Perhaps we're truly asleep when we think we're awake, and those things that give us pleasure and pain are mere dreams?

Guerdon Can you wake her to dream?

Yates I must, else she'll sleep till Resurrection Day.

Guerdon Why you, not me? I love her and the power of love should bring her back to life and dreaming.

Yates As long as a man sees himself above other men he has limits and God cannot pour His holiness into him – for God is without limits. But I'm not proud, standing five foot ten in what's left of my stockings, curing carbuncles and hemorrhoids and capering up and down in the gutters of the world. And so God pours His glory into me.

Guerdon Wake her, and I'll caper in the gutters with you.

Yates *takes out a piece of quartz on a chain.*

Yates This quartz must pull her back. As the magnetised earth and all its bodies are attracted by lodestones in secret and invisible ways, so the polary power of this humble rock will attract the soul of Sister Abegail from shadow . . . (*He dangles the pendant over* **Abegail**'*s face.*) Fix your heart and mind on quartz, Brother Guerdon. Fix and move it. Together we will make it move . . . God's will through our wills . . . And so it begins . . . (*His hand remains still but the pendant trembles and starts to swing gently to and fro above her face.*) Now call her, Brother Guerdon . . . gently . . . gently . . . call her back . . .

Guerdon Abegail . . . Abegail . . . Abegail . . .

Yates Abegail, there's darkness above thee, below thee, darkness around thee . . . no world . . . no people . . . only empty corners . . . for the Lord hangeth this world on nothing and nothing is what and where you are . . . He sucks thee back, back, through endless night . . . Hear the sounds, Abegail? . . . A cock crows . . . a dog barks . . . Now see that single spark of light ahead . . . there, Abegail . . . there . . . It grows . . . Darkness lifts and the sun, the sun bursts through the last mists and see, oh see, the colours of our world . . . You are home!

Abegail *sits bolt upright.*

Guerdon Christ is merciful!

Yates His love shines like flowers on their stems.

Abegail *speaks in a strangely deep voice.*

Abegail Who raised me from the dead?

Yates Only Christ can raise the dead, so it follows you were but sleeping.

Abegail Died August 4th in the year of our Lord 1653. Noon, the sun shining through the bedroom window and the fields of wheat and the apples turning red.

Guerdon Sarah?

Abegail They gathered round my bed, watching my last breath, weeping, and my soul left me.

Guerdon Sarah! That's Sarah's voice.

Yates Sarah? Who's Sarah?

Guerdon My first wife.

Yates Your first wife?!

Guerdon She died August 4th, 1653. You've brought back the wrong one!

Yates Ah, yes . . . well, that can happen.

Abegail Who disturbs my rest?

Guerdon That's Sarah.

Yates She has possession then.

Guerdon Possession of who?

Yates Sister Abegail.

Guerdon Abegail is possessed by my first wife?

Yates Complete.

Guerdon Why didn't you tell me?

Yates How could I? I didn't know you had a first wife. I'm not privy to your domestic arrangements, Brother Guerdon.

Abegail Who disturbs my rest?

Guerdon No one, Sarah, it was Abegail we wished to disturb, not you.

Yates I see it plain now. It was Sarah who called Abegail to shadow on her wedding day; made her sleep and now takes her place here. We must discover why, else Abegail will be returned to sleep and sleep eternal.

Guerdon Sarah, 'twas God's will you died but Abegail cannot die on your will. She loved you as I loved you.

Yates *dangles the pendant in front of* **Abegail***'s face.*

Yates Please, Brother Guerdon, we have certain set ways of doing this. She'll only answer under the spell of quartz . . . Call to her, Brother Guerdon . . .

Guerdon Sarah . . . Sarah . . .

The pendant begins to swing gently to and fro.

Yates Sarah, answer your husband, Jonathan.

She answers in a deep voice.

Abegail Jonathan? . . . Jonathan? . . . Are you my husband Jonathan? Did you weep when I died? Yes, I saw thee weep and Abegail weep, holding my hand till it turned cold. How long did you weep, Jonathan? How long did the salt rivers run? How long, Abegail, till they froze? Was she still weeping, Jonathan, when you first kissed her?

Guerdon We wept as long as it was possible to weep, till the waters dried, and we could weep no more, Sarah.

Abegail I welcomed her into our home an orphan, raised her as our own daughter. You were away preaching and fighting to make a new land of this land for the Lord. Money scarce, prospects poor, as we suffered to endure. Then the pleasant beams of prosperity broke through the clouds between. Good years stretched ahead, years of ease. All lost, stolen from me. I had only the worst years, Jonathan.

Guerdon The best, Sarah. The years of struggle when we were up and doing, full of pith and purpose while the spirit shone in excellency around us. We were young! There's a word now – 'young'.

Abegail Young.

Yates Young . . . Lovely word, 'young'.

Guerdon Remember those years, Sarah, they were the good years. Years that can never be bettered, never come again.

Abegail I remember the April when God struck me down with the hot sweats. Abegail took on my duties as I lay stricken, gaining strength even as I was losing mine. She bloomed and I withered. I knew my death-day was near and my spirit grew heavy, husband, for we had so little time together . . .

Guerdon So little.

Abegail Yet you said love was a durable fire.

Guerdon Sarah.

Abegail Despite our love, I knew you would raise another in my place after my death. And it came to my heart that you would choose Abegail. She is so young, so fair . . .

Guerdon Sarah.

Abegail I grew envious as my last hour came and I called thee both to me and you saw me dying and your souls over-flowed with the sorrow of it. And I asked you to take an oath on the Holy Book would that thou would not marry Abegail. And you swore. And I died, my soul fled with rushing wings and my life-breath returned to the place from whence it came . . . But even before my shadow faded from the house you looked into her eyes as once you looked into mine, and you understood her

as once you understood me and you could not let her go as once
you could not let me go . . .

Guerdon Sarah.

Abegail And you pledged yourselves to each other, breaking
your pledge to me, forgetting thy oath and my darkness. I could
not lay quiet in my death. My strong will came to claim my
rights and my spirit tore at Abegail's soul pulling her into sleep
and shadow.

Guerdon Sarah, release her for our love's sake.

Abegail I keep her for our love's sake.

Yates So much cruelty and all for love's sake. Brother
Guerdon, did you by word, act or thought, look on thy ward
Abegail, profanely whilst Sarah lived?

Guerdon Never. I swear it. There is no deceit here to be
brought to daylight. I feel no guilt because there is no guilt in
me.

Yates *holds up the pendant in front of* **Abegail**'s *face. It swings.*

Yates Abegail! Look on this rock and come home. In the name
of the god who dwells in you in darkness and in light, answer.
Abegail! Did you look on Brother Guerdon whilst his wife,
Sarah, lived?

Abegail (*lighter voice*) Never. I swear it.

Guerdon Abegail!

Yates Sarah, do thou know this to be true?

Abegail It's true. I know they did not look on each other
whilst I was alive. But after I was gone, wishing to be together
they broke their holy oath to me.

Guerdon Yes, we broke it.

Abegail (*lighter voice*) That is why I am guilty and so Satan
drags me down. Sarah took me in as her child, gave me her
home, made me her family. And I betrayed her love, broke my
promise to her and God as Eve did in Eden. I am guilty.

Guerdon You are innocent.

Abegail Yet God punishes me.

Yates No, we do it to ourselves.

Guerdon You are not guilty, Abegail.

Abegail Yet there is no punishment harsh enough for me to suffer. Believe it.

Yates I never believe a mind in pain. Guilt and punishment, punishment and guilt. God is tired of guilt in every corner, punishment in every room. Why nurture tortures within thee? Sting 'em out! You have liberty to love and marry and nothing shall hinder you in this world or the next. Follow me! Follow me! Whoring is the essence of the joys this world affords and there is no human pleasure richer and truer so I've kissed and hugged the ladies and made the fiery chariot mount in me, without sin and guilt. Not a trace! Not a trace!

Abegail (*deeper voice*) You are ranting.

Yates And you are dead.

Sarah Justice. Give me justice. They betrayed my love.

Yates You are dead, Sarah. Justice is with the living. We owe no loyalty to the dead if it means betraying the living. For their sakes and your soul's sake, let Abegail go.

Sarah I suffer.

Yates It's natural.

Sarah I'm no longer loved.

Yates It's natural too. Time, not the heart puts an end to love. You are remembered with love. You cannot ask for more.

Sarah Oh it's hard, it's hard.

Yates It isn't easy . . . Light fights darkness, love – selfishness, life – death. So give liberty to the inward woman, Sarah. Let her go.

Sarah I can't. I want someone to blame!

Yates This is the hardest of all. There is no one to blame!

Sarah *Eeeeeeeeee.*

Yates Let God speak and confirm it . . . (*He cups his hands round his mouth.*) Oh my children, my sweet Sister in Christ, I am God, the First Mover and am moved now to give my verdict . . . Abegail, you are not guilty. Sarah, let her go.

Sarah Why?

Yates Out of love, you poor fool.

He kisses her. She shudders convulsively.

Sarah Jon . . . a . . . th . . . an!

She slumps forward. **Guerdon** *catches her.*

Guerdon What have you done?

Yates Acted. It's by action whereby we shine in glory, Brother. So I acted.

Guerdon But does Abegail live or sleep forever?

Yates God knows.

Guerdon I know God knows but do you know?

Yates No.

Guerdon I know. Sarah's love was too strong. Abegail's gone back to dark and I am alone.

Abegail Jonathan . . .

Guerdon Abegail?

She gets up and speaks now in a lighter voice.

Abegail I was dressing before a mirror . . . thought of thee . . . and of Sarah . . . felt fingers round my heart . . . couldn't breathe . . . I was tired . . . Did I sleep, Jonathan?

Guerdon Deep but now you wake.

They embrace.

Yates When you slept, Sister Abegail, what did you see or hear?

Guerdon This is a friend, Master Israel-of-the-Ten-Tribes-No-Less-Yates, the Lord's true servant who wondrously guided thee back to life. You were sleeping near to death, Abegail, so we both ask did thou see or hear anything on the far side?

Yates Did God, the Master of Dreams and Death, transport you to far places? Did you travel through Egypt?

Guerdon Did you see Noah's Ark, Rachel's Tomb, and talk with the prophets?

Yates Did Moses stutter and Elijah come down on a rope or in his fiery chariot and show you all the heavens, worlds and spheres?

Guerdon Did you see Jerusalem?

Abegail No, only darkness . . . But now I come to think of it, I heard a voice. Such a voice. Oh my Brothers, a voice exultant, sweet and treasured, fine and true.

Guerdon ⎫
Yates ⎬ God's voice?!
⎭

Abegail If the voice of Him who made the world has a voice, yes.

Guerdon What did He say?

Abegail 'Oh my child, my sweet Sister in Christ, I am God, the First Mover and am moved now to give my verdict. Abegail, you are not guilty. Sarah, let her go!'

Guerdon Oh, that was him.

Yates Yes, that was me.

Abegail That was you?

Yates You are disappointed?

Guerdon No, Abegail, it was still the voice of truth. You were judged innocent. There's no guilt in thee, Abegail.

Abegail No guilt in me?

Guerdon None.

Yates Whatever is done by you in light and love is light and lovely. No matter what the Scriptures, Saints or Churches say, if that within you does not condemn you, you shall not be condemned. So live and love and remember to praise the Lord with a full heart.

Guerdon Just as I'll remember to praise thee, Brother Yates. You have saved us both. If Abegail had stayed in that dark limbo, I too would have lost the light, despaired and died.

Abegail My love.

Guerdon So I'll proclaim thy worth through the streets of Southwark and the lanes of Middlesex.

Yates *stuffs the feathers back into his pocket.*

Yates Do not, Brother Guerdon. We've met in strange circumstances just as we live in strange times when people dreamed of infinite liberty.

Guerdon And building Heaven here on earth.

Yates Those coming after us will wonder if it happened, that Englishmen turned all things topsy-turvy seeing no reason why some should have so much and others so little.

Abegail And Mistress Joan Hoby of Colnbrooke could tell Archbishop Laud to his face, 'I do not care a pin or a fart for my Lord the Grace of Canterbury.'

Yates What days we have lived through, Brothers and Sisters. But they are already fading. And such ranting, holy imbeciles as Israel-of-the-Ten-Tribes-No-Less-Yates will soon be gone too. People's great desire now is to say nothing. They see their new won freedom taken from them one by one. But they do not care, Brother Guerdon, consumed by the greatest sin of all – indifference. They want to be left sitting in front of a warm fire, toasting their toes and purring. But my thorny conscience will never let me sit. The Commonwealth has no more use for my kind. We roused the people to throw off the old orders but new ones take their place. And we Ranters who cling to the bright light of liberty and love, are obsolete and worse dangerous, and must be pulled out by the roots. So stay clear of me, friends. I am of that company. Soon there is no safe place left for my kind.

Guerdon There will be one here.

Yates My thanks, Brother Jonathan, but offers of help wound the pride of those whose cause is lost.

Abegail What will you do?

Yates Continue to act. Without acting, no life, without life, no perfection.

Guerdon Call on us, Brother Israel-of-the-Ten-Tribes-No-Less and what you would have us do, we will do.

Abegail And gladly.

Yates 'Gladly'. That's a good word, Sister Abegail. To do things gladly lifts the heart. (*Singing.*) 'And there can be no happy glad-man, compared to a madman. For his mind is free of all care. His fits and fancies are above all mischances. And joy is his favourite fare. So be mad, mad, mad let's be. Nor shall the sad fiend be madder than me.'

Guerdon Brother Yates?

Abegail Are you well?

Yates I am shaking off melancholy soul-dust, Sister. Come join in. I would have you both sing-a-long with me.

Guerdon Sing-a-long?

Yates And caper too.

Guerdon Dance?!

Abegail But is it proper?

Guerdon I was rigid with righteousness but I've learned the only way to save your life is to sacrifice your reputation.

Yates All together now . . . (*Singing.*) 'We laugh at all wise men . . .

Slowly and awkwardly at first but with increasing confidence **Guerdon** *and* **Abegail** *join in singing and dancing.*

All (*singing*) 'We laugh at all wise men who really despise men. Their wisdom we always decline. Follow me and you'll see, what you say is frenzy. Is really but rapture divine. So be mad, mad, mad, let's be. Nor shall the sad fiend be madder than we . . .'

Quick fade out.

III

THE NIGHT OF THE SINHAT TORAH

The Night of the Sinhat Torah was first broadcast by
BBC TV as the third part of the trio *The Spirit of Man*
on 23 August 1989 with the following cast:

Seer of Lublin   Ian Cuthbertson
The Maggid of Kozhenitz   Harold Innocent
Rev Mendel of Riminov   Peter Jeffrey

Directed by Peter Barnes
Produced by Richard Langridge
Music by Stephen Deutsch

A night sky.

1st Voice Let us worship fire.

2nd Voice No, better worship water, that puts out fire.

1st Voice Good, we'll worship water.

2nd Voice No, better worship clouds that carry water.

1st Voice We'll worship clouds.

2nd Voice No, better yet worship the wind that scatters clouds.

1st Voice We'll worship the wind.

2nd Voice No, better still worship man who withstands the wind.

1st Voice That's too much. I'll worship fire and throw you into it!

A Cantor chants Psalm XXII in Hebrew.

Lights up on a bare wooden House of Study with large darkened double windows and lit by big tallow candles in each corner.

The black-clad figures of the **Seer of Lublin** *and* **Rev Mendel of Riminov** *wait in the centre of the room. Behind them is a tall seven-branched candlestick with unlit black candles.*

The Maggid of Kozhenitz, *also in black, enters.*

Seer You are late.

Maggid They said I died last night but I don't believe it. I'm here as I promised I would be.

Seer Let us begin.

Each man steps forward and opens his mouth and shouts but there is no sound.

The unheard cry echoes in the far corners of the universe. This is the most important night in the history of the world, the Festival of the Sinhat Torah, Lublin 1812, when the laws of nature change, the axis of eternity shifts and mankind is finally redeemed. As the Seer of Lublin, descendant of Shelo, disciple of

Shelke, I lived seven years in silence, not wishing to abuse language; seven years with my eyes closed, not wishing to see what the world had to show me. Now they're open but I am still in darkness. So I've gathered my holy friends, Rev Mendel of Riminov and the Maggid of Kozhenitz here, to join me in this plot against You, the Lord God Almighty.

Mendel Locked in the habit of trusting in the triumph of right over wrong, living as if good will defeat evil when all things are against it and God hides His face from us, we find believing in you, Lord, is like climbing up a straight wall with nothing to hold on to.

Maggid Lord, Lord, how long have we known each other? So long it's been I don't like to count. Yet still the earth churns in blood and fury, cruelty and death. So let me ask You, is this the way You rule Your world? If it is, what am I still doing in it?

Mendel Lord, You looked at the world and found it good. I don't. I'm more demanding. I've no use for this world as it is except to wipe my tuchas on.

Maggid A fool looks at the lightning, the wise man on the landscape lit by it. We've prayed and waited but redemption hasn't come. Is it because we don't obey Your commandments? You knew we wouldn't when You gave them to us, but still You gave them. We can't bear the injustice of it in silence.

Seer We are going to make you speak to us and change it.

Maggid We know how. You've given us great powers, Lord. One day I was forced to inaugurate the Sabbath in an open field. A flock of sheep was in the pasture nearby. When I pronounced the hymn to greet the coming Sabbath the sheep rose on their hind legs to listen.

Mendel On a winter's day I went to the bath with a disciple. It was so cold icicles hung from the roof. But as soon as I stepped into the water it grew warm. We stood for a while until the candle began to splutter and go out. There were no others so I ordered my disciple to take an icicle from the roof, and light it. It burnt brightly.

Seer At noon one holy Sabbath I was sharing a meal with friends in Lizensk, eating soup from a communal bowl. On the eighth spoonful I suddenly tipped the bowl over shouting 'Trust the Almighty!' At that moment in Vienna the Emperor was about to sign a decree forcing young Jews into his army and at the same time I tipped over the soup the Emperor tipped over the ink-stand. The ink drowned his decree as the soup drowned my tablecloth. The Emperor said it was a bad omen and refused to sign the document. I upset the soup in Lizensk to upset the ink in Vienna.

Maggid See we've been given great powers, Lord, though they're weak compared to the Baal Shem Tov who could light the fire, say the prayer, know the place and so perform miracles. All we can do is say words, tell stories, sing and dance to gain the Lord's attention.

Mendel Before we can put our case, show Him the injustice of life, we must first gain God's attention. And we'll do it by singing, dancing, telling stories, saying words.

Seer Words were born from snow-white sheep. The frost wind is its own guardian and the hail wind is a messenger and the dwelling place of the dew-breeze is in the extreme ends of Heaven where Angels go down in the River of Fire to bathe forever and forever.

Maggid And the mountain shall dance and the face of the Angels glow with joy when He commanded there be lamps lit on the heavenly circles forever and forever.

Mendel For He has judged the secret things and by His oath the sea was created, likewise the winds, as the Sons of God chant His praises forever and forever.

Seer These are our words, Lord.

Silence.

Maggid God doesn't answer. Words do not attract his attention. And they were words of praise too, just as He likes them – thick and in buckets full. What does He want?

Mendel Stories. He wants stories. Here's one . . . Solomon once asked an old eagle what would happen to the world after they both died. 'One terrible winter,' replied the eagle, 'I was starving to death when I landed on a temple with a lead roof where a ceremony was in progress with men with long white beards. They saw me and someone shouted, "It's a hungry bird. Let's feed him." I was saved. Years later there was another terrible winter and I landed on a temple with a gold roof where a similar ceremony was being held. Only this time with men with long black beards. They saw me and someone shouted, "It's a hungry bird. He wants to share our food. Kill him!".' The world changes and usually for the worse . . . Come down, Lord, and change it for the better.

They look up.

Seer Mendel, Mendel, that story was too bitter.

Mendel Bitter? It was meant to be bitter.

Maggid Let me try. Wanting to punish his son, the king, his father, sent him into exile. The prince wandered for years suffering hunger and cold until the king finally relented and sent him a messenger who would grant him anything he wanted. 'What do you want?' the messenger asked. 'A piece of bread and a warm coat,' replied the prince. That's all he asked for. He'd forgotten he was a prince and could return to his father's palace . . . We all ask for too little from God and from life. We forget we are all princes in exile, Lord. Help us remember.

They look up.

Mendel No, no, that was too sad for the Lord.

Maggid Sad? I always thought it was beautiful.

Seer Let me tell Him my story. For months, the people of Chelm were driven mad by worry. They worried on getting up in the morning and going to bed at night and they worried about everything. So the Council held a meeting and a motion was passed to call in the local beggar Saul – the one who saw Baron Rothechild in a magnificent tomb in Frankfurt cemetery and said, 'Now that's what I call living.' Saul was to be employed at one rouble a week to do all the worrying for the whole of Chelm. Everyone was relieved until the Patriarch of Chelm asked a terrible question, 'Tell me please,' he said, 'if we gave Saul one rouble a week what the devil will he have to worry about? . . .' Come down, Lord, and wipe away our worry.

They look up.

Mendel God still doesn't answer. It was too funny, Jacob.

Maggid Our stories are either too bitter, too sad or too funny. He's very hard to please.

Seer That has always been the trouble.

Maggid We've failed with words and stories so we must try songs for one fragment of melody contains all the joy in the world and reverberates in the holy spheres.

Mendel I know very few songs. I could never hold a tune. When I tried some people called it singing, I called it neuralgia.

Seer In my youth I heard a sweet melody *The Beautiful Country Maid*.

Mendel I know that song. But it's hardly suitable.

Maggid We must sing *King of Kings*. In time, please.

He takes a tuning fork out of his pocket and hits it against his knuckles.

All (*singing*)

> 'King of Kings, God of Gods, wrap the
>   Heavens in His glory.
> See His beauty glow.
> All the trees rejoice, the grass exults.
> And when He speaks sweet perfumes flow.'

They look up.

Seer No answer. Perhaps we should have tried *The Beautiful Country Maid*.

Mendel Song does not stir him.

Maggid Yet the rock fish and the flounder sing, enjoying every kind of music except 'a catch'.

Seer We must try dancing. For the Universe is a dance and the rhythm of the dance determines the shape and pattern of Creation.

The three men softly chant the hymn Hitkabbezu mal akim zeh el zeh.

As they sing they produce Holy Scrolls from their coat pockets and dance with them. Jumping and whirling they hold the scrolls higher and higher and end with a great leap.

Panting hard, they look up.

Mendel Words, stories, songs and now dances are too weak to batter down the granite gates of His heart.

Seer We cannot even gain His attention.

Maggid Do not force us to use force, Lord.

Seer We swore we'd not shrink from it though it may snuff out our light and cast this world back into chaos.

Maggid Before we take that last step we must be certain the fault isn't within ourselves.

Mendel That's hard to know. Our God is a terrible God who seeks out our hairline faults and weaknesses.

Maggid Surely we three, above all others, have been tested and purged in the fires of faith.

Seer Yet one small part of our souls could still be stained by that last sin – pride.

Mendel No, I've singed and starved out pride.

Maggid And I have kept it from me.

Mendel If it lingers on in anyone, Jacob, it is in you.

Seer Me?!

Mendel You are the most famous of us, Jacob, therefore the most vulnerable to king-tyrant pride.

Maggid You've always been the most worldly of us, Jacob. And that's where pride has its home.

Seer No! When Rabbi Azriel Horowitz accused me of deluding the people with my holiness and told me I should declare I was not a saint, I agreed. Next day I proclaimed before the whole

congregation I was indeed no saint, only a sinful man. The
congregation chanted back, 'What humility!' 'What
humbleness!' So is it my fault my fame increased? Then
Horowitz said, 'You must show the people you aren't humble.
Tell them you *are* a saint!' 'Never,' I replied. 'I refuse to lie.'
Pride has left me, Mendel.

Mendel Nothing in nature is all of a piece and so pride prowls
deep in humility. Jacob, perhaps God wanted you to proclaim
yourself a saint knowing you weren't one. Yet you were too
proud to lie for Him.

Seer That's very subtle . . . but true. Satan covets the humble,
the conceited are already corrupt enough.

He falls on his knees.

Mendel You were tested as I was tested when my beloved son
Nathan lay dying. The Lord wanted that sacrifice and I was
wracked but ready, my tears washing out the gall in my heart.
As I prayed the bedside candle finally guttered down to
darkness. My Nathan lay still as death. But the flame suddenly
flared up star-bright. Nathan stirred and called out my name.
He had been saved and I rejoiced in the Lord.

Maggid But in the rejoicing you failed, showed weakness. God
asked for the sacrifice of your son and then asked for a sacrifice
even greater – to sacrifice your sacrifice. But you were too
proud for that sacrifice.

Mendel That's even more subtle . . . but true. Instead of
rejoicing at my sacrifice I rejoiced my son had been spared, I
loved him so.

He falls on his knees.

Maggid I was tested young. I was fourteen when my father
arranged a marriage for me with Sarah from Krasnograd. On
the wedding eve I asked to see my bride. They were surprised
but I quoted the Talmud and Sarah was brought, and lifted her
veil and she was beautiful like a fawn. God spoke to me and I
shivered. I couldn't marry her and I fled to another country
weeping for the love I had lost for the love of God. I had been
tested and was not found wanting. Later Sarah left her own

people and married a Gentile. I had seen that betrayal in her sweet face and shivered.

Seer Perhaps you shivered at her beauty soon to be lost. You were too proud to see if you hadn't rejected her she wouldn't have married the Gentile and betrayed God.

Maggid That's subtle too . . . but also true.

He falls to his knees.

Mendel What are we but bundles of wet straw, three old fools, dreaming mad dreams in an obscure town in Eastern Europe, 1812.

Maggid We're flawed. We can't answer the simplest questions like when you knock a nail into the wall where does the mortar go or when you eat a bagel what happens to the hole?

Seer We are not the holiest of holy we thought we were . . . Yet we have the power to try to impose our will on all Creation.

They help each other up.

Mendel God doesn't compromise, neither should we. What is important is to accept the challenge.

Maggid Pharaoh too knew how to fight and when the blows fell he didn't give up. I'm less than dust but believe the Universe was created for me alone.

The three link hands and breathe deeply. Each in turn expels his breath loudly.

Mendel We now bring God Himself to Judgement.

A long note on a Zopha horn is heard.

Seer Let the palaces of Heaven quiver.

Maggid As we force open the gates.

Mendel And stand amid the cohorts of flame, girt with fire, crowned with light.

Suddenly the candles in the seven-branched candlestick all light spontaneously.

Maggid The Talmud speaks of 25 punishable offences. We charge You Almighty God with offence number 13: through Your acts You have caused men and women to curse God Almighty.

Mendel And they do it with reason for You have created a world where evil triumphs and goodness is crushed amid blood and cruelty and the closed heart never opens.

Maggid A world made in Your image where sickness, poverty, sorrow, mourning and trouble of all kinds are man's daily lot.

Seer So they curse You. The charge laid before Your representatives on earth is that You have caused men and women to curse thy name, Lord . . . What is your verdict?

Maggid Guilty.

Mendel Guilty.

Seer Guilty.

Maggid It's hard, Lord, but no harder than the verdict You have passed on all mankind.

Drumbeats.

Seer We three, the Seer of Lublin, the Rev Mendel, and the Maggid of Kozhenitz, now deliver our sentence – that You, Lord God Almighty, Creator of the Universe, be hereby excommunicated. You are excluded from the community of Thy children till the end of time.

Mendel
Maggid } That is the sentence of us all!
Seer

The drumbeats stop. The candles are suddenly snuffed out to a great sucking noise as a vast wind swirls through the room and bursts open the double windows and sweeps out into the dark.

Pitch blackness. No light. No sound. Then, as clouds drift slowly from the face of the moon, faint glimmers of light reveal the three men standing by the open window looking out at the night. Their hair has turned white.

They look up at the same night sky as the opening.

Maggid We've driven God away. We tried to imagine the world without God, now we know. And the horror is, it's just the same.

Mendel We've turned Him out but no one will notice the difference. For there is none. He never revealed Himself so who'll know He's no longer here? Only we know and no one will believe us.

Seer They did not believe us when we said He was here. So why should they believe us when we say He's gone? Nothing's changed.

Mendel It's the final end.

Maggid What do we do?

Seer Continue, of course.

A Cantor chants Psalm XXII in Hebrew as the lights slowly fade out.

Nobody Here But
Us Chickens

There are so many conditions which are handicapping in the widest sense – being an Arab in Israel, a Jew in Syria, being a woman, gay, black or poor anywhere. These handicaps prevent people making the normal responses to their surroundings, stifle their opportunities and create prejudices in others. Yet we all make sure we suffer disabilities to some degree or other.

These plays, however, deal with handicaps in the more limited sense of mental or physical disabilities such as blindness, deafness, palsy, mental deficiencies; handicaps that are primarily motor, mental or sensory deprivations.

No special sympathy is shown for these disabilities, as that would merely emphasize the differences between the disabled and those without such handicaps, whereas the object is to emphasize the similarities. Acceptance is needed, not sympathy.

It is true that the strengths, weaknesses, loves and hates of a disabled person will often spring from their disabilities. But not always. Someone may be blind but can be a marvellous lover, deaf but handle a complex computer brilliantly, mentally defective but be a good athlete or journalist.

A specific handicap does not imply one specific problem. Some, born disabled, have stable homes. Others come from broken homes and would have difficulties due to their background *despite* their handicap.

Authorities label the disabled as 'the blind', 'the deaf'. It is easier to think of them as part of a group but the disabilities are not always simple in their effect. Within each group there is a whole range of varying responses of how to cope. For a group is made up of individuals, each one absolutely unique. Their similar disabilities do not make them the same. The disabled are not a different species but, like the rest of us, absurd and ridiculous; only they have it harder. They have so much more to overcome. Cripples are the rest of us, dramatized.

Peter Barnes
1989

Nobody Here But Us Chickens was first broadcast by
Channel 4 in September 1989 with the following cast:

Nobody Here But Us Chickens

Allsop   Jack Shepherd
Hern   Daniel Massey

More Than a Touch of Zen

Carver   David Suchet
Hills   Nicholas Farrell
Powell   Michael Maloney

Not As Bad As They Seem

Berridge   Stephen Rea
Judith   Janet Suzman
Sefton   Norman Rodway

Directed by Peter Barnes
Produced by Ann Scott

I

NOBODY HERE BUT US CHICKENS

*Darkness. The sound of a man crowing 'Cock-a-doodle-do!'
repeatedly.*

*Dawn light up on a bare, totally white room with a heavy door. A
small table with a plate of sandwiches and clothes over a chair.*

George Allsop, *in his underpants, crows and talks urgently to
himself as the light grows steadily brighter.*

Allsop *Cock-a-doodle-do!*, my crowing drives away the night.
Every morning I cock-crow and the day comes again, *cock-a-
doodle-do!* Without my crowing there'd be no light. None at
all. Darkness always. I know to casual eyes I'm just another
farmyard cockerel – an ordinary White Leghorn. I say
ordinary, but of course, one White Leghorn is worth a
dozen Rhode Island Reds, Buff Orpingtons, Jersey Giants or
Grey Dumpies scuttling about, bare rumps dragging in the
dust. We Leghorn Whites are supreme. More popular than
all other breeds combined. Pure Mediterranean – nothing
Asiatic about us. Not a feather or a beak, *cock-a-doodle-do!*
Whites are supreme, *cock-a-doodle-do!* But it's still a
problem . . . I strut like a cockerel. (*He struts around with a
high-stepping leg action and jerking his neck up and down.*) I eat
maize, ground oats, bran and mash like a cockerel, *peck-peck-
peck.* (*He pecks the ground.*) I flap my wings like a cockerel.
(*He flaps his arms.*) And I crow like a cockerel, *cock-a-doodle-
do!* It's obvious I look every inch a cockerel, I do, I do. And
yet they don't believe I am a cockerel. They're convinced
against the evidence of their eyes I'm a man. Yes, a man!
Can you credit it? They have an acute identity problem but
instead of changing themselves they try to change me.
Words like schizophrenic and paranoia are used to weaken
my reason . . . Oh they try, how they try . . . They produce
variations and undulations to harass my brain cells. But I
know what I am, *cluck-cluck-cluck.* I told 'em I lost my body
but not my mind, didn't I? It happened when the wet
creature slid in and a power acted on me. I asked myself the
question 'Who am I?' Am I an obstacle or an opening, a wall
or a door, man or chicken? I'd been with the firm of
Harcourt and Ridley, man and boy, but I slipped out of
orbit; couldn't cope. My story got chopped about somewhere
along the line. Bits and pieces, purges and vivisections, guts

over the sawdust. So I was taken away to rest. What a day!
No more whistles and roars from inside. I was in the
country walking with trees and grass and so I found myself
in the world of the farmyard. I touched peace, at last, in the
order of the henhouse, *cluck-cluck-cluck*, *cock-a-doodle-do*! I
saw the top birds pecked all the others and those in the
middle ranks pecked those below but respected those above,
whilst the fowls at the bottom took it from everybody. This
was the England I knew and loved! I was completely at
home. So I came out of the closet, wardrobe and coal-hole,
no longer ashamed to let everyone know I was a true White
Leghorn, *cock-a-doodle-do*! But I'm more than just a rooster.
Oh we know that don't we? . . . (*He laughs to himself.*) No
Chicken Little me. Even if I am alone I can still only
whisper it. Quietly, little puffs, little puffs . . . I'm not really
a cockerel, I'm *the* cockerel of myth and legend, the real live
rooster booster – I'm Goldcrest, the original Cock of the
North! I can't tell those with the white coats and rubber-
soled shoes. They'd think I was mad, the pages turning,
nutcases together. Instead, I play it canny, and say I'm a
common White Leghorn and let it go. They don't believe
that so why bother 'em with something that's too big for 'em
to grasp. Another secret locked away inside . . . They try to
break me, Dora, day after day in this room, but breaking's
taking place in rooms and prisons like this all over the world
at this very moment – it's all normal, nothing special. That
fumed frog of a man, Dr Exley's the worst. But he won't
break me, no, not me. We cocks are famous for our
courage. Lions are afraid of us, and we frighten away the
night and death. They hurt, Dora, oh they hurt, but what's a
little suffering? Suffering doesn't matter that much. It
happens all the time . . . Dr Exley keeps saying I'm a man
like him, as if that's something to be proud of.
I agree I thought I was a man once, mea culpa. I made a
mistake, what's their excuse? I know I was only fooling
myself then but we can all convert. Towns and cities change
their names, I changed my being, blotted out, no roadsigns,
not even a station. I won't go back to living a lie. Now I
stand newborn, consumed with faith in my chickenness, my
rock and my anchor. Let me say it once and for all, loud
and clear, in plain English: I'm a *cluck-cluck-cluck, cock-a-*

doodle-do! Nothing could be plainer than that!

There is the sound of a key being turned in the lock. The door opens and **Charles Hern** *strides in dressed in his underpants and carrying his clothes in a neat bundle. He drops them as he sees* **Allsop** *for the first time. The door bangs shut behind him.*

As the two men stare at each other **Allsop** *starts to move cautiously round, with a high stepping action, poking his neck in and out and clucking softly.* **Hern** *continues to stare at him, then moves round in the opposite direction with exactly the same movements. He too clucks softly.* **Allsop** *stops in surprise.*

Hern *makes tiny jumps at him like a fighting cock and starts to crow.* **Allsop** *immediately jumps too and crows. The jumps become higher, faster and fiercer, and the crowing louder. They kick out at each other as they jump. Leaping, kicking and crowing they finally crash straight into each other in mid-air and fall exhausted.*

Allsop *Cock-a . . .!*

Hern *Doodle-do!*

Allsop Steady the Whites.

Hern They're trying to sweat my identity out of me. I don't know you.

Allsop And I don't know you.

Hern That makes two of us.

Allsop You're sailing through the middle of my dream.

Hern I'm not dreaming.

Allsop I am, I can give you the grid reference.

Hern Who are you? What are you?

Allsop I've nothing to hide. I'm a cockerel.

Hern I can see that, pullet-head. What breed?

Allsop Pure White Leghorn.

Hern Commonplace stuff.

Allsop What makes you so special?

Hern I'm a prize Jersey Giant. Basildon Poultry Club. Best of the Best Breed '66, *cock-a-doodle-do!*

Allsop Best breed? You Jersey Giants are all duck-footed, dropped-tail and dropsical.

Hern And you Whites are all lungy and liverish; narrow-necked, canker-combed, dusty-shanked and moulty, *cluck-cluck.*

Allsop This is a restricted area, off limits to all birds, *cluck.*

Hern I didn't fly here because I wanted to. I've a snug henhouse in Basildon. I was forced out.

Allsop They forced me out of my place once, high up on the sixth floor with a view over the gardens. Vermin! Dora took it hard but it didn't worry me.

Hern It didn't worry me.

Allsop Whites're above worrying where they perch for the night. Just so no foxes get near me, I'm all right.

Hern I can see it now. They've set up this meeting hoping the sight of a scraggy rooster like you will drive me out of my mind.

Allsop They could, they're crafty. They try things like that. One hundred and fifty volts and convulsions. Leave your birth certificate on the table and you never see it again.

Hern And the injections. Don't forget the injections.

Allsop With the thirty-foot needles. They try, oh they try.

Hern The more they try the stronger I become. I was a bank teller for twenty years before I found myself. People would come to my window for money. I'd count out five – ten – twenty – fifty – hundred; quick – quick – quick – quick. Two tellers to a cage. Caged birds cramped and grey. Then the light came and I spread my wings.

Allsop Up and away! Top of the dunghill!

Hern Joy and peace, thanks to the great Lord Cockerel Almighty. Oh righteous Father, the world does not know Thee, but I know Thee, *cock-a-doodle-do.*

Allsop I know Thee, I know Thee. But no one accepts it here. They call themselves doctors but they're really white slavers. That's why they wear white coats – it's advertizing.

Hern They're worse than white slavers. Most're into factory farming on the side.

Allsop Save me, Lord, save me!

Hern They try to counter my conversation with drugs, pumping in phenothiazine daily. But religion is my rock, they can't shake my chicken beliefs. I tell them St Catherine was yellow all over and the first Quaker, George Fox, ran barefoot through the winter streets, shouting 'Woe to the bloody city of Lichfield' and Cardinal Richelieu's sister knew she was made of glass and couldn't sit down because she'd crack. So why pick on me? *Cock-a-doodle-do!*

Allsop You fight the unbelievers with words, I do it with silence. I thunder at them silently and when they assault me I enter the silent zone, zilch, where they can't follow and counter their power with the power of silence.

Hern You're deluding yourself. You've got no power. You're just another poor White Leghorn.

Allsop *flaps his arm slowly.* **Hern** *does likewise.*

Allsop You're wrong. Look behind this beak, this comb, these cockerel eyes.

Hern I'm looking.

Allsop It's all fake nooks and crannies, false exits, zigzags, disguises. I've never told this to another living cock before, Jersey, but I'm not just another Leghorn. I'm Goldcrest.

Hern Goldcrest?

Allsop The legendary Cock of the North.

Hern Oh, that Goldcrest. Then this must be the time for revelations. Hang onto your comb and tail-feathers, Whitey, you're the first to know it but I'm no ordinary Jersey Giant either. I'm Chanticleer!

Allsop Who's that?

Hern Chanticleer! Chanticleer! The magical cock from the Roman de Reynart.

Allsop Ah, yes.

Hern I'm the black cock that crowed the night Christ was denied, *cock-a-doodle-do*!

Allsop And I crowed the morn he was born in Bethelem, *cock-a-doodle-do*!

They stop slowly flapping their arms.

Hern We're the Yin and Yan of it, magical roosters.

Allsop Cock heroes.

Hern We must join forces and make sure the liars, cheats and bullies called men, don't win.

Allsop
Hern *Cock-a-doodle-do*!

Allsop Usually two cocks in the same barnyard fight. It happens all over. But there's room for two styles, crawl and breast-stroke. You're a bird of the right plumage. You're no fake.

Hern You have to be on guard every second for fakes. A dubious psychiatrist of my acquaintance dressed up as a chicken to fool me. Dyed his moustache and eyebrows, but I knew. His legs were too thin. And you should've heard his accent. I'm hungry.

He struts around, pecking the air.

Allsop That's a problem in this henhouse. I ask for ordinary chicken meals, maize, sunflower seeds or mash – nothing fancy, but all I'm sent is beef sandwiches. Look there.

Hern You're lucky it isn't chicken sandwiches. We're not cannibals! Not cannibals! Still, beef is quite tasty. (*He picks up a sandwich from the table and eats.*) As I said, you have to be on your guard night and day else they'll trick you. Geese, ducks, fighting bantams, they can really be social workers in disguise, *cluck-cluck*. Why're you staring, Whitey?

Allsop You're eating a beef sandwich!

Hern With mustard.

Allsop Roosters don't eat beef sandwiches.

Hern This rooster does. Needs must.

Allsop You're not even pecking it like a rooster. You're eating it like a man! It's a trick to delude me, the stories drip venom, paranoia lays in wait destroying whole cities and fields. You're one of them in disguise. You're no Chanticleer, no Jersey Giant, no proper cock. You're an agent provocateur!

Hern Feather-legged carbuncle, you're the agent provocateur. Real cockerels are damn smart birds but you're duck-dumb. No true cockerel would believe if he eats like a man, he stops being a cockerel. The Duchess of Macini's favourite cock took tea in the morning on her bed and dined on beef at her table every day. He was still a cockerel, *cock-a-doodle-do*! *Cock-a-doodle-do*! (*He struts around, crowing loudly.*) I can eat a thousand beef sandwiches a day and I'm still the great Chanticleer, a pure Jersey Giant, a real life rooster. But are you, Whitey?

Allsop Of course I am!

Hern You can't prove it.

Allsop Prove it? I don't have to prove it. I don't have to prove anything. No, not me. I am who I am, and I fling my message into the wind. That's the way it is.

Hern Take a good look at yourself.

Allsop I do every morning. My father said I was too ugly, I should grow a beard, but I'm still top of the pile. Cock of the North, *cock-a-doodle-do*!

Hern Better. At least there's a real life crow-note in your crowing. That can't be faked.

Allsop What if there is or there isn't? Crow-notes don't matter. I'm not on approval here, Jersey, pro or con, left or right. You're the one who eats beef sandwiches, not me. Beef, I said beef. It's junk-food!

Hern Beef, pork or salami, outward forms are nothing, Goldcrest, so long as you keep your inner cockerelness. I'm an old bird, as birds go, and that's not far, and I know men lie, cheat and betray – it's in their nature.

Allsop Bullies, liars, blackmailers, wheedlers, toadies, fools who brawl and swagger.

Hern But cunning with it. We fowl can't afford to cling to our animal purity and honour. We must adapt to survive, change with the changing times. If need be take on protective colouring. Though fowl we must behave like chameleons.

*He takes **Allsop**'s clothes from the chair and hands them to him. Then he picks up his own clothes and starts putting them on.*

Allsop *Cluck-cluck, cluck-cluck, cluck-cluck.* What are you doing?

Hern Changing with the changing times.

Allsop Those are *clothes*, Chanticleer.

Hern Protective colouring. I'm becoming a chameleon.

Allsop You're becoming a man. It's the first step down the road to sin and degradation. Down, down, down, down.

Hern Have faith. Believe. Do as I do.

Allsop I can't Chanticleer . . . The roof is falling on the world . . . New York . . . Singapore . . . Dartmouth . . . all covered with dust . . . trembling on the edge . . .

Hern Don't be chicken. Believe in yourself. Remember, dressed like a man you'll still be a cockerel. You're still a cockerel. Still a cockerel. Say it – I'm still a cockerel, I'm still a cockerel.

Allsop I'm still a cockerel. I'm still a cockerel.

*Trembling **Allsop** starts to put on his trousers, shirt and jacket.*

Hern A White Leghorn, no less. Never believe because you eat and dress like a man you are one and stop being what you truly are – Goldcrest, the one and only original Cock of the North.

Allsop I am, I am! Yes, I am!

Hern It's not enough for a pure cockerel to behave like a man to become one – oh no, oh no! You can do anything in man's tarred world and still be that rooster booster you magnificently are. So crow you feathered fool, crow. Crow! Crow!

Allsop *Cock-a-doodle-do*!

Hern You hear that outside? You white-coated look-a-likes, there's nobody here but us chickens!

Allsop *Cock-a-doodle-do*!

Hern You're dressed. Do you feel like a man?

Allsop *Cock-a-doodle-do*!

Hern Of course not. Proves my point. Now step out and follow me.

Both fully dressed **Allsop** *follows* **Hern** *round with the familiar high-stepping action, like cockerels.*

Allsop I haven't changed.

Hern You have.

Allsop I'm still a bird.

Hern But smarter, much smarter. You can move in their world without danger.

Allsop I'm camouflaged all over.

Hern You can fake being one of 'em.

Allsop Easy, nothing easier . . . shelling peas . . . rob 'em blind and they wouldn't know . . . Wait, stop the minute hand . . . Why should I? Who should I, would I, want to fake being a man?

Hern Because it's your duty.

Allsop I have no duty except to be what I was born to be – mad as the world says but true to myself.

Hern I've been watching you and I've come to a decision.

I'm recruiting you into the service. I think you're made of the right stuff, fowl through and through. The Chicken Brotherhood needs agents like you in the field.

Allsop The Chicken Brotherhood?

Hern First, I must swear you to secrecy.

Allsop I swear. I'll make my scratches on the Official Secrets Act if you like.

Hern Not necessary. Take your word. The Chicken Brotherhood is an Intelligence Operation. We must monitor mankind, Goldcrest. If we don't, we'll be defeated. Look at Factory Farming. We didn't know the horror of it, couldn't believe it could happen. But it did. We weren't prepared. We're fighting it now but it's late. So many millions of our brethren have suffered and died in agony. What new terrors could mankind be dreaming up? One day they'll manufacture synthetic eyes and chickens out of soya beans and we'll be for the chop. They'll exterminate us like they did the Great Auk and the American Buffalo. They don't care, Goldcrest. They don't care.

Allsop I can see the purpose of it but I've never heard of the Brotherhood.

Hern Good. That proves how successful we've been. We've tried to keep it very quiet. It has to be all underground, undercover, underwraps. If they once got wind . . . well you can guess the rest . . . Kaput.

Allsop Yes, we're cursed and marked down for destruction.

Hern I've been an agent for years. Incognito and then some. It's a strain I can tell you.

Allsop I know about strain.

Hern Sometimes even experienced operators like me crack and break cover. They reveal their true identity and start strutting and crowing. And then they're locked up, double-bolted and put away. It happened to me. That's why I'm here.

Allsop I wondered why you were put in with me.

Hern I thought you might wonder. I yearned for the security of a normal henhouse. I found it hard keeping up the pretence of being Charles Hern, Mister. I broke cover last Thursday at a Chinese Restaurant. Chicken Chow Mein, Chicken Chop Suey – it was too much! The menus dripped with the blood of our brethren. I stood up and crowed my defiance.

Allsop Understandable in the circumstances.

Hern Weak. Especially for an experienced operator like me. You'll have to be stronger, Goldcrest.

Allsop Stronger?

Hern By the power invested in me by the Chicken Brotherhood I deputize you Feather Agent Four Five Eight.

Allsop Why me?

Hern Because you're here and not there.

Allsop But what do I do?

Hern Discard your beak and feathers. Act like a man, talk like a man, think like a man.

Allsop It's horrible.

Hern Someone has to do it. Duty, Goldcrest, duty. Once you're mingling amongst them, accepted as a man, keep watch on them and report to me.

Allsop But to go back into their world . . . surrounded night and day by human kind. Never to see any of our own species again. To be completely alone out there. It's more than feathers can stand.

Hern You won't be alone. We've hundreds of thousands of chicken agents in the field. And it's not just us. Other species have their intelligence operators at work too – pigs, foxes, buzzards, vultures and the like.

Allsop Nobody told me.

Hern Didn't know you could be trusted. There's a whole army of animals in disguise and they're working for the overthrow of that evil strain called humanity.

Allsop But how will I know them?

Hern By a certain animal look in the eyes, an animal turn of the head, an unfinished animal gesture. Jackals, hyenas, wolves, behaving like men so well no one can tell them apart. But you will. You'll learn to. You must. It'll keep you sane, knowing there are others like you doing a dirty job because somebody has to do it. But remember, you must never reveal yourself. It's too dangerous. Once started you can't stop pretending to be a man.

Allsop For how long?

Hern As long as it lasts. Your whole life perhaps – or longer.

Allsop Can I do it?

Hern Of course. We're the best. In this whole wide world only chickens can unscramble omelettes.

Allsop How?

Hern By eating them, dummy.

Allsop That's so right.

Hern So you're 'cured' of your so-called delusion, aren't you?

Allsop Absolutely. If I can't fool those emaciated white-coated dwarfs I deserve to be par-boiled and pot-roasted.

Hern They'll think it's a triumph. Because you act like a man they'll believe you're no longer a rooster. It's acting normal that counts with them. They're not interested in what you are inside.

Allsop Inside I'll be a rooster and still they'll preen themselves on their success. But we'll know the truth, *cock-a-doodle-do*!

Hern *Sssshh.*

Allsop Sorry.

Hern No more cocking and doodling, please. You have a higher purpose now.

Allsop That's good. No more drifting here to there at the mercy of the tide. Dora would be proud of me.

Hern Are you ready Mr . . .? What's your given name?

Allsop Allsop.

Hern Mine's Hern. Ready Mr Allsop?

Allsop As I'll ever be Mr Hern.

Hern *bangs on the door.*

Hern We want to talk.

Allsop Open the cage and let us out.

Hern It's Charles Hern.

Allsop And Gerald Allsop. We know who we are!

The sound of a key being turned in the lock and the door swings slowly open and arm-in-arm **Allsop** *and* **Hern** *march out, smiling to themselves as lights fade out to a triumphant 'cock-a-doodle-do!'*

II

MORE THAN A TOUCH OF ZEN

Darkness. The sound of Japanese wood-blocks being banged together.

Lights up on a seedy gymnasium in semi-darkness. Mats on the floor, some chairs in the far corner Left. Sitting sprawled in the shadows, against the side wall Down Left in track-suits are **George Hills** *and* **Douglas Powell**.

The instructor **Joseph Carver** *enters briskly Right, in a Judo outfit, and addresses them from a pool of light, from a solitary skylight.*

Carver Harai-gosphi, O-gosphi knoshi-nage, yoko-goke, wan-kam-setsu, kata-ha-jime Judo is the Path, the Way, the Do, the harmony of circles, efficient use of mind and body, the controlled movement executed with speed, lightness and precision, *aya!* . . . (*He assumes a Judo position, arms straight above his head, right leg bent, left straight out.*) Virabhadrasana One or the First-Warrior Pose. But Judo is more than just a formalized method of combat – it is a way of life. The Judoka is consumed by the cosmic currents. His freedom from fear doesn't spring from his strength or power but from balance and clarity of purpose *aya!* (*He assumes another Judo position, arms stretched out either side of his head, right leg bent, left straight out.*) Virabhadrasano Two or the Second Warrior Pose. There are three basic principles of Judo laid down by the great Kensho Abe. One – all things in the universe're in motion. Two – this motion is flowing. Three – all things flow in harmony. And all this was said by a man only five feet tall. If your balance is right it needs only a little finger to be raised a fraction, a foot to shift an inch and the biggest fall, *aya!* (*He kicks out with his right foot.*) The Ke-Age or the kick to the testicles. Barton Wright developed his own Judo system called Bartitsu, which Sherlock Holmes used to destroy Moriarty. I've developed my own system too, called Bujutsu-Carver. It's Judo sprinkled with T'ai Chi Ch'uan, a smidgeon of Shiatzu – that's Japanese finger pressure for energy, sexual vitality and relief from tension – and more than a touch of Zen: trees have no voice but when the wind blows they sing. Bujutsu-Carver takes the best of the East for the West, *aya!* (*He executes a thrust to the eye.*) The Ryogan Tsuki or Eye-thrust. You can gouge out an eye in a

flash with that move. But remember Judo is a spiritual
discipline. We reach out beyond ourselves, see the unlit
flame, hear sphere music. Heaven's in a single breath, the
universe in the movement of a hand. And all for £8.50 a
session, plus V.A.T. I've no idea what your backgrounds are
but they couldn't be worse than mine. I was born in
Chingford and now I'm a Fifth-Dan. Judo is available to all.
There can be no barriers here on the Dojo. No barriers in
you either physical or mental. The most formidable
opponent you'll ever meet on the mat is yourself. But if you
have an open mind you'll take everyone and everything in
your stride. Now, gentlemen, this will be your first session so
we'll concentrate on posture. On your feet and we'll begin a
voyage of discovery. But we'd better get some light on the
scene and see where we are first.

As **Carver** *crosses to the right wall and switches on the lights,* **Hills**
and **Powell** *use the wall bars to drag themselves upright, their
limbs and torsos shaking violently now that they are moving.*

Carver *turns back to see them twitching and lurching
uncontrollably. He stares and deliberately closes his eyes in disbelief.
When he opens them again they are still there, still shaking
spastically, and trying to stand upright.*

Powell Something wrong Mr Carver?

Carver Wrong? . . . No . . . no, no, no . . . What could be
wrong?

Powell Is it because you think we're cripples?

Carver Cripples? Oh I wouldn't put it quite like that.

Powell Spastic paralysis. That's paralysis marked by tonic
spasms of the muscles and increased by tendon reflexes.

Carver Ahhh, yes . . .

Hills J-j-judoooo! . . . finger pressure . . . UOKO-gake-wan-
ka – soup . . . SHIFT a foot . . . AYA – keee – age . . . pariiii
goooooshi . . . Let's get at it . . . aya-aya-AYYAA.

He nearly falls over in his enthusiasm.

Powell Spastic dysphonia. George suffers from a speech

disorder as well as spastic paralysis – well at least he's not a tenor. It's comforting to know however bad you are you can always find someone worse off than you. Count your blessings, one by one, two by two, eight by eight.

Hills Nooo barriers here on the Dojo-jo-jo-jodo, *aya!*

He attempts the First Warrior Pose and ends up entangled in his own feet.

Carver No barriers but we do have a few technical problems. Nobody told me about you. I could kill Bristow in Admin *aya!* (*He mimes a knife thrust.*) The Tsuki-Koni or Knife-Thrust. (*He breathes in slowly.*) Acki-do . . . acki-do. I breathe in the spirit of acki-do for inner calm . . . Gentlemen, before we actually start you'd better tell me why you want to take up Judo. (*He crosses and picks up two chairs.*) I'm tired of teaching men and women who only want to break bricks with their heads, who have no appreciation of the deeper meaning of martial arts. Will you be able to obtain 'shin' which means heart? Do you have 'ki' which is energy? (*He places the chairs and* **Powell** *and* **Hills** *slump onto them with difficulty.*) Frankly, at first sight, you're not obviously suited to the spiritual disciplines involved.

Hills W-w-weeee're n-n-n-ooot?

Carver No, but that's only at first sight. Tell me something about yourselves.

Powell Handy handicappers – Number 8973 George Hills there and I'm Number 4539 Douglas Powell, Streatham Institute for the Physically Handicapped. I'm an institute man born and bred. I smell of carbolic and quicklime. Years of stone walls, hard beds. But I've been lucky, George here lived soft with his parents till they decided to shuffle off their responsibilities and die. Parents can always be counted on to do that in the end. So he never grew callouses like me. When he joined us he didn't know beans.

Hills Now I'm in an Institute I h-h-have to lick my PLATE clean and p-p-praise the COOK.

Powell You have to learn to surround yourself with yourself to survive. I'm the Institute's Wonder Boy.

M.A.PhD. My fame echoed from one end of Streatham High Street to the other, a distance of some twenty linear feet. Now I write school text books. But I want to develop my body as well as my mind. I always want more. To go to Samarkand as well as stay at home with a family; to sleep alone in a bed and have a woman there too; to have the cherry blossom as well as the timber from the tree; to be famous and unknown.

Hills I want to be a BRAIN-SURGEON.

Carver A brain-surgeon?

Hills I k-k-know I can't be a brain-surgeon, anyone c-c-can see . . . I haven't got the patience.

Carver Ah, no . . .

Hills I'm Judoing because I've had noooo success for sooo long I'm growing UGLY. You need harmony and happiness and circles NOT toooo grow UGLY. A Judok-a-a-a has a clear mind plugged into currents, zzzz, balanced, controlled, LAID-BACK.

In his excitement he topples off his chair.

Powell I'm here because they said I shouldn't, wouldn't, couldn't.

Hills *clambers back into his chair.*

Hills Therapy's no good, they want me too make TABLE-MATS and baskets. I want Bujutsu-Carver.

Powell Not forgetting Zen and Shiatzu up your finger for sexual relief.

Hills But we've both got GET up and GO-GO-GO.

Powell Yes, we'll always have a go, go, go won't we George? Hum 'The Blue Danube'.

Carver Hum?

Powell 'The Blue Danube'

*Startled, **Carver** hums loudly. **Powell** grabs **Hills** and they attempt a waltz, their arms and legs still shooting out in all* *directions, but vaguely in time to the music.*

Powell Well?

Carver Very impressive. What I was going to say was I
don't want you to waste your money. It is £8.50 a week plus
V.A.T. and it'll take you at least six months.

Powell To learn Judo?

Carver No, to get you into First Position.

Powell Money can be found. George was left a little and I
have something from my books.

Carver Let me be honest. Bujutsu-Carver is just becoming
more widely known. I have three former pupils right now
teaching the method under licence. It hasn't been easy: part-
time jobs and bedsitters in Bayswater, six hours practice
every day for years. Sacrifices had to be made. My wife left
me and took everything including the pin-cushions. She was
married in white you know – what a memory that woman
had. Still I can't blame her for leaving, she only ever saw me
in Judo positions. That's why I've included Shiatzu sexual
finger relief in Bujutsu-Carver. Nobody believed in me then.
Even my mother said I'd end up in a Tokyo gutter pissed
on by little Japanese dogs. When you're a visionary that's the
sort of stupid comment you can expect. Especially from your
own mother. But I'll live to see Bujutsu-Carver clubs all over
the country; accountants and housewives, bankers and
bishops taking an hour off every day to do their Bujutsuing.
Stripping away body flab, mind flab. British men and
women fit in mind and body – now there's a vision for you.
And you two could wreck it.

Hills Hooow? Whaaa soooo SPECIAL about UUUUS?

Carver A year ago I let a Mr Gooms join one of my classes.
He was extremely enthusiastic and fit – for a 79 year old.
The first exercise he did he broke he broke two ribs. We
settled out of court.

Powell We're not 79 and we fall easy like drunks fall. If we
didn't we'd be permanently in traction. Our bones're
rubbery, not brittle like Mr Goom's.

He throws himself off the chair.

Hills And I'm even better aaat FALLING. I've had more practice. Bones aren't i-i-important.

He falls over the back of the chair.

Carver What is important?

Hills W-W-Whatever we happen t-t-to BE doing at the moment.

Carver A good Zen answer. But gentlemen I can't teach you. I'm only a fourth Dan. You need a sixth or seventh Dan at least. Besides, one breath of scandal, one hint of failure reflects back on Bujutsu-Carver. I've made a desert of my life for it. I can't risk the risk.

Powell You're putting up barriers, Mr Carver. You said the most formidable opponent you could meet was yourself. If you have an open mind you take whatever comes in your stride.

Hills You've juuust got an attack of NERVES – a c-c-crisis of confidence.

Powell Think of the prestige if you pull it off. We'd be the ultimate test of Bujutsu-Carver – a very Everest. You have to tackle us because we're there.

Hills We need y-y-your HELP.

Carver And I need you two like I need a giraffe . . . But, gentlemen, I'm touched – I must be touched to agree to take you on . . . for one session. We'll see how it goes. It's true you are the ultimate test for Bujutsu-Carver to say nothing of Shiatzu and Zen. There'll be more than the sound of one hand clapping if I pull it off.

Hills Whaaa's the sound of ONE hand clapping?

Carver Snow falling, grass growing, dead sparrows; it's soundless sound. Mr Hills, Mr Powell, put your chairs out of the way and we'll start . . . (**Powell** *and* **Hills** *pick up their chairs and immediately bang into each other: disentangling themselves they stagger over to put the chairs down over to the left.*) Zen masters say: 'The Most Valuable thing in the world is the head of a dead cat.' I don't know what good that is to us of course. But I'm sure Zen has something to say that is helpful – if I could just think of it.

Powell *and* **Hills** *come back and stand in front of him, their bodies twitching continuously.*

Carver Hhmm . . . Good posture is the basis of Bujutsu-Carver.

Hills Gooo posture . . .

Carver Yes, it's the basis of all creative Judo. And the essence of good posture is the Tanden. The Tanden is a point, here, two inches below the navel . . . (*He points.*) All physical movement stems from the Tanden.

Powell Is it Shiatzu sexual finger relief?

Carver No. It just means that if you're aware of your Tanden you bring your body's centre of gravity down to a new low. And if your centre of gravity's low it's difficult for anyone to throw you off-balance. So always think of the Tanden . . . (*He points to it again.*) Now show me where your Tandens are.

Powell *and* **Hills** *try to point to their Tandens. But, because they are shaking so,* **Powell** *ends up pointing to his chest and* **Hills** *to his groin.*

Carver N-e-a-r-l-y right. Two inches *below* your belly-button Mr Powell. Up a little Mr Hills.

Hills U-U-Up, up.

They try desperately to point to the right spot.

Carver Awareness of the Tanden is as much psychological as physical. So concentrate your minds on that point. Control the mind and the body follows. Hold the Tanden in your mind. Feel your weight shifting down. Hold the Tanden . . . Hold . . .

Powell I'm holding.

Hills Tanden . . . T-T-TANDEN . . .

They are now vaguely pointing to the right spot.

Carver Yes . . . Now let's take up a Shizentai posture which is the simple standing position. First breath deeply and regularly . . . Now just stand upright – I know that's difficult but try. Your feet should be about shoulder width apart. (*He takes up the position;* **Powell** *and* **Hills** *imitate him though their feet skid about under them.*) Now the body weight is down to your toes. Knees slightly flexed . . . easy . . . easy.

As **Powell** *and* **Hills** *copy him they find themselves slowly topping forward.*

Hills E-E-Easy.

Carver Now, hands open, fingers curling inwards, wrists flexible, arms at sides ready to grapple, elbows below the level of your hands . . . (**Powell** *and* **Hills** *fling their arms about uncontrollably.*) Head up, eyes alert . . . And you're ready.

Carver *is in the Shizentai position but* **Powell** *and* **Hills** *are twisting themselves into knots trying to imitate him.*

Hills KNEES . . . HANDS . . . fingersss . . . e-e-elbows . . .

Powell Head . . . eyes . . .

Carver It's knees flexed, hands open, fingers curled, elbows low, head up, eyes alert. . . . Hhmm . . . Take a break . . . Well, you could've been worse.

Powell How?

Carver You weren't stiff. No, you weren't stiff. Stiff-armed, stiff-arsed Judo is worse.

He closes his eyes and breathes deeply.

Hills Whaa you doing?

Carver Contemplating non-existence.

Powell Control the mind you said and the body follows, you said. I control my mind. I can pin you to the wall with differential equations. My mind moves with speed and precision – it's a fifth Dan mind. But this body of mine can never be more than half a Daniel.

Carver (*opening his eyes*) And I'm afraid not all the Wisdom of the East, not Zen Masters, Encho Ekai or even Shaku can change a hair of it. I believed with the five-foot nothing Kensho Anbe, that all things flowed in harmony and one candle could light the Universe – Bujutsu-Carver should be a system for all mankind. What good is it if it's only for the fit and the whole? What good is it if some are left outside? What good is it if you can't even Shizentai, can't hold?

Hills Weee can hold onto pain, sickness, loneliness and death – wee're experts of all that. If we didn't HOLD we'd s-s-shake ourselves to pieces. No rest for us, I guess we must be wicked. I wake up EVERY e-e-every morning saying 'Hold. Don't let go.' I let go-o-o once when my PARENTS d-d-died on me. I tried tooo listen to the birds b-b-but they wouldn't put u-u-up with ME. I couldn't look out of the RIGHT window. Sooo I bought a razor to cut my throat. I ended up s-s-slashing my k-k-kneecap instead I was shaking so much. NOW I hold. There's no-one in the world like us handicappers for H-H-HOLDING.

Powell George's right. I was so busy thinking I was forgetting.

Carver Zen Master Joshu always said, 'If you've got nothing on your mind, throw it out. And if you can't throw it out, carry it out.'

Hills Whaa did he mean?

Carver Who knows? Those damn Zen Masters were always saying things like that . . . We'll give it another try. Shizentai . . . But first the Tanden . . . (*He points.*) It's here. Hold it in your mind's eye. And point. Hold and point. (*This time* **Powell**'s *shaking finger points to his thigh and* **Hills**'s *to his right side.*) No . . . No . . . I'll show you exactly.

He moves forward and takes **Hills**'s *hand to direct his waving finger to the correct spot. As he does so* **Hills** *judders convulsively sending* **Carver** *crashing to the floor.*

Powell *and* **Hills** *look down at him in horror.*

Hills Oooh . . .

Powell He didn't mean it, did you George?

Hills Nooooo!

Carver That's the first time I've been off my feet since '68.

Hills I-I-I feel in a p-p-pretty p-p-palsy state. W-W-Weee've BLOWN it, eh Mr Carver?

Carver *Aya!* (*He jumps up and mimes a Judo hold.*) The Gyaku-juji-jime or Reverse Cross Strangle! I was forgetting the great Zen principle of turning disadvantages to advantage. The famous one-armed fighter Kusunda became a supreme Judo champion because he followed the advice of his Zen teacher and secretly practised Hanemakikomi holds. Now the Hanemakikomi's can only be countered by grabbing your opponent's right arm. But Kusunda didn't have a right arm. By the time his opponents had adjusted to his empty sleeve he'd thrown them.

Powell But we haven't got empty sleeves.

Carver No, you've got the shakes, which is better. I made the mistake of trying to overcome them instead of using 'em. Most Judoka are well-balanced, low-slung, poised fighters. You'll be the opposite – off-balanced, high-strung and a shambles. They won't be expecting that. Good Judo is sneaky. Oh, it's sneaky. You see a Judoka tries to anticipate his opponent's next move. They can sense if it's going to be a hip throw, an ankle sweep or a shoulder wheel. But in your case they won't know your next move because you're moving all the time. Take the simple Shizentai position . . . (*He assumes the position.*) Now you . . . (**Powell** *and* **Hills** *try to imitate him despite their shaking.*) That's good . . . Now as your opponent I come forward to grab your arms. (*He moves forward to take* **Powell**'*s forearms but keeps missing them because of* **Powell**'*s shaking.*) See, see, it works! Whilst I'm trying to catch hold you could ankle sweep me. (*He finally catches hold of* **Powell** *and finds himself juddering and shaking as well.*) I'm disorientated . . . I've lost my Tanden. You could Seri-nage me or give me the old Hiza-guruma. The possibilities are endless. (*He lets go of* **Powell**.) You'll have to be taught the moves of course. But I can see you as champions.

Hills C-C-Champions? Bujutsu-Carver CHAMPS, sexy finger CHAMPS, heads of dead cats C-C-CHAMPS?

Powell Are you sure we really look like championship material, Mr Carver?

Carver With practice. But all those shakes and twitches. Not good enough gentlemen.

Powell We know.

Carver They're much too small.

Powell Too small?

Carver I want strong shakes, convulsive twitches, titanic lurches.

Hills } W-W-What?
Powell

Carver *imitates* **Powell** *and* **Hills***'s movements violently shaking and flinging out his arms and legs with exaggerated wildness.*

Carver No half-measure, gentlemen. I aim to make spastic paralysis a fighting force to be reckoned with, *aya!* (*He thrusts out his right arm and leg.*) The Ago-Oshi Palsey or the Palsey-Punch to Groin and Throat.

Powell But we've spent our lives trying to shake less.

Carver I want more, not less. You hit the target by aiming in the opposite direction – that's sound Zen. I want bold, full-blooded convulsions . . . (*He jumps and shakes violently.*) You were born to shake, rattle and roll. Don't fight it, go with it. Go, go, go!

Powell But it's different.

Carver Of course it's different. You've got to start thinking like winners.

Hills H-H-HARD. W-W-We've always been LOSERS.

Carver The difference between winners and losers is that winners always expect to win and they do, even when they lose. And remember you'll win not despite your handicaps but because of 'em – that's true Zen, gentlemen.

Hills Up t-t-till now OUR h-h-handicaps haaave generally been a HANDICAP. I-I-I m-m-must s-s-say I like THIS w-w-way better. Whaaa about holding our b-b-belly button TANDENS?

Carver Forget your Tandens and hold your shakes. At all times I want you to have a clear mental picture of how you shake, twitch and shake. It's your biggest asset.

Powell Nobody's ever said that to us before.

Carver Because they're not into Bujutsu-Carver or dead cat Zen – the fools. All you'll ever get from them is sympathy.

Powell *and* **Hills** *shudder in horror.*

Hills S-S-S-S-Sympathy . . . *uggghhh.*

Carver Right, assume the Shizentai position again, gentlemen . . . Wait, I've just thought of a lovely opening gambit. Oh when you're on song, the ideas swarm in like bees to honey. Listen, don't shake for the first few seconds. It'll be a bluff. Your opponents'll think you're just ordinary fighters, then we'll hit 'em with our Spastic Variations . . . Oh, it's so beautifully sneaky . . . Right, into the Shizentai *(The three take up the Shizentai positions, arms out, knees flexed.)* Keep it still . . . *(They are still.)* That's good . . . Now shake it. *(The three shake more wildly than ever before.)* That's good, *ahh!* *(In his eagerness,* **Powell** *has blundered into him and has convulsively brought his knee up into* **Carver***'s stomach.)* Ooooh-ah!

Powell Sorry!

Carver No, don't apologize. That's good. We'll call it the Hari Hiza Spastic or the Spastic Knee Into the Stomach, *aya!* *(He jerks his right knee up.)* Hold those shakes, men! Hold!

But **Powell** *suddenly stops shaking so violently and looks across at* **Hills** *who also slows down.*

Powell We didn't shake at all just now.

Hills Noooooo, weeee didn't . . .

Carver Because I told you not to. Part of the plan to throw your opponents off balance and keep 'em guessing.

Hills B-B-But weeee didn't SHAKE!

Powell Not once – once, once! Not once! For the first time in my waking life I was at rest.

Hills W-W-We're WINNERS.

Carver Not if you rest. That's not the idea at all. It's just a ploy. We only use it – briefly – at the beginning of a fight. Mustn't overdo it. Anyone can rest. Keeping still isn't important. What's important is getting power into those twitches, shakes and turns. I want every muscle working. No resting, *please* . . . So let's have a full five minutes of shakes. Shizentai and shake it *aya*!

Powell *Aya*!

Hills *Ayaaaa* !

Carver It's all for Bujutsu-Carver. Remember the dead cats. Shake and hold. Now – shake! Shake! Shake!

All three are shaking and twitching furiously as the lights slowly fade out.

III

NOT AS BAD AS THEY SEEM

Lights up on a bedroom. Late afternoon. **Paul Berridge** *and*
Judith Sefton *are in bed. Door Left, window Right.* **Berridge**'s
clothes are placed neatly over the back of a chair nearby. **Judith** *is
smoking a cigarette in bed.*

Berridge My ex-wife never smoked in bed after we made
love. She said one drag was enough. She was kinky, kept
asking me to hurt her. So I told her her budgie was dead.

Judith Harvey was like that too. He said he had marks all
over his body from women touching him with ten-foot poles.
The man was either mad or both. I knew he was a lousy
lover in just eight seconds flat.

Berridge Actually, I've never thought of myself as a great
lover, not since the day they caught a Peeping Tom booing
me.

Judith Rhino horns're supposed to be the best aphrodisiacs
but they have one side-effect – you keep charging Morris
Minors.

They laugh.

Berridge They broke the mould before they made you.
You're funny and you're beautiful.

Judith As what?

Berridge As a system of complex numbers.

Judith To be beautiful you need happiness and fulfilment.
When I was young I had ideas I'll never catch again. Why
do you say I'm beautiful?

Berridge Because I see your shape in the sound of your
voice, because my world isn't quite so dark now.

Judith Paul, if we're going to be lovers we shouldn't get too
personal. We'll only stay together if we stay independent. It's
hard but I'm me because I'm me and you're you because
you're you. But if I'm only me because you're you and
you're only you because I'm me, then I'm not me and you're
not you.

Berridge You're right . . . I had another fight with the

Faculty this morning. That bunch would try switching on a light to see how dark it was. Ernest kept saying 'This is only a suggestion, Paul, but don't let's forget who's making it.' He'll have to go, as Head of the Department he isn't smart enough to be an idiot.

Judith But he is my husband.

Berridge That's no excuse. How did you come to marry a man like that? You're intelligent and he has a room temperature I.Q.

Judith I'm so intelligent I was working as a hotel switchboard operator. Sixty-two hours a week, five hundred calls a day. At the end of an eight-hour session I'd pick up the cords and they'd slide out of my hands. But it's a job where you learn how to judge people just from their vocals.

Berridge So what happened, you got lonely?

Judith Tired. I wanted to grab a handful of cords and pull. Instead I pulled Ernest. I didn't want to end up sleeping alone with a hot-water bottle and blackheads. So I married Ernest though I didn't love him.

Berridge I'm glad. Morals don't bother me much but taste *is* important.

Judith We went to Worthing for our honeymoon. It was so dull there, the tide went out one Sunday and didn't come back.

Berridge Believe it or not, when I was a student I worked in a hotel. As a bar pianist, five thirty to midnight, to pre-recorded applause by professional mourners. Maths and music're close even if it's music to drink by. Customers always wanted to tell me their troubles, as if I hadn't got enough of my own. But I never got friendly. They don't tip if they think you're a friend. I earned good money playing. Being working class my family thought I should make it permanent. But I was lucky. I was bright and I knew what I wanted.

Judith Me too – home, security, money and the respect money brings. Now every morning I sit down and eat my cornflakes. I don't know how many I have, fifteen, sixteen, seventeen – who's counting?

Berridge If you plan, the trajectory is always up. At first I thought I'd teach Economics, be a learned professor of usury and selfishness. But I saw the field was overcrowded. So I switched to Maths. A good choice. I'm a creature of order, first, last and always, obsessed with precision and neatness. I keep my pencils sharp and my passions blunted.

Judith I wish Ernest did. He's too passionate for a man of his weight. It's all hot air and heavy breathing in the Groves of Academia.

Berridge Passion blurs. It's like walking in a high wind. You don't know where you are. I've always stayed clear.

Judith What about your ex-wife?

Berridge Ahh, that was a sudden rush of blood to the, er, head. I can't say I planned that in my waking dreams. Sarah was vain and greedy; she'd eat her cake and yours too. But she was vivid. She was *there* . . . Sorry I'm talking about her. Though a marriage dies letters still come.

Judith The past rots. It should be treated with stain remover. Why did it end?

Berridge I heard the weasel sound of pity in her voice. We threw a last party and when it was over a guest said, 'I'd like to say goodbye to your wife.' I said, 'Who wouldn't?' Neat. The rest was messy and a real waste of energy.

Judith I hope I won't be. I mean at the very least it can't do your career any harm having an affair with the wife of the Departmental Head.

Berridge Provided he doesn't find out.

Judith He'd better not. We're both in safe harbour. If Ernest ever looks like finding out we end it. Much as I'd hate to.

Berridge Why? I know I can imitate falling leaves and tall buildings but why pick me?

Judith You're a good listener and when a woman finds a man who actually listens to her she usually lets him into her bed out of sheer gratitude.

Berridge You're good to listen to. And don't worry about the rest. I'll see you twice a week – Tuesdays and Fridays, three-thirty to six, when Ernest has classes and I haven't. It appeals to my sense of order.

Judith I don't see how he can find out. He's so wrapped up in himself he's quite blind.

They laugh. There is the sound of someone coming into the living room. **Ernest Sefton** *calls.*

Sefton (*off*) Judith! . . . Are you in?!

Judith *and* **Berridge** *'freeze' in horror.*

Judith (*low*) It's·. . .

Berridge (*low*) Yes . . .

As **Sefton** *is heard in the living-room,* **Berridge** *leaps out of bed and stumbles forward, putting his hands out in front of him. He feels desperately for support along the edge of the bed to the end. He is blind.*

Berridge (*low*) Clothes? . . .

Judith (*low*) Chair . . .

Berridge (*low*) Where? . . .

Judith (*low*) Left . . .

As she clambers off the bed dragging the blanket off in her panic, **Berridge** *bumps into the chair. He catches it before it topples over, but his clothes and white stick, which we see for the first time, fall in a heap. He goes on his hands and knees to pick them up.*

Judith (*low*) Where are you?!

She has picked up her white stick on the floor behind the dressing table, lurches forward and cannons straight into him. She is blind too.

They quickly disentangle themselves and **Berridge** *puts on his* *trousers. When he tries to zip them up he finds he has them on back to front.* **Judith** *frantically helps him on with his shirt but in her haste rips the front. She suddenly points excitedly, poking a finger in his eye.*

Berridge (*low*) Arrrx.

Judith (*low*) Shh, he's coming – surround Asia – run for your lives!

Sefton *is heard approaching the bedroom. As* **Berridge** *scoops up his things,* **Judith** *grabs her white stick and dives for the bed – and misses it, landing on the blanket on the floor.*

Undeterred, she jumps back into bed whilst **Berridge** *veers off to the Right as the door opens and* **Ernest Sefton** *stands in the doorway. He stares at the dishevelled* **Judith** *who is lying full-length on the bed, but the wrong way round, and ignores* **Berridge** *who is standing in a torn shirt, trying to hold up his trousers.*

Sefton Judith? What're you doing?

Judith (*pretending she was just woken up*) Sleeping . . .

Sefton Sleeping?

Judith I didn't hear you come in.

Sefton Obviously.

He crosses straight to her and trips over the blanket on the floor.

What the devil was that?

He scrambles around on his hands and knees trying to get his bearing. **Sefton** *too is blind.*

Judith It must be my blanket. You *do* need a guide dog.

Sefton It's your fault, Pet. Anything out of place and we blinders're sure to crash into it.

Judith Sorry. I think I've got a cold coming.

Berridge, *slowly and with extreme care, stuffs his socks and shoes in his pockets as* **Sefton** *sits on the edge of the bed to talk to* **Judith,** *unaware he is actually talking to her feet because she is still lying the wrong way round.*

Sefton I'm not feeling myself either, Pet. That's why I got Tomlinson to deputize for me. I've been teaching at the Henly School for the blind for eighteen years and it's the first time I've missed a class. I got a blinding migraine then this extraordinary thing happened . . . Judith, I think I'm beginning to see again!

Judith *jerks upright and* **Berridge** *lets go of his trousers in fright.*

Sefton Of course when I say see, I don't mean *see* see. I saw shadows and no shadow is black. So there was light. You've been blind from birth but I was struck blind so I kow what light is. Maybe I've been granted second sight.

As **Judith** *quietly turns round on the bed to face the right way,* **Berridge** *pulls up his trousers and moves to the wall Right, and feels his way along it.*

Sefton I'm hoping against hope, but I shouldn't hope. I must turn a deaf eye to all that. But to see a candle burning, girls bathing, *blue.* To see blue again.

Pressing himself against the wall, **Berridge** *has worked his way round to the bedroom window which flies open and he disappears straight out of it. There is a muffled cry and crash.* **Judith** *and* **Sefton** *turn.*

What was that?

Judith Mice.

Sefton Mice? Mice! You can't fool me Judith. I know what it was. It's that marauding cat you're always protecting – not the Siamese. Siamese have a different cat tread. I've got *ears.* I can hear the sound of walls . . . (*He gets up and crosses to the window.*) The window's open, feel the breeze. (*He stands in front of the window and shouts as* **Berridge**'s *dishevelled head appears outside.*) Damn cat! Get off!

Berridge *flinches.* **Sefton** *slams the window shut on* **Berridge**'s *hands. His face contorts in pain. He opens his mouth to yell but with a heroic effort suppresses it.*

There's something wrong with the catch.

Judith Leave it. You've thought you could see before.

As **Sefton** *crosses to the bed,* **Berridge** *clambers inside as quietly as he can, blowing on his numbed fingers, and clutching his trousers.*

Sefton All I can tell you is that it wasn't all black. I felt I had the power to bend spoons with my mind.

Judith When I see Dr Palmer about my cold, you'd better come along and have your eyes checked. But right now could you be an angel and get me a glass of milk?

Sefton Certainly, Pet. Colds're *the* worst for blinders. With nose and ears clogged, who can judge distances, people or things? Nothing's what it sounds like, cats're mice, mice men, and everything's micky murky.

He exits, closing the door behind him.

Judith (*low*) Hello? . . .

Berridge (*low*). Hello . . . I thought he'd recognize me by the air I was breathing. I've got to change my trousers.

He sits on the edge of the bed and starts to put his trousers on the right way round.

Judith (*low*) This isn't the time to think about being well dressed! Just grease your shoes and slip away. Did you hear? He might be able to see.

This time he has got his shirt sleeve caught in his trouser zip. He hops about bent double.

Berridge (*low*) Congratulations. I feel like I've got both feet in one sock . . . (*Groaning.*) Oh Lord, lay me in some tacky bit of earth that is forever England. I must look an idiot.

Judith (*low*) How do I know? I can't see. I never could. Ernest had years of sight.

Berridge (*low*) That's why he isn't one of us. We're not people who can't see. We're a different species – we're blind from birth, perfectly adjusted, aristos of the dark . . . I'm lost. How do I get out?

He finally disentangles his shirt from his trousers.

Judith (*low*) The door's thirteen feet four inches directly left, the window ten feet three inches from the end of the bed. Follow my pointed finger.

The door opens and **Sefton** *stands in the doorway with a glass of milk in one hand and his white stick in the other.*

Sefton Judith, I feel there's somebody else.

Berridge *jumps onto the bed and cowers down beside* **Judith.**

Judith Somebody else?

Sefton I have this extraordinary feeling I'm being watched by another pair of eyes.

Judith You're upset. You'll probably imagine all sorts of things.

Sefton *taps his way to the bed.*

Sefton I hope I didn't imagine the light and the shadows. I'm using my stick in case you've left anything else about. Here's your milk.

He holds out the glass of milk for her. She edges over **Berridge,** *half lying on top of him to take it.*

Paul . . .

Berridge *reacts, jerks* **Judith**'s *arm and gets a glass of milk in the face.* **Sefton** *sits on the edge of the bed and chuckles.*

Paul Berridge is responsible for all this. He gave me that blinding migraine and afterwards I saw the light. He'd be furious if he found out. The first time we shook hands I knew he was after my job. Smooth. When he sheds his skin he can send me the rattle . . . (**Berridge** *reacts but* **Judith** *quickly pushes him down.*) Berridge has had it too easy. I've had to fight all the way. Everybody was against me. The authorities always favour teachers blind from birth. Oh don't think I don't know what's going on. I know – everything . . . On top of that if you're born sighted, like me, you can't ever forget it. You carry the sun around in your pocket always. Berridge was lucky he was born stone-blind.

Judith So was I and I don't feel lucky. *You* may be though. You'll see dusks and dawns, tigers, mountains and mirrors. I don't even know what a dusk or a dawn is. I can't see what I can't feel. My eyes're at the end of my fingers.

Sefton I don't care about the tigers and the mountains. What I miss is the moment when you wake up in the morning and one world disappears and another comes into being.

Judith You'll be able to see me.

Sefton See myself too for the first time in years. I had a young face then. I'll be older, but I'm pretty confident I'll be a fine figure of a man. You can tell by my voice.

Judith I may have angry wrinkles.

Sefton Nonsense. I've felt you all over so I can see you're beautiful. Kiss, Pet.

He bends over to kiss her. **Berridge** *partly under her reacts, pitching her forward so she and* **Sefton** *crack heads. Undeterred,* **Sefton** *kisses her.* **Berridge** *takes the opportunity to slide off the other side of the bed and goes into a cupboard by mistake.*

Judith I think I'll get up. We'll go in and have tea.

Judith *sits on the edge of the bed and picks up her white stick as* **Sefton** *makes his way out. He suddenly stops as he hears* **Berridge** *come out of the cupboard.*

Sefton Judith, there is somebody else. There!

He points with his white stick vaguely in the direction of **Berridge**, *who tries not to breathe.*

Judith That's me.

Sefton No, the shadow's moving. Ahha!

He takes a mighty swipe, misses and the momentum whirls him round as **Berridge** *turns to avoid the unseen blow.*

Though they are now facing in opposite directions, they assume fencing positions for a moment. Shouting 'En Guarde', **Sefton** *lunges at the empty air and* **Berridge** *parries a non-existant thrust.* **Judith** *rushes over to blunder into* **Sefton**'s *stick.*

Ahh! Touche! . . . Plie! . . . (*The two men fence, backs to each other.*) It's a touch of the toledo steels!

Judith Ernest, it's me!

As **Sefton** *stops fighting,* **Berridge** *tiptoes away, stumbles on his jacket and picks it up.*

Sefton Judith?

Judith What's the matter with you?

Sefton It must be nerves. Today's shaken up my whole nervous system.

I'm going to lie down for a minute.

Judith Will you be all right?

She crosses to the bed with him whilst **Berridge** *finally finds the open door by hitting the door frame.*

Sefton What was that?

Judith I was clearing my throat. Lie down, Pet.

They are both by the bed as **Berridge** *exits and is heard crashing into something in the living room.* **Judith** *reacts instinctively, clasps her hands over* **Sefton**'s *ears, pulls his face to her and kisses him.*

A series of crashes and muffled curses from the living room marks **Berridge**'s *progress to the front door as* **Judith** *continues the kiss. Only after she has heard* **Berridge** *leave does she finish it and take her hands away from* **Sefton**'s *ears. He gasps.*

Sefton I've stopped breathing. You smell good.

Judith 'Desire'.

He pulls her onto the bed.

The front doorbell rings. **Judith** *gets up.*

You rest. I'll go.

She exits into the living-room. **Sefton** *takes off his jacket in the fast-fading light.*

Judith *is heard opening and closing the front door.*

Sefton This dark of mine is full of eyes . . . I blame it on these short days and long winter evenings . . . I'll see Dr Palmer, maybe he can help . . . in medicine, where there's money there's hope.

Judith *appears in the doorway with* **Berridge**, *who tries to pose elegantly despite the fact he has no socks, his trousers are half done up, his shirt is out and ripped and his jacket torn. He and* **Judith**, *however, force themselves to speak with exaggerated calm.*

Judith Look who it is, Ernest. I mean, guess who it is?

Sefton Aunt Sarah from Grimsby with the elastic-sided boots.

Judith No, it's Paul Berridge.

Sefton The vultures're gathering already.

Berridge I trust I'm not disturbing you, Ernest. I heard you'd been taken ill. It's so unlike you we all got a little anxious. Is there anything any of us can do?

Sefton Oh no, nothing. This is most thoughtful of you and the others Paul.

Berridge (*low, to* **Judith**) I've lost my keys.

Berridge *drops on his hands and knees and feels the bedroom carpet.*

Judith Yes Paul, most thoughtful.

Sefton How did you know I'd been taken sick?

Berridge *jumps to his feet to answer whilst* **Judith** *goes on her hands and knees to continue the search.*

Berridge Tomlinson. He made it sound as if you were really bad.

Sefton No, I was upset. I thought I saw light.

Berridge Did you?

Sefton Who knows? I've been fooled before. But it shook me up like nothing else could. I'm touched you came to see me Paul, and I'm not a man to say that lightly, am I, Judith?

Judith *springs to her feet to answer and* **Berridge** *goes down to search.*

Judith You say nothing lightly, Ernest.

Berridge *finds his bunch of keys.*

He scrambles up and puts them into **Judith***'s hand for a second to show he has found them.*

Outside the window the winter light has almost faded.

Sefton Yes, given half a chance people are kind. I sometimes forget blindness brings out the best in others. They know forebearance is typical of the blind as irritability is of the deaf. I think that's why there're comedies about the deaf, none about the blind.

Judith (*low*) Till now.

Berridge Sorry I disturbed you, Ernest. I'll leave you to rest.

Sefton Don't go, and please don't apologize. It's good to discover one's colleagues care a little. And I know by your voice the concern is sincere. We blinders have ways of seeing the truth the rest're blind to.

There is no longer any light from the window. It is completely dark so we cannot see **Sefton, Judith** *or* **Berridge***. We are now as completely in the dark as they have been all along.*

Judith I used to believe we had new ways of seeing too. I was sure I saw a universe of meaning in the sound of a door slamming shut – bang. I thought I could tell if it was the end of a marriage, a job, a friendship or a life. I had a sixth sense developed to the seventh degree. But now I wonder. Maybe we fool ourselves and we're as much in the dark as those who can see – only we're in a double darkness.

Berridge I always thought I knew what I was doing. My life has an orderly shape. Now look at me . . . I mean, I lost my way and fell, coming here. I was so sure of where I was going.

Sefton We all make mistakes, it's human. I was sure I was being watched just now and heard phantom footsteps.

Berridge Suddenly things conspired against me. I felt betrayed.

Sefton Betrayed? I'm the one who's been betrayed.

He is heard getting up.

Berridge You?!

Judith Who? Who betrayed you?

Sefton Hope.

Judith
Berridge Ahhh . . .

Sefton I hoped, though I shouldn't've hoped, I was going to see. But the world's gone invisible again.

Berridge The world's a cheat. We can't be certain of anything.

Sefton That's something. We have to find consolation in order to survive: if the text is lousy admire the binding. Look at me. I don't think of the light I lost but the friends I've found, eh Paul. Let me shake your hand . . . Do you know you've got something hanging down in front of you? . . . Here . . .

There is a loud ripping sound.

Berridge I think you've just torn off the sleeve of my jacket.

Sefton It's all right, I've got a spare sleeve I always carry for emergencies.

Judith (*laughing despite herself*) This is a pretty kettle of fish and it's a funny place to keep them. You probably tore it when you fell. You'd better stay for supper and clean up. You must look a sight.

They are heard moving to the door.

Berridge (*laughing*) Lucky no-one here'll ever know, we're as blind as bats.

Sefton (*laughing*) Lucky we're as blind as moles in a mist.
You see, things never are as bad as they seem.

Judith Why not?

The door is heard slamming behind them as they exit.

Sunsets and Glories

Sunsets and Glories was premièred on 28 June 1990 at the West Yorkshire Playhouse, with the following cast:

Characters

Nicholas IV	Dennis Edwards
Malabranca	Marius Goring
Gaetani	Jimmy Logan
Orsini	Ian Barritt
Cholet	Peter Whitbread
Colonna	Bob Cartland
Morrone	Freddie Jones
Sala	Timothy Bateson
Charles II	Michael Mears
Queen Maria	Geraldine Fitzgerald
Montefelto	Jeremy Sinden
Jacopone	Murray Melvin
Sophia Aldesca	Susie Baxter
Gina	Sarah-Jane Holm
Maifreda	Tricia Kelly
Guard	Shaun Prendergast
James of Aragon	Peter Whitbread
Elijah	Dennis Edwards
Verrier	Trevor Laird
Lucera	Shaun Prendergast
Roffred	Michael Brogan
Bartol	Peter Whitbread
Isobella	Tricia Kelly
Benvenuto	Sarah-Jane Holm

Directed by Stuart Burge
Designed by Fotini Dimou
Music by Stephen Deutsch
Movement by Eleanor Fazan
Lighting by Tim Thornally

It is all imagined: the Middle Ages, Waterloo, 1066. History is not history unless it is imagined. No one I know was present in the distant past, so the past, like the future, is an act of imagination. The ghosts are all here and now and with us always. We conjure them up, clothe them with historical facts and call them Caesar and Alexander and say they are real. But even those of us who live in the past only live there in our imaginations. It is not real – not even yesterday.

'Life is like a river.'
'Why?'
'How should I know. Am I a philosopher?'

I am coming to feel all the big ideas about God, faith, free-will, and the rest are fascinating games but not something, in the end, you should, perhaps, commit yourself to; live or die for. Particularly when, it seems, they answer nothing in a soulless universe.

All I can do is tell stories and leave the big ideas to priests and politicians who will steal the whites of your eyes if you let them get close enough.

'Eureka, it's finished! It's a winner, I can smell it!'
'What're you going to call it, Signor Boccaccio?'
'I thought, maybe *The Decameron*. That has a ring to it. It may be just a collection of filthy stories to you, Fred, but mark my words, it'll be a classic.'

Have you heard the story of the death of the Emperor Claudius? It seems that he 'bubbled up his ghost' at a banquet when he was listening to a troupe of comics. Which just goes to show how dangerous comics can be.

In the middle of a joke, Claudius farted, and cried out before he died, 'Oh dear, oh dear! I think I've done a mess.' Whether he had or not, nobody is certain, but it is likely, after all he always made a mess of everything.

Talking about comics, the American entertainer, Eddie Foy, lost a court case and was berated by his lawyer: 'When you were in the witness box and they asked you your occupation why did you say "The greatest comedian in the world"? Don't you see it completely antagonised the jury?' Foy looked at him in astonishment. 'But I had to say that,' he replied, 'I was under oath.'

In another court case, the courtesan, Phyrne, a native of Thespiae, was prosecuted on a capital charge of corrupting the citizens of Athens. They did not mind Athenians corrupting Athenians, but were presumably incensed at foreigners taking all the best jobs. Her lover, Hyperides, defended her but it was obvious the judges were about to condemn her, when she tore open her tunic and showed her breasts. She was acquitted of all charges. But others, like the poet Posidippus, say this is all a pack of lies. What Phyrne really did was see each of the judges separately and in private and there was consequently never any doubt that she would get off.

Which reminds me of the Athenian prostitutes who followed that 'great statesman' Pericles when he laid siege to Samos and they made a fortune. Afterwards they presented the politician with a large sum of money – raised by subscription – as a token of their appreciation for the trade he had put their way.

In contrast, one hard winter in Bologna, Leopardi encased himself in a sack of feathers to keep warm whilst Thorstein Veblen, on the other hand, said he studied foreign languages by staring at each word until he knew what it meant. Ezra Pound claimed he understood Chinese ideograms the same way. Is this gift hereditary?

Then again Shakespeare, seeing Jonson on a toilet and reading a book, said that he was sorry Johnson's memory was so bad he did not know how to shit without a book. This is probably the only remotely half-decent joke Will ever made – if he made it. Certainly it is the only one that does not need footnotes.*

Whereas there was Oscar Wilde dying in a hotel room saying 'Either that wallpaper goes or I do.'

Apropos of nothing, what about the saint who became Pope? That story, however, needs rather more space to do it justice.

Peter Barnes, 1990

---

* John Barrymore said that footnotes are like going downstairs to answer the doorbell on your wedding night.

Act One

Maria Maggiore Palace. Rome, 1292. A shaft of light shines diagonally onto **Pope Nicholas IV** *downstage centre in full regalia. Five cowled* **Cardinals** *in purple robes stand in a semi-circle behind him. Behind them in deep shadow upstage centre is a life-size crucifix.*

Nicholas IV *holds up his hands and rings slip off his fingers.*

Nicholas IV Death hour. Two a.m. the 4th April in the year of our Lord, 1292. Rings slip from me. Weak, bent, heavy with the weight of heavy silks and heavier crown, I stand before God's high altar and give account of my reign as Pope Nicholas IV, 1288 to 1292. I did what was expected, needed. No monster me, sadly no saint either. A middling sort of man. No high noons, low midnights, I saw no orbs, no fiery bushes, no crosses in the sky. I did not change the world into something greener. I lost God when I gained St Peter's chair. Goodness drained from me when I became supreme Pontiff – oh what a loss is in that word, supreme. (*Singing.*) 'Now I die,/Plunged into dark./Plunged into God who is dark with too much light for us to see./I do not know what God is./Only what/He is not./And He is not near, not here, not in me.'

The **Cardinals** *step from the shadows, surround him for an instant, then step back to their places leaving* **Nicholas IV** *stripped naked except for a loin cloth.*

Nicholas IV Sotto . . . sotto . . . I crouch. I cannot bear the sky or the warts on my face. I'll soon be dust, my deeds already are. There must be a way for God's truth, Christ's reign of love to begin. I tried and in the trying is my only comfort. (*He straightens up.*) I'll try again. There's still time to try again. Still time for change. The world's ripe for it. And if not with me, Christ's Vicar, who else? Yes. I give the great cry, yes . . . yes . . . yes to life. Do you hear me, Lord? I do not believe in death.

God's massive foot stamps down from the flies squashing **Nicholas IV** *flat with a loud squelch. Spot snaps off as a funeral bell tolls.*

Scene One

Lights on **Cardinals Latinus Malabranca, Benedict Gaetani, Matteo Orsini, John Cholet** *and* **James Colonna** *in a Vatican ante-chamber. The life-size crucifix upstage centre is still in shadow.*

Colonna   Turd-eating Guelph!

Orsini   Beshait Ghibelline!

Colonna   To sword, Ghibellines, for God and the People!

Orsini   To sword Guelphs for God and the Papacy!

They draw their swords from beneath their Cardinals' robes.

Malabranca (*holding up his bible*)   Whilst Christ bleeds and His holy blood waters the Holy Land – Acre and Tripoli are lost to the Infidels 'cause we hate.

Orsini   Imbecile dribbler, years pass but you don't!

He snatches the bible and jams it into **Malabranca***'s mouth. As he resumes fighting savagely with* **Colonna**, **Gaetani** *throws a small bag of gold on the floor. The fighting stops immediately.* **Malabranca** *removes the bible from his mouth.*

Gaetani   Thirty-five thousand florins a year certain; two hundred and fifty thousand computed possible. It's income we lost. There's death, misery and civil war throughout Italy. The head stinks, the body rots because we unhappy few haven't been able to elect a new Pope to succeed Pope Nicholas IV. Two years gone since his death and still we talk.

Cholet   Two years arguing and now there's plague in the streets. Flesh turns black, bubos sprout and men laugh who have no reason to laugh, laughing before they fall; ripe wheat before the reaper. Two years of fear and still we cannot elect a new Pope.

Orsini   Whose fault that? When Cholet here submitted my name a year ago as the next Vicar of Christ, you rejected it.

Colonna   You should've voted for me when Cardinal Malabranca put forward my name. I have qualities. I don't walk on my knees to give my feet a rest.

Cholet Being so few, decimated by war and plague, we must now go outside the Cardinals College and seek new names worthy of St Peter's chair.

Orsini There's danger in names: too many names and so few of them the same. Names make people think they're different. True worth lies in blood, not names.

Cholet (*laughing*) New names, old names, no matter. I used to know so many names.

Colonna Why're you laughing, Cholet?

Cholet (*laughing*) I'm not laughing. My shoes're laughing but I'm not. I'm shivering but not laughing . . . (*Laughing.*) Why should I laugh? Laughing without reason's a sign of approaching death. A dying man's free to laugh because he's no longer in bondage to seriousness. (*He wrenches at his nose to stop himself laughing.*) 'Tis pain that makes these sounds, not laughter. (*He hits himself in the face and a red boil appears on his forehead: the others shrink away from him.*) So the plague boils have come. (*He laughs louder.*) Why me? Why now? We've only just begun electing a new Pope. I had a big role to play: the worldly-wise prelate – ironic, passionately detached. I've the makings of a fascinating character; cut this early, who'll remember me by the last act? Cardinal Cholet, who's he? (*Laughing in pain.*) Malabranca, Malabranca, there's no sunset in your soul, day is always there, pray for me . . . (*Laughing.*) What waste. Everything you learn from life goes for nothing in the end. Did you know dying men reach up to God till they can hear His words? . . . Come closer . . . I can hear God say . . . aeeehhh eerrrggh, neeekkk.

He falls dead. The others make the sign of the cross.

Malabranca No time even to confess him. Death is now here . . . there . . . there . . . or there . . . he hovers in the middle air. (*They all start moving fearfully.*) Jump, slide, slither, in moving away we only move closer to Death.

They jump and zig-zag about with increasing desperation.

Colonna Hell gapes but we cannot move far till we choose a new Pope.

Gaetani Quick, it must be quick.

Malabranca We cannot. God can. We empty ourselves, Lord, of pride; become a hollow vessel to be filled by Thy spirit. Almighty God, name him. Pluck one name from out this wild world. Name us a good man worthy to wear the ring of Peter . . . (*He chants softly as lights become brighter.*) Peter . . . Peter . . . Peter . . . de Morrone . . . de Morrone . . . Peter de Morrone. (*The others take up the chant.*) Peter de Morrone . . . Peter de Morrone!

Orsini Peter who? Do you mean that old, raggedy-arsed hermit who lives in the Abruzzi mountains?

Malabranca (*falling on his knees*) In the name of the Father and the Son and the Holy Ghost, I elect Brother Peter de Morrone ruler of the Church of God.

He hums the 'Te Deum' softly.

Orsini Peter de Morrone is a peasant, untutored in worldly affairs with no experience of ruling. He's a man of wondrous sanctity and goodness, but . . . (*He suddenly falls on his knees.*) In the name of the Father and the Son and the Holy Ghost, I elect Brother Peter de Morrone ruler of the Church of God.

He joins in quietly humming the 'Te Deum'.

Colonna A Guelph trick, Orsini, but I'll not fall. Elect your infirm Hermit of Sulmona as Pope?! Your wits're addled. True he's performed miracles and his piety is known throughout Christendom, however . . . (*He suddenly falls on his knees.*) In the name of the Father and the Son and the Holy Ghost, I elect Brother Peter de Morrone ruler of the Church of God.

He joins the others humming the 'Te Deum'.

Gaetani I see the attraction, submitting our necks to the sweet yoke of Christ in the name of sweet Peter de Morrone but we need a leader with the strength to hold and command monarchs and men, so . . . (*He falls on his knees.*) I elect Brother Peter de Morrone ruler of the Church of God.

The **Cardinals** *sing exultantly.*

All (*singing*) 'Te Deum laudamus: we acknowledge Thee to be the Lord./To Him we sinners cry aloud: the Hermit of Sulmona!/To this Holy Man true Christian: continually we cry./ (*They rise and exit, singing, stage right.*) Save us, save us, save us: dry the tears of Mother Church.'

Scene Two

The light has built to a cold white intensity now, whilst, amid mist, a white carpet unrolls to cover the entire stage. We are on top of Mount Majella and the edge of the mountain is upstage. The life-size crucifix upstage is fully seen for the first time as the Christ-like figure on it climbs down from the cross. It is **Peter de Morrone,** *a gaunt man in a loincloth. He puts on a tattered habit, picks up a small bowl and a piece of stale bread from the foot of the cross and comes downstage, shaking his arms and legs to rid himself of cramp. He kneels and eats.*

Morrone   Voices. Living on top of a mountain, it's easy to hear voices. And I always hear voices when I've been at my devotionals. Hanging out on snowy mountain tops you hear the best voices, see the best visions; best and worst . . . (*He bites the bread.*) This bread's middle-aged. I've told Brother Sala I want old bread, so when I bite it, it bites back. He'll bring me half-dead water too. I used to eat bread as hard as living rock when I was young. That's when I saw the answer to the suffering of the world was to break with everything that justified man in the world – knowledge, possessions, friends, family. Fifty years on, I'm still happy . . .

Father Robert Sala *appears upstage centre, shivering with cold and dressed in a brown habit, large fur boots and carrying a water jug.*

Sala   Another cold coming, Brother Morrone. Why aren't you in your hut? Tradition decrees hermits live in desert caves, roasting under a hot sun, not shivering on top of the highest mountain in Abruzzi.

Morrone   The higher, the nearer I am to God, Brother Sala. Do you hear voices?

There is a faint sound of murmurings below upstage centre as **Sala** *pours water into his bowl.*

Sala   Yes, I hear. You've been crucifying yourself again and so conjuring up Satan's legions. It sounds like the full complement of 13,330,663 of Hell's demons led by fiend Beleth this time.

The noise grows louder. It is a vast crowd far away out of sight, below upstage centre.

Morrone   Beleth? No, Beleth appears riding a pale horse amid trumpets. I hear no trumpets. Belephegor could be leading them.

Sala Easily verified, Belephegor's a female demon with a fine pair of bubies.

The light turns snowy white, the mist increases as a figure shrouded in a grey robe appears upstage centre.

Sala 'Tisn't Belephegor, no bubies.

The figure staggers about gasping for breath as **Morrone** *and* **Sala** *whip out crosses for protection. The wind decreases.*

Morrone Fiend of Satan, I, Peter de Morrone, command you in the name of Jesus Christ reveal thyself.

Gaetani (*gasping and throwing back his cowl*) No demon, Brother . . . but Cardinal Gaetani . . . This is so high . . . I can hardly . . . breathe . . .

Sala Demons cannot breathe the air of Christ. Reveal thy demonic nature, thy cloven-hoof and tail.

Gaetani (*lifting his robe*) I'm whole-hoofed. (*Turning and bending.*) And whole-arsed. A flock of Cardinals follow up behind me as quickly as their very close veins will let them. Below, a great congress of people wait in the name of the Father and the Son and the Holy Ghost.

Morrone No demon could say those words.

Morrone *and* **Sala** *lower their crosses.* **Gaetani** *kneels.*

Gaetani They wait to kneel as I kneel before the reverent Brother, Peter de Morrone of the Order of St Benedict, now by Divine Providence elected Bishop of Rome, Holy Father, Supreme Pontiff.

Morrone *and* **Sala** *quickly hold up their crosses again.*

Morrone You are a demon, come to tempt me as Christ was tempted once in high places.

Sala He's Phul, demon of the moon and waters.

Gaetani Brother Morrone, believe. You are elected Christ's Vicar on earth.

Morrone I'm a simple man of prayer and fasting. Go tell thy Master, Satan, he's misjudged me. I could've been tempted more with a small fire, warm bed, mittens, underwear. Times past, I'd've been tempted to sell my soul for a bowl of hot chicken broth. But the chair of St Peter's outside the range of my temptations.

Sala *and* **Morrone** *advance on* **Gaetani** *as Cardinals* **Orsini, Colonna** *and* **Malabranca** *lurch on upstage centre, desperately gasping for breath. They stagger drunkenly.* **Malabranca** *crawls over to the large cross and collapses against it.*

Sala There's more of 'em. Close your eyes, bolt your ears and pray for salvation.

He closes his eyes and puts his hands over his ears.

Gaetani Cardinal Orsini, Cardinal Colonna, tell Brother Morrone news of his election to St Peter's throne.

Orsini *and* **Colonna** *open their mouths but can only wheeze painfully and nod.*

Morrone I know Cardinal Malabranca of old. Your Eminence, swear you are the true Cardinal Malabranca and not a phantom in his shape, in the name of the Father, Son and Holy Ghost.

Malabranca (*gasping*) Naaahh . . . Father . . . uggh . . . Sooo . . . Hooly . . . Ghoosht . . .

Orsini *shakily hands* **Morrone** *a document.*

Orsini The Decree of Election signed by the Sacred College of Cardinals.

Morrone Is this real?

Colonna Is this carpet of snow real? This mountain top? This earth? This sky?

Morrone Men and women come to me with gangrenous limbs, carcinomas of the breast and spine, screaming under the butchering knife. And they ask, 'Why me? Why me?' Now I ask, 'Why me?'

Gaetani Because your goodness can save us. Nations grow more powerful daily. All that holds this exploding world together is the Holy Church of Rome. We must become one community under God's Anointed, not a hundred different warring States.

Morrone I am not worthy.

Malabranca Let God be the judge.

Morrone Do you hear, Brother Sala?

Sala (*taking his hands from his ears and opening his eyes*) I hear nothing, see nothing. Do not be tempted, Brother Morrone.

Malabranca Do not defy God's will. Take Peter's ring. Seal of your authority.

He offers **Morrone** *a ring.*

Orsini
Colonna } Take the ring!
Gaetani

Morrone I'll pray, Your Eminences. Wait for me down the mountain. If God commands me to take up the Cross of the world, I'll join you. If not, I'll stay here in bliss. Ask the people to pray for me . . . in silence, so I can hear God's word.

They all exit upstage, disappearing down the mountain. The murmuring of the crowd below quickly dies away.

Morrone (*singing*) 'Lord, I am tired and I am old. It's snowing and my feet are cold. Why me? Why me? If I leave, it will never be the same. No end to misery or to shame. Lord, answer me if you can. I'm led to slaughter like a lamb. Why me? Why me?' (*He kneels.*) Peter de Morrone, born in Isernia 1210 or was it 1209? Since I was taught the bible by a wandering scholar I wanted to be a solitary. I obeyed you, Lord, and came to this silent wilderness – losing myself to find myself!

Echo Find myself . . .

Morrone Breaking myself to remake myself.

Echo Remake myself . . .

Morrone God commanded – abandon everything except your desire for God.

Echo Desire for God – abandon that too . . .

Morrone Then I would truly be as nothing. Can I go down, mix with the mass of men, not be of this world but in it?

Echo In it – up to your neck. To have no Pope is worse even than having you.

Morrone I cannot resist God's command. But I ask again, why me? Why me?

Echo Why me? Why me? Because you're there, goosehead.

Morrone *laughs. As he gets up, a chorus chants 'Sancti, Sancti'. He moves over to the cross, lifts it up and exits with it upstage centre. As he disappears down the mountain, a triumphant cry goes up from the unseen crowd below, who roar again and again, 'Christ has come! Christ has come!'*

Scene Three

The shouts fade out. Lights go up to a hot brightness as the white carpet is pulled off upstage and a huge crown is lowered from the flies above the great hall of the Castel Nuovo, Naples. There is a fanfare of trumpets and **Charles II** *and* **Queen Maria** *enter upstage centre. As the fanfare stops,* **Charles II** *lifts the robes, lets out a high-pitched whinny of triumph and capers around joyfully.*

Charles Who's a clever boy then? Who's a clever boy? Me – Charles II, King of Naples and Sicily, Count of Anjou, the fairest, brightest of the French Angevin kings. Peter Morrone is our only true native born holy man and my policy has always been to encourage native products. I supported him and his poor followers in their obscurity. Now I reap the rewards of my unselfish act. He's Pope and he's here in Naples.

Maria How long before he moves to Rome?

Charles Our task is to hold him. The moment he settles in the Holy See, he's no longer our Pope. The Curia will claim him, show him no mercy.

Maria Lookee, you're now the close friend of the Vicar of Christ, fulcrum of the world. Use it, turn it into crowbar, broadsword, that we may hack off more than our share. We've young mouths to feed. King's don't have sons, they have heirs, who need kingdoms to devour.

Charles We must make the saintly Morrone stay in Naples beguiling so there will be no banquets, masques or festivities. Luxury and lust must be kept in dark corners, distant bedrooms and Sicily will be ours once more.

Maria And Provence, Piedmont, Lombardy and the Papal States.

Charles And Flanders, France, Aragon . . .

They kiss passionately.

Maria Acre, Tripoli, Jerusalem, the Holy Land.

Charles The Roman Empire, Christendom, the World – not tomorrow – today! Today!

They fall and roll on the floor kissing and tearing at each other's clothes. Trumpets sound and they quickly scramble to their knees and pray. Cardinals **Orsini** *and* **Gaetani** *enter downstage right, whilst* **Colonna** *and* **Malabranca** *enter downstage left. They kneel facing upstage centre as* **Morrone** *enters dressed in the magnificent white Papal robe. He lifts his hands for silence; he has St Peter's ring on his finger.*

Morrone I said grass will grow from out my jaws before I clad myself in these rich trappings, but I obey God in this and all things. I've come down in the world from high Majella to low Naples. I entered on an ass like Jesus entered Jerusalem. Happen I'll meet an easier fate than the Saviour's; vain hope. I am already crucified. We came down to this place, so stinking in the hot sun, that even the wind fled from us. Only the poor stayed waving palm leaves to cool us as we passed, their faces lit with hope; hope I will speak of peace and life everlasting. Though the future is full of holes, I'll never destroy their hope, which is heavenly. And so, I take the name Celestine, meaning 'heavenly'. I will be called Pope Celestine V.

The others chant 'Celestine V!'. As they get up from their knees, **Morrone** *recognises* **Charles II** *for the first time. In his excitement, he darts over to him and right out of his magnificent but oversize white robe. The robe itself is so stiff, it is left standing upright but without* **Morrone** *in it.* **Charles II** *bends to kiss* **Morrone***'s ring but* **Morrone,** *in his dirty tunic, embraces him.*

Morrone Rise, my son. You befriended me and my followers when there was no reward in it. You asked me then if there was anything I wanted of you – there was nothing. Now 'tis my turn. Is there anything you want of me?

Charles Nothing, Holy Father – except that you stay here, with us in Naples.

Morrone Granted, my son.

Orsini Holy Father, you cannot rule without the organisation created for ruling – the Roman Curia. And that's in Rome.

Colonna The Roman people need you, Your Holiness. You bring them spiritual and material comfort. A thousand pilgrims a day come to the Capitol to kiss your feet. Without those feet to kiss that revenue's lost.

Malabranca The Pope's in Rome all's right with the world. You'll be safe behind Vatican walls.

Maria Which can be breached by any marauding army. Here you have Neapolitan battalions to defend you, Holy Father.

Morrone I'd forgotten the sound of a woman's voice in fifty years' solitude. Soft, soft, not an angel voice but soft, Your Majesty, soft. I must choose, it seems; hard when God's always chosen for me. Cardinal Gaetani, how do I choose?

Gaetani If you choose to stay in Naples, you will be vulnerable to French influence, Holy Father. On the other hand, the centre of Christendom is where you are – Rome or Naples makes little difference.

Morrone A lawyer's answer. After training my will to destroy itself, it must now assert itself. After rooting it out, I must now replant it and decide to go or stay. Go. Stay. However. Perhaps. On the other hand, I could do neither . . .

A fanfare and shouts of 'Montefelto! Montefelto!' off. The others react.

Charles Montefelto? My father would never have allowed that excommunicated butcher in. I'm surrounded by incompetents!

Maria You're not terrifying enough, Charles. I've told you never to shuffle about in soft slippers.

Morrone I granted Count Montefelto audience.

Orsini Holy Father, Montefelto was excommunicated by Pope Nicholas for attacks on the Church. He killed my brother-in-law, Guido, in a sudden fury. In that instance he had some justification. Guido brightened the world just by leaving it.

Colonna Montefelto has fired monasteries and churches, raped, ravaged and mutilated whole areas of Sienna. His temper's close to madness.

Malabranca He's the man of blood, a tyrant's tyrant. Run, hide, the sky's falling!

Count Guido Montefelto *enters upstage centre in black armour, huge sword and spiked ball on a chain hanging from his belt. He clanks over to* **Morrone**'s *free-standing white robe. Not realising it is empty, he bows his head and kneels beside it.*

Montefelto Holy Father, I kneel contrite before you. Wash away my sins. Our wives're dead, our sons idiots, our daughters whores and there's so little life left to be alive in. (*He takes the sleeve to kiss and finds there is not a hand in it.*) Ahh, God rot, empty as Christ's tomb. (*He gets up and lashes out with his spike ball and chain.*) Skomers! You mock my despair!

Morrone Satan is tempted into despair. Why should you be different?

Montefelto I've fired whole cities, gutted provinces, deserts turned red with blood in the Holy Land: Cross against Crescent. Infidels, Jews, Heretics cut down – infinities of death. I was the Lord's good and faithful servant then, slaughtering for Christ. But when I went into business for myself – anathema. And they laugh!

He bites his chain in fury.

Morrone They laugh at me too in dark corners. And with cause. They elected me Supreme Pontiff, Pope Celestine V.

He capers up and down. **Montefelto** *lashes out at him.*

Montefelto Senile rackenback, I've no sense of humour.

Charles This is no jest, this is truly Pope Celestine.

The others shout agreement.

Montefelto I've dirtied my hands on three Popes – they needed me then. This is no Pope. I know Popes. This one hasn't the true disdain, the malignant cunning, the bone-crushing power of a true Pope. He's too milky; he doesn't look like a Pope.

Morrone And you don't look like the man of rage and blood, Guido Montefelto.

Montefelto (*whirling round*) Arrrrhhhh – that's me!

Morrone That's the reds. The hate-demon moored in the middle of your forehead – there. (*He points.*) See, see, it's scaly, tailed and horned, suckered to you – there. It draws up all the hate in your soul and spits it out – streams of hate – there. There!

Montefelto Where? Where?

He tries to knock the demon off his forehead with his spiked ball.

Morrone In the world of evil, like cannot destroy like, only its opposite will do that as light drives out darkness. Stand, my son, I come to spear the scaly red one with St Peter's ringed forefinger. So, I impale hate on the stretching finger of love . . .

He lunges and places the tip of his forefinger on the centre of **Montefelto***'s forehead.* **Montefelto** *drops his weapons. As* **Morrone** *continues pressing,* **Montefelto** *goes into violent convulsions.*

Maria Gentlemen, don't stand like sclerotic mice, call for assistance.

Morrone None's needed. Count Montefelto's purged. I absolve him.

Montefelto*'s convulsions stop.*

Montefelto (*singing*) 'I rise up amazed that I once yearned/For daylight to appear/Now there is no darkness in my soul/Day – day – day is here!' 'Tis a miracle, a good man sits on St Peter's throne. The shell's broken, the kernel found. I submit to the power of goodness, surrender myself to find myself. I renounce the world, throw down my arms, take up St Francis' girdle and dedicate what's left of my life to Christ.

Morrone Monkish robes will become you, my son. Leave the world, thousands will follow you into the wilderness, sleeping on hard stone, eating harder bread, burning by day, freezing by night. It's the only way to live. (*He steps back into his white robe.*) Charles, my son, behind Vatican walls I would not have been exposed to this dangerous intrusion. Sinners sicker even than the once murderous Montefelto can reach me here. My voices tell me it would never happen in Rome. Therefore, I shall stay here in Naples, open to the sins of the world. (*Singing.*) 'I rise up amazed that once I yearned/For daylight to appear/Now there is no darkness in my soul/Day – day – day is here!'

He leads them off upstage centre, singing 'Day – day – day is here!' as the crown above them is taken up.

Scene Four

An ante-chamber. **Enrico Jacopone** *enters muttering, downstage right, with towel, bowl and pitcher of water.*

Jacopone Www sss beee iii Roo.

Sophia Aldesca *enters downstage left carrying a portable bed, with a very young girl,* **Gina**, *dressed in white and singing sweetly.*

Gina (*singing*) 'How long, how long shall I pine for love?/How long shall I sing in vain?/How long like the turtle dove/Shall I ceaselessly complain/Oh fye, oh fye, oh fye, how long will the mill go round?/How long will the mill go round, the mill go round again?'

Sophia Master Jacopone, will His Eminence be needing both of us tonight? There's a special rate for doubles.

Jacopone Aaassk Hiiiiss EEmmineen.

Sophia We expect to have our hands, and other parts, full now the Papal Court is in Naples. It will provide needed employment for a hundred different trades.

Jacopone (*handing her a bag of money*) Thiii ssshouu bee eennouu.

Sophia (*weighing the bag in her hand*) Enough to accommodate you too, Master Jacopone, provided the Infidel Turks only cut off your tongue and nothing else.

Jacopone (*laughing*) Oooo mmme tttooo.

Gaetani *hurries in excitedly stage right.* **Jacopone** *helps him strip to the waist.*

Gaetani Jacopone, Jacopone, I want to soar on angel's wings. I was raised to be a church lawyer, I do nothing on impulse. Now I'm seized by love, swept away by goodness.

Sophia Goodness? Who's selling that commodity, Your Eminence?

Gaetani The Holy Father, Celestine – a cleansing wind from the mountains. With it he drove out the beast in Montefelto.

Jacopone Thaa waa ooull oon maan, Youu Emmineen.

Gaetani Yes, Montefelto's only one man but what he can do for one warring man, perhaps he can do for warring nations. Cure them as he cured Montefelto with his purging pity and goodness.

Sophia I've fallen too poor to be good. Never seem to be able to afford it. I've lived off the vanity and selfishness of men and the fears of 'good' women – and I sleep like a baby with my big toe in my mouth. As for pity, it's something the strong give to those who they refuse to help.

Jacopone Doon'tt taa too Hiisss EEmmineen, liik thaa.

Gaetani *flicks a little water on his face and chest and towels himself.*

Gaetani No, speak freely, Wagtails. I listen, I learn. I do not demand conformity in private only obedience in public. (*He takes* **Gina***'s face in his hands.*) Child, child, so young, so seeming fair, what Hells have you seen and crossed in your short years? What indignities endured, sins committed? What do you say to life and virtue?

Gina Drink and women killed my father – he couldn't get enough of either, so he hung himself. I would've liked to have danced on the green and played mumbly pegs with the other children. But I was lucky. I was a white ewe, pretty enough to be a half-florin hackster before I was ten, else I would be working in the fields, dawn to dusk, pulling a plough, yoked with oxen. Life has us in its grip, Your Eminence. There's no time for virtue.

Gaetani The Holy Father will make time; have faith, take heart.

Gina I'll take anything, Your Eminence, that's what you pay for.

Gaetani No copulation tonight, Mistresses. Chastity follows virtue.

Sophia You see, Gina, with every attack of morality, we lose money.

Gaetani Keep the gold.

Sophia You're generous, Your Eminence. But I've found nothing ever comes free. All free gifts have strings, so I always pay for them – it's cheaper. I'll give you some hard wisdom, learnt the hard way, on my back. You're right to forgo copulation, if you can. I've spent long hours thinking about the problem. I ask, what good is copulation? What good is exploring forbidden orifices? What good is ecstasy? Satiety is quick and final. After the most sublime buttock-balling, everything returns – anxieties, debts, memories, old age, bad luck and worse breath. The consolations of the carnal are fixed and short. Power is better than your best copulating. That's valuable advice from a true Lady Abbess, Your Eminence, and so, goodnight.

Sophia and **Gina** *pick up the portable bed and exit stage left.*

Jacopone Soooo soorrr I brrouu thoos twwoo hee tooniighh, Youu EEmineen.

Gaetani 'Twasn't your fault, Jacopone. I didn't indulge for practical as well as spiritual reasons. The Holy Father is a saint. But he'll be destroyed 'less I can protect him. To do that, I must stand by him but he'll not allow it if I stink of lust. To become his friend, I'll become Cardinal Clean. Jacopone, music for the fading light. Sing me a lullaby.

Jacopone (*singing*) 'Hooo looo hoo loo shaa III piinn foor loov/Hooo looo shaa III sinn iii vaaiin ssss iiii aaa . . .'

The lights fade out to darkness as **Jacopone** *sings the song* **Gina** *sang.*

Scene Five

Spot up on **Morrone**, *upstage centre, with a small writing board and inkwell strapped to his side.* **Charles II** *and* **Sala** *in a white and black habit stand on his right and left side respectively, placing documents on the board.* **Morrone** *signs them simultaneously right and left handed as the light comes up on the hall of the Castel Nuova with the crown above. There is a pile of wooden slats on the floor upstage left.*

Charles Sign this . . . this . . . this . . . this . . . this . . .

Sala And this . . . this . . . this . . . this . . . this . . .

Morrone I'm a small man in a big world and my hair has turned to white. What am I signing?

Charles Grants to cardinal prelates, kings, magnates, of benefices, lands, stipends, honours, Holy Father.

Sala Dispensation to your followers so they can leave the Benedictine order and form their own new religious order – the Celestines, based on piety, prayer, fasting and poverty – God's own.

Morrone But these documents all seem to be blank.

Sala So I can fill in the details later, like the head of the new Celestine Order – John of Castroceoeli. There's nothing deceitful there, Holy Father, everyone knows John is a close friend of mine and, therefore, trustworthy.

Charles Likewise with the twelve new Cardinals I've asked you to create, Your Holiness. All Frenchmen like myself. 'Tis all in the family, not a stranger amongst 'em.

Sala I serve you now as I served you then, bringing bread and water and defeating the Cardinals you thought the demons Thammsey, Zavebe and Yamyael.

Morrone The final verdict is not yet in, Brother Sala. Perhaps this is but a dream Satan's dreaming for me.

Sala It's real. You can trust me, Holy Father. I climbed the mountain for years but never the ladder of success, I've never kissed the arses of those above me, or kicked the heads of those below. I owe no man.

Charles Neither do I. I began at the top. Even when my father was almost alive, I could cast a subject down on a whim – life and death were in my baby fingers. Power brings no rush of blood to my head. You can trust me to use it for the Church's good.

Morrone I trust you both. All's new, you see – signing, judging, ordering – it's a great annoyance ordering when I took such pleasure in doing things for myself.

Sala Now they are done for you. (*He poses.*) Dost like the cut of this habit I designed for the new Celestines, Holy Father? I think the colours most becoming.

Morrone They are the colours of life, Brother Sala. So I'll sign this . . . this . . . this . . .

As **Gaetani** *enters downstage right,* **Orsini** *and* **Colonna** *hurry in upstage centre with papers and start placing them on* **Morrone***'s writing board.*

Orsini And this . . . this . . . this . . .

Colonna This . . . this . . . this . . .

But the weight of the documents sends **Morrone** *slowly toppling forward. They just manage to catch him before he hits the floor but the papers spill onto the ground. As* **Colonna** *and* **Orsini** *kneel to sort them out,* **Morrone** *takes off his writing board and joins them.*

Charles Holy Father! Floorwork is for servants.

Sala Your Holiness! The creator of the glorious Celestines does not scramble.

Morrone I am on my knees. A man who's afraid to kneel on his prayer-bones is no friend of Christ – or me.

Charles II *and* **Sala** *immediately drop on their knees and help sort out the papers.*

Orsini Ah, that's mine.

Colonna And that's mine, sapskull.

Charles Mine, I believe.

Sala How do you know mine from thine when every paper is blank?

Orsini Mine are blanker than the rest. I use larger and better parchment, naturally.

Gaetani *crosses to the group as they snatch papers from each other.*

Gaetani Your Holiness, would it not be fairer if each had an equal number of blanks?

Charles Equal? The word has no meaning for kings. I had more blanks than the rest, my need is greater.

Morrone But equal seems fair. Perhaps you can have more of an equal share of blanks, son Charles.

The others get up but are too busy sorting out the right number of blanks to notice **Morrone** *has difficulty in rising and is helped by* **Gaetani.**

Morrone Ah, I must have help. I need good men close about me.

Charles You have one, Your Holiness. But now I must take my leave. I've a kingdom to rule and these documents should be completed.

Sala And quickly, before others take advantage, Holy Father.

Morrone *nods.* **Colonna** *and* **Orsini,** *seeing* **Charles II** *and* **Sala** *backing away, quickly do likewise. All speed out by different exits.*

Morrone Years past, I saw that the absolute rule of one high priest was the curse of Christianity. Being the source of all privileges, all bow down to him. Now I'm that high priest, sanctified head of the apparatus of a mechanical religion.

Gaetani Change it into the true blood and flesh of Christ.

Morrone *gestures to* **Gaetani** *to help him and they cross stage right and carry the wooden slats stage centre.*

Morrone I am not equipped. So much I don't know. Why is the sky? Why are the stars? Did the force that made these spots on the back of my hand make the universe? Sometimes I wish I were an arrow shot into the air which never falls to earth.

Gaetani There was a Rabbi in Paoli who disappeared into a flooded cellar. When they drained the water away he'd vanished. Sometimes, I think, lucky Jew, lucky Jew.

Gaetani *copies* **Morrone** *tying the slats together to form partitions.*

Morrone As a boy I tended sheep, visited only by phantoms and silent voices.

Gaetani When I was young I wore my hair short, dressed myself in black, studied Roman Law by sunlight and tallow-light and as a lawyer, learnt to question every statement except the legitimacy of my own birth.

Morrone I never trusted my youth.

Gaetani Nor I. We're both solitaries, Holy Father, you out of the world, me in it.

Morrone Bind the slats tighter, Your Eminence, so they hold firm. I can move standing stones but what do I know of prelates, scholars, princes, kings?

Gaetani Know that if you give them a free hand, it will end in your pockets. This world is covered with daggers. Let me help, and be your true friend, Holy Father.

Morrone Raise the walls high, my son, high, high. (*They raise the bound partitions and lock them together into the four walls of a hut with an entrance.*) Now the roof . . . (*They put the last partition on top of the others as a roof.*) It looks strong.

Gaetani Yes, but what is it for?

Lights go down to a spot on the hut.

Morrone Soul's rest. My retreat from the pinking eyes of the Court, where I can crouch cramped in the dark, feasting on stale bread and staler water: I want paradise all to myself. (*He crawls into the hut.*) Yes . . . yes . . . oh yes . . . I can't invite you in, Your Eminence, it's too small. Oh, but years drop from me. I hear voices. I kneel in darkness, safe with my God.

Spot out.

Scene Six

Amid the sounds of hundreds of insects, **Orsini** *and* **Colonna** *appear in white nightshirts out of the darkness stage left and right. They come downstage, arms outstretched as if sleepwalking.*

Colonna Neapolitan corridors are treacherous not stern and straight like honest Roman passages, they bend and twist.

Orsini But we must go down them unafraid. Extraordinary lives call for extraordinary actions.

Colonna Which is why I agreed to this secret meeting. But it doesn't mean Guelph and Ghibelline are in any shape or colour reconciled.

Orsini Never. I still head the party of sound men of property, influence and blood who support the status quo.

Colonna And I head those without property, influence and very little blood. We Ghibellines still fight for bread, land and justice for every poor Roman.

Orsini Good, our firm hatred is still intact.

Colonna But as this is a secret meeting, I secretly confess, I often hunger for a role-change. 'Twould be exhilarating to briefly lead the successful Guelphs. The poor never seem to win.

Orsini It's no jest heading the aristo-party, Your Eminence. Never expect gratitude; the rich have long pockets and very short arms. If I lead the poor and oppressed I'd have gratitude. I'd have nothing else but I'd have gratitude. All foolishness, we meet to talk of the Holy Father.

Colonna The twelve newly created Cardinals are all French. The Sacred College splits. We Romans're in a minority. We must conclude a private alliance even if we seemingly stand opposed in public.

Orsini Agreed. Cardinal Malabranca is old and dying, and Cardinal Gaetani plays his own hand.

Colonna Did you note how he doesn't ask for anything? He's so greedy.

Orsini But the Holy Father himself is the true cause of our discontent. I've never seen his like and I've seen Popes come in all shapes and sizes.

Colonna He frightens me and I'm not easily frightened . . . (*He starts.*) Footsteps!

They immediately resume their sleepwalking pose – arms outstretched.

Colonna Where's the East Wing?

Orsini Opposite the West Wing . . . I think . . .

Arms outstretched in front of them, they disappear into the darkness stage left and right, as **Charles** II *and* **Queen Maria** *appear upstage left and right in white nightgowns, also 'sleepwalking', arms outstretched.*

Charles I've lost myself twice already.

Maria Because we haven't used this castle since your father died. 'Tis absurd meeting like thieves in the night. Husbands and wives share rooms and beds: we are married.

Charles Which St Paul says is better than burning in hell-fire – but only just. The Holy Father is possibly of that mind too;

we cannot risk his displeasure. So we must keep separate and meet beyond the reach of a hundred Court eyes. He's made twelve new French Cardinals for me . . .

Arms raised, obviously lost, **Orsini** *and* **Colonna** *suddenly appear 'sleepwalking' out of the darkness.* **Charles II** *and* **Maria** *immediately stick out their arms and move around in a circle 'sleepwalking'.* **Orsini** *and* **Colonna** *see them and immediately turn stiffly and 'sleepwalk' off upstage left and right.*

Maria Twelve Cardinals are not enough. You must persuade His Holiness to have Sicily returned to you. If the meeting with James of Aragon comes to nought, he could proclaim a Holy Crusade in your favour.

Charles A Crusade to liberate Sicily from the Sicilians. His Holiness will do what I ask.

Maria He'll do what everybody asks.

Charles Yes but Brother Sala's concerned with souls and so is of no account. And though we saw them sleep-walking together, Cardinals Orsini and Colonna hate each other, so can be used. Cardinal Malabranca's decayed. Cardinal Gaetani is the one.

Maria He asked for nothing. That man is dangerous. He should be stopped. Be a despot, Charles.

Charles How can I be a despot if the people love me?

Maria Do away with executions and they'll hate you. If I hadn't shrunk to wife and mother, I'd show you the way. But bearing children slackens the sinews, makes you consider the consequences – fatal.

Charles I have men about me who'd wield the knife but most're low-born, not Cardinal-killers. Since Montefelto turned holy, there's been a dearth of class assassins who could thrust in deep and silent. Thrust, slide and slit. Hard blade, soft flesh . . .

They embrace passionately, pulling off each other's nightgowns.

Maria Squirming . . . under the hard blade . . . *ahhh!* (*She stops.*) Something's coming!

Charles Yes! Yes! . . . (*He stops.*) You're right – footsteps!

Both immediately raise their arms and assume a sleepwalking pose.

Maria Which way is back?

Charles II *points uncertainly and they 'sleepwalk' stage left as* **Cardinal Malabranca** *appears out of the darkness in a white nightgown, arms outstretched, eyes closed. He bumps into* **Charles II** *and moves on: he really is sleepwalking.*

Maria (*low*) What's he doing here?

Charles (*low*) I think the old fool really is asleep.

They exit into the darkness.

Malabranca Down what dream corridors, dream paths do I wander, flecked and furry. (*Behind him* **Orsini** *and* **Colonna** *cross and recross, still 'sleepwalking' and still hopelessly lost.*) I am lying in bed dreaming and standing in the dark in the Sacred College of Cardinals, electing a new Pope . . . 'In the name of the Father and the Son and the Holy Ghost, I elect Brother Peter de Morrone ruler of the Church of God' . . . And the Hermit of Sulmona is elected Pope. (*He chuckles.*) Such things could only happen in a dream. Only in a dream could I lead and enthrone him. Poor fool. We only dream what we want to happen, fear will happen, never what has happened, alas. This is rich, God must be rewarding me with such a rare dream. A good man on the throne of the world . . . enjoy . . . enjoy . . . I'll never dream its like again.

He sleepwalks upstage into the darkness to join **Charles II, Maria, Orsini** *and* **Colonna** *still wandering about, arms outstretched and lost as* **Jacopone** *enters downstage right.*

Jacopone Whaa caa yoo dooo wii theem, IIII aasssk yoooo? (*He spits.*) Theeey ruull thiii woorll aaa thh woorll heeree – aaffteer . . .

He claps his hands rhythmically and the sleepwalkers move in time to his beat. They skip and touch hands in a short impromptu ballet before all exit.

Scene Seven

A cock crows. Lights up on **Morrone**'s *hut in the centre of the great hall.* **Gaetani** *enters downstage left with the Pope's red robe.*

Gaetani Holy Father, God has granted us another day.

Morrone *crawls out of the hut and gets up. He is bent double.*

Morrone A glorious night, Your Eminence, on my prayer-bones talking with God.

Gaetani *gives up trying to put the robe on him, takes his shoulders from behind, places his knee in his back and pulls. There is a loud crack,* **Morrone** *stands upright and* **Gaetani** *helps him on with his robe.*

Gaetani You've received messages of congratulations and obedience from King Edward of England and Philip of France, addressing you as Father and Lord in Christ.

Morrone How kind of them to write. After all, I don't know them personally – not at all.

Gaetani Today you begin talks to end the Sicilian war. King James of Aragon and his entourage have just arrived.

Morrone No, I cannot begin talks with him, I haven't finished my talks with God.

Gaetani Holy Father, I've arranged it so's James and Charles talk with you alone without Courtiers and Ministers.

Morrone My days used to be sublimely empty. God gives us time to live in, not use.

Gaetani But we must. The Inquisitor General of Milan has sent the persistent heretic, Mistress Maifreda, for you to question direct. And more important, even than heresy or peace, is the new Papal accountancy system which ensures greater care with the enforcement of taxes. Our clerics extort monies for private gain. Eliminate individual corruption in the Church and your reign will be blessed.

Morrone What has Christ's Church to do with monies and taxes?

Gaetani Everything, Your Holiness. Everything.

Mistress Maifreda *is brought in by a* **Guard.** *Her hands are chained. The* **Guard** *kneels and kisses the ring on* **Morrone**'s *finger.*

Gaetani Mistress Maifreda, 'tis custom to kiss St Peter's ring and kneel before the Vicar of Christ.

Maifreda Yes, you should kneel before me. Kiss and kneel, kiss and kneel while the light hovers round.

Morrone No, my child, you are Mistress Maifreda and I am Christ's Vicar on earth.

Maifreda The Inquisitor of Milan split my left eardrum. Could you repeat that?

Morrone I am Pope Celestine V.

Maifreda You look less like a Pope than I do and no one believes me, so why should I believe you? By the tomb of our Lady Guglielma miracles abound and her followers saw the light shining and plucked me from thousands to become Pope. I didn't want it but God's voice confirmed, and they made me Pope Maifreda I.

Morrone There's no heresy here, Your Eminence, only a poor mad, moon loon.

Maifreda This man's a false Pope. Fire kindling wood, so his eyes melt from his sockets and he weeps his urine upwards. The true Pope lives in poverty, not in marble palaces, rich gowns, shoes shining bright as slick stone.

Morrone There's truth in her falsehood, sense in her madness. What do you say, Guard?

Guard Me?

Morrone Yes, what would you do with her?

Guard I don't want to choose but for choice, I'd say, burn her to ashes. People are easier to blow away when they're ashes: dust on the wind.

Maifreda I've God's work to do not with the warm smile but the cold sword. Sucking dog leeches feeding on the body of Christ must be burnt off. Yes, burn the false Pope.

Cardinal Malabranca *shuffles in excitedly upstage centre.*

Malabranca Cardinal Gaetani, I had the most fantastical dream last night. The Sacred College was choosing a new Pope when I was seized with a frenzy of the spirit and led them into electing a good man as Pope. We named the poor Hermit, Peter de Morrone, Pope for his piety. What a glorious dream.

Gaetani It wasn't. We did, don't you remember, Your Eminence, this is the Holy Father, Celestine V, late Peter de Morrone.

Malabranca My bowels don't function like they should, so I can't explain myself clearly. 'Twas all a dream.

Morrone Though it reads like a dream, we're awake and I was chosen.

Maifreda And they say my wits're gone, claiming to be Pope.

Morrone I am ruler of Holy Mother Church, Christ's Vicar on Earth, Supreme Pontiff, Pope Celestine V.

Trumpets sound off.

Gaetani That will be King Charles and James of Aragon.

Morrone *dives into the hut in fright.*

Maifreda What has the Pope to do with kings? Take me back to my cell to pray.

Gaetani *gestures and the* **Guard** *escorts* **Maifreda** *away followed by* **Malabranca.**

Malabranca I drool now but I know you cannot be Pope – you're a woman.

Maifreda Only on Tuesday.

They exit stage left.

Gaetani Holy Father, come out, there's nothing to be afraid of.

Trumpets sound again. **Gaetani** *picks up the whole hut and carries it off stage right as* **Jacopone** *enters stage left with a large round table and places it exactly where the hut was, over the crouching figure of* **Morrone.** *As* **Gaetani** *returns and* **Jacopone** *exits stage left,* **King Charles II** *and* **James of Aragon** *enter upstage centre.*

Richly gowned, they each carry a pile of documents and **James** *has a stuffed monkey on a chain.* **Morrone** *is heard praying under the table.* **Gaetani** *taps on it respectfully.*

Gaetani Your Holiness, we beg to interrupt your devotionals. King James of Aragon and Charles of Naples crave audiences.

Morrone *crawls out, stands and holds out his hand.* **James** *and* **Charles II** *kiss his ring.* **James** *makes his stuffed monkey do the same. Lights go down to an overhead spot on them as they take up positions round the table.* **Morrone** *himself stands upstage with* **Gaetani. James** *to the right,* **Charles** *to the left; both have their documents in front of them.*

James The Holy Father swore a binding oath to give the kingdom of Sicily to me forever. Isn't that true, Thomas? (*He pulls the stuffed monkey up onto the table.*) These documents are proof, Holy Father.

Charles Pope Martin released me from that oath, made under duress, and crowned me king of Sicily instead. These documents prove it.

James Read my pleas, Holy Father.

Charles Read mine, Holy Father.

Morrone In my youth, I walked beside lakes and streams learning the art of listening. Now I must find the right word, the needed gestures. (*He suddenly spins the table top round so* **James'** *pile of documents is in front of* **Charles II** *and* **Charles II**'s *is in front of* **James**.) Read me proof of the justice of your enemy's cause and judge its worth.

Charles Holy Father, I cannot read his case 'gainst me.

James Or his 'gainst me. It will lead nowhere.

Morrone All paths lead somewhere if God is present at the start.

He falls on his knees to pray.

James This is moon madness. Don't you agree, Thomas?

Morrone King Solomon was the wisest king not because he mastered every tongue but because he understood the language of madmen. Read the proofs.

Gaetani Come, Your Majesties, the Vicar of Christ asks it of you.

He kneels beside **Morrone.**

Morrone (*praying*) Lord, we are unworthy of addressing our prayers to you. Instead, we shall whistle.

He starts to whistle softly. **Gaetani** *joins in.*

Charles I feel a bigger fool than I look, which is difficult, but as the Holy Father commands it . . . (*He reads a document.*) 'I, Charles II, Count of Anjou, captured by the Aragonese, do hereby swear by the blood of Christ to renounce the crown of Sicily in return for my freedom . . . signed . . . dated . . .'

James (*reading a document*) 'I, Supreme Pontiff, Pope Martin IV, by the power invested in me by God do hereby release Charles II, Count of Anjou from his oath to the Aragonese and crown him King of Sicily . . . signed . . . dated . . .' All the words ring true.

Charles But the sounds lack conviction.

James Thomas agrees. Yet when my father read your binding oath, it seemed worth fighting for. I hated my father.

Charles Now you come to it, I hated mine.

James Ah, but everyone did.

Charles But none more than me. After all, I knew him best. (*Low.*) The Holy Father is a friend but he's no idea how to conduct a meeting of this importance between kings.

James (*low*) He's some kind of saint, I'm told, but no natural authority. You have it. I have it. Born with it, weren't we, Thomas?

Charles (*low*) I believe two wise rulers like ourselves should be able to reach a sensible accommodation. But in another place. I fear 'sense' is in short supply here.

James (*low*) The Holy Father's the kind of man who stands in front of a mirror with his eyes closed to see what he looks like asleep.

They giggle. **Charles II** *puts his finger to his lips and they tip-toe out stage right.* **Gaetani** *and* **Morrone** *stop whistling.* **Gaetani** *gets up.*

Gaetani Your Holiness seems to have put two royal fools on the road to talking peace. But at what cost to your dignity? It matters. The Pope's power lies as much in his image as in his canons. The mask is more important than the face.

Morrone No, it's more important to *be* than to appear. I should've remembered all men are princes and not fear them. (*Lights down to a spot on him.*) The Universe hinges on God's Will alone which decides how many times the dry leaf turns in the dust. One tear, Your Eminence, one prayer, can change it all.

Scene Eight

Another spot slowly up on a throne behind him, upstage centre with an iron crown suspended from the flies above it.

Morrone Lord, let one man attain perfection and mankind is saved. I have been chosen.

Amid smoke, the demon **Verrier** *slides from behind the throne in a robe made up of mirrors.*

Verrier I am Verrier of the Second Hierarchy, Prince of Thrones: Verrier the demon of Pride. Why are you afraid of me, Master Morrone? Why're you bare-arsed, dirt-loving saints so afraid of pride? What've you got to be proud of? Now I grant it is different. You are this world's fulcrum. Use it to lift the Church out of the mire. Though I am a demon, this time I am on the side of sense. I speak for the good of the Church. Soon, in Wittenburg a nail will be hammered in and the split will be made visible. There'll be no more need for us poor demons. Men will commit evil enough without our help. If you sin through pride to prevent that split, then you will sin for all our sakes. You can change the destiny of the world.

Amid smoke, the bearded figure of **Elijah** *emerges from behind the throne, dressed in a tattered loincloth and carrying a staff.*

Elijah God heard your silent scream from the farthest corner of heaven, Brother Morrone, and sent me down to oppose this pride-demon. The Prophet Elijah, Elijah the Tishbite, has come again. We have much in common, Peter, I was a desert solitary who rose to power in Judah. So I know you cannot change the world by the world's means. Rid yourself of pride, be the naked nomad again, show them the worthlessness of possession, be the fool and show them the uncertainty of reason. Become what man can be, should be, wants to be. By refusing everything, you refuse nothing. Submit.

Verrier Submission to God without understanding the meaning of submission diminishes Him. Revolt.

Elijah To understand Him is to reduce Him to our own level. Submit.

Morrone *holds his head.*

Verrier We're not strong enough pro and contra to persuade him. Would Lucifer have done better on my side, Moses yours?

Elijah Moses? Why Moses? Hairy crawler. Pharaoh's favourite. Him and his burning bush. I tell you he couldn't even light a fire.

They move backwards towards the throne. As they disappear behind the throne, lights up on the throne-room. Large double doors upstage left. **Sala** *and* **Montefelto** *enter downstage right as* **Morrone** *gets to his feet.*

Morrone Brother Sala, you missed a visitation from the pride-demon Verrier and my good spirit Elijah.

Sala A mighty voice, Holy Father, perhaps he came to remind you of the bare-boned severity of the desert whilst you lap this luxury.

Montefelto When I was leading armies across the killing grounds of Europe I heard no voices. Now I lead the soft pious life, I hear them loud in my inner ear. The battlefield dead, slaughtered in forgotten wars repeat their names else they be forgotten – Harmannus Bartol, pikeman; Johannes Imola, cavalry; Pierre Lanquet, archer . . .

Morrone Voices are our familiars daily. How goes the holy life, Brother Montefelto?

Montefelto I control my rage, Holy Father, put it in my pocket and never pull it out.

Sala Brother Montefelto's proved invaluable. He's organised the Celestine order into regiments, companies and battalions spiritually armed to the teeth.

Montefelto We've taken Monte Cassino Monastery from the Dominicans and made good Brother Angelarius abbot there.

Morrone Is that Christian?

Sala It is necessary. Living in the ways of Christ and the Gospels, prayer and poverty, the Celestians is the fastest growing order in Christendom. And we must have a monastery of fitting worth from which to send out our messages of the Lord proclaiming a new age of the Holy Ghost.

Morrone I am about to proclaim it too.

The sound of drumming. **Morrone** *crosses upstage and stands in front of the throne with* **Sala** *and* **Montefelto** *either side of him. A* **Drummer** *enters downstage left beating a large drum and leading in* **Orsini, Colonna, Gaetani** *and* **Malabranca.** *All kneel before* **Morrone.**

Morrone Brethren, too many stand between God and His Church – priests, monks, friars, nunners, pleaders, pardoners, priors, deacons, cardinals, Popes. Christ was poor, we are rich. Christ was meek and low, we are tall and proud. Christ forsook worldly glory, we hold it fast. Christ washed his disciples' feet, we make men kiss ours. Christ came to serve, we seek to be served. Christ purchased heaven, we give the earth to the rich. Christ rode on an ass, we on fat palfreys. Christ gave power, we grapple it close. Christ loosened, we bind. Christ brought life, we bring death. I have the power to change it, yet I doubt. I ask; when you all honour me, that means you are all more humble than I am, which means you are all better than I am. So why should you all honour me when I should honour all of you? I am not worthy.

The drumming stops. The throne and dais revolve quickly with **Morrone, Montefelto** *and* **Sala** *to reveal an identical empty throne on the other side.*

Malabranca One spin and everything disappears at the same speed and no sediment left. I still dream a Pope proclaims Christ's reign on earth. Do not wake me, let me dream a little longer.

Orsini Beat your toothless gums together, Malabranca, your dream is our nightmare. If you hadn't seen the light in conclave, we wouldn't be in this darkness. Your Eminences, the new French Cardinals arrive at any moment. The Celestine Order devour Dominican and Franciscan alike. We must act. We know what he'll dream of next.

Colonna He's milk-and-water-weak. Yet he frightens me more with each drum beat.

Orsini You heard him say he'll strip the Church of her raiments and power. It's wrong, Your Eminences.

Gaetani The Church, and its head, who speaks for the Church, cannot be wrong. If there were a power which possessed the right to say it was wrong, it would be a higher power than the Church which is God on earth. But God cannot recognise a superior.

Orsini Don't confuse the issue with logic and reason, Gaetani. The Holy Father puts us all at risk with his return to the Gospels.

Colonna Universal poverty is not the most inspiring message for humanity. Thanks to the Holy Father's zeal, true religion is creeping back into the Papacy. They'll turn to other creeds.

Malabranca One man's dream becomes another man's reality.

Gaetani Catholics are forbidden to rebel and there is no appeal to outside authority.

Colonna You have a fine, treacherous lawyer's mind, Cardinal Gaetani; is there no way out?

Orsini Find it, and Guelph and Ghibelline will prove grateful.

Gaetani We found our way in. Let me brood on it.

Orsini, Colonna and **Malabranca** *exit stage left.*

Gaetani The Holy Father would pray to God for guidance but I'm not certain if God is that interested in our prayers. Perhaps He prefers our doubts, tears and suffering. Choices have to be made now, here, by us. Let my heart splinter, shoulders shake, I am created for truth not happiness. I must examine experience in the light of truth whatever the cost. The Holy Father has done good – brought peace to Sicily – though wars are what nation states are for. He has cured Montefelto and by so doing lost a soldier for Christ. And Guelph and Ghibelline are united – thus making them doubly dangerous. Good is Janus faced. What is the link between man and God, man and man? Fear. God wants to be feared rather than loved. So does man. And if that is man, what is the good of saving him? But that's another question. The Holy Father is good but isn't feared, so he cannot hold and who knows what hellish chain of events will result from just one act of unconsidered goodness? (*He sits on the throne.*) A Pope is too much in this world, of this world, to risk being good. Lord, if I'm wrong, give me a sign.

Jacopone *appears from behind the throne.*

Jacopone (*low*) Sooo wheeee dooo weeee mooo agaaa aagaa Hii Hoolliiii?

Gaetani I cannot move against him, betray him Judas-like in a garden crunched and crucified.

Jacopone Whhhh?

Gaetani Because he's my friend.

Jacopone AAccc.

Gaetani I cannot act against the laws of man and God. The blessed Peter sits like a rock on St Peter's rock, if needs be, till the seas dry, the sun blacks, the light fades. (*The light fades to darkness.*) Only a Pope can pull down a Pope.

Scene Nine

Spot downstage right on the **Archangel Gabriel,** *in white breeches, doublet, wings, mask and golden hair.*

Gabriel
    I am the Archangel Gabriel
    Whose rays stain the unclouded sea.

I come to tell you, Holy Celestine,
To give up St Peter's ring.
Pride and lust for power creeps into
     every corner of a man
And trickling down into his beating
     heart
Every sin has its reasons except pride.
Give up St Peter's throne and be worthy
     of God's . . .
Or something like that.

Gabriel's *wings droop.* **Jacopone,** *who has been listening, comes into the spot as* **Gabriel** *takes off the mask and wig, to show it is actually* **Sophia Aldesca.**

Sophia The wings shake every time I move.

Jacopone IIttsss nooo gooood enooo. Toooo floooweee.

Sophia It's too flowery?

Jacopone Soooffff aaa sslllooowee.

Sophia Softer and slower? The usual advice is louder and faster when I'm playing whore-games for my clients. I've played the shy virgin, lascivious nun, big bellied duchess but no one has asked me to tumble backwards as the Archangel Gabriel.

Jacopone Gesstuuus. Doon't juuuss taaalkkk. Gesstuuu . . . 'IIII aaamm thhh Archaaa Gaabb . . .' (*He gestures upwards.*) 'Prrrii aaa luuuss foo pooooweer . . .' (*He points downwards.*) Gesstuuu.

Sophia Gesture. Yes, I shouldn't be just a talking angel-head . . . 'I am the Archangel Gabriel.' (*She points upwards.*) 'Pride and lust for power' . . . (*She points downwards.*)

Gaetani *enters the spot.*

Gaetani I approve the costume. It's some years since I've seen an angel. But the Holy Father knows them well.

Sophia Whores must be paid before the carnal act but I want no money for my part in this scheming, Your Eminence.

Gaetani No money? You're asking that much, are you? What is it you do want?

Sophia Respectability. I've always respected myself, now it's time for others. If we succeed, give me a titled husband with a small estate in Italy.

Gaetani Done. If we succeed and I become a villain.

Jacopone Ooonleee iiff eeeee faaaill.

Gaetani Failure or success, I seek to destroy a man I love.

Sophia Men loved me yet still sought to destroy me. How do you know you'll be a villain when no one can distinguish between truth and lies, love and hate, good and evil?

Gaetani I can. I smell myself burning.

Spot out. Spot up downstage left on a second **Archangel Gabriel** *dressed exactly like the first one, winged, masked and in white.*

Gabriel II
I am the Archangel Gabriel
Come to tell you, Holy Celestine,
To continue God's work; do not be tempted
To give up the burden; remain Supreme
    Pontiff.
You are a man with pure hands
Needed to guide the Church of God
Back onto the path of righteousness.
And that's an order! . . .

Charles II, *who has been watching, steps into the spot as* **Gabriel II** *takes off the mask and wig to reveal* **Queen Maria.**

Charles II Somewhat commanding, Madame. But then Gabriel is Commander of the Host, used to giving orders. Try it louder and faster.

Maria And no gestures. Angels do not need gestures: their meaning's plain. They are talking heads, or, perhaps, singing heads. Should I sing Gabriel?

Charles No, no, I've heard you sing. Remember, the Holy Father knows angels. But if you stay back and do not come close to the light, 'twill pass. One visitation is all that's needed. When the new French Cardinals arrive we'll be safe. But until then, I fear the Holy Father may have a sudden attack of humility and give away all we gained. We have to cheat the old man into staying Pope though it hurts. I am a man of honour and he's proved a good friend.

Maria You can afford neither. You're a king.

Charles And you're a queen who shouldn't have to play the mummer's part.

Maria Who else can you trust? We go to trick a Pope. Besides, I love being active. Oh Charles, Charles, soon we'll flaunt our names across the known world and I'll never again shrink back to being a wife with a bright future behind her.

Charles A kiss, a kiss, my sweet.

Maria No, Sire, no lechery. I must be an angel now. (*She puts on the wig and mask.*) I am the Archangel Gabriel.

The spot fades out.

Scene Ten

Lights up on the chapel, shrouded in thick incense. Pulpits upstage right and left, either side of a stained-glass window, with organ pipes and altar in front of them upstage centre. **Morrone** *prays in front of it as* **Maria**'s *voice continues.*

Maria's Voice
   I am the Archangel Gabriel . . .

Maria *appears as* **Gabriel** *out of the incense from behind the pipes.*

   Come to tell you, Holy Celestine,
   To continue God's work; do not be tempted
   To give up your burden; remain Supreme
         Pontiff.

Sophia's Voice
   I am the Archangel Gabriel . . .

Sophia *as* **Gabriel** *appears out of the incense from behind the organ pipes.*

   Come to tell you, Holy Celestine,
   To give up St Peter's throne . . .

She stops and sees the other **Gabriel** *opposite staring at her. They both jump back in horror.*

Morrone Two Gabriels?

Sophia *and* **Maria** *are nervously circling each other making the sign of the cross.*

Maria Adjuro ergo te omnis immundissime spiritus omne phantasma . . .

Sophia Adjuro ergo te omnis immundissime spiritus omne phantasma . . .

Morrone Two Gabriels. A singular honour, Lord. None has been visited by two Gabriels.

Sophia There's only one. I am the true Gabriel, the Angel of Mercy.

Maria I am the true Gabriel, the Angel of the Power of God.

Sophia I am that Gabriel sent to Daniel to explain the meaning of his vision and to warn you, Peter de Morrone, of false pride, obey God's command and give up St Peter's throne.

Maria I am that Gabriel sent to strengthen Our Lord in the garden, as I strengthen you, Peter de Morrone, to obey God's command and remain Supreme Pontiff.

Morrone Two Gabriels sent by God with directly opposite advice. God certainly moves in mysterious ways.

Maria That's a false Gabriel. I am the Archangel of the Lord. I'll prove it – list. (*She sings a piercing high note.*) *Aaaaaa* . . . there!

Sophia (*singing a high note*) *Aaaaaa* . . .

Maria (*singing*) 'He who can soar, one instance at the most, most, most. Will sing and join the angelic host.'

Sophia (*singing*) 'He who desires nothing has all, all, all. He who desires all, will fall.'

Maria 'I am *Gabrieeell*.'

She hits such a high note, **Sophia***'s wings and her own fall off.*

Sophia (*singing*) *Gabrieeeelll*.

She hits an even higher note and the stained-glass window above the organ pipes shatters. At that moment **Verrier** *and* **Elijah** *appear in the pulpits stage left and right.*

Morrone My visions come legion-strong: whole armies of 'em.

Verrier *and* **Elijah** *stare down at* **Maria** *and* **Sophia** *picking up their wings and start hitting each other with them.*

Elijah It must be the last Battle before the Last Judgement, why else would God send two Gabriels.

Verrier He never plays fair. I can't cope with two Gabriels and an Elijah like you. I can't win the soul of this man 'gainst these odds. Leaf-bright Lucifer send my thy Seraphims, Cherubims and Thrones, for this battle.

Elijah Lord of the Universe send my Thy blessed troop of Prophets, Saints and Martyrs.

The light trembles to the tramp of bare-footed armies approaching stage left and right, whilst the two Gabriels fight violently below amidst incense and feathers.

Verrier The hollow ground breaks and the heavens split.

Elijah The army of the good is on the march.

Verrier The light shatters, 'tis Lucifer burning as he comes!

Elijah Light brighter than the brightest dazzles my eyes. It's Christ!

As the two Gabriels fight more fiercely and the light oscillates violently and the sound of approaching armies grows thunderous, **Morrone** *suddenly holds up his hand and snaps his fingers. The light and sound is instantly cut off except for a spot on* **Morrone.**

Morrone Too many shapes, too many voices, some things can be told by language, others only by silence.

Scene Eleven

Lights up on **Morrone** *and* **Gaetani** *in the throne room.*

Morrone Your Eminence; I've been plagued by sad voices, demons, dead saints and martyrs. Verrier, Elijah and two Gabriels.

Gaetani Two Gabriels? Do they usually come in matching pairs? How do you know good angel from bad, if they turn and turn again? Whose voice do you listen to, Your Holiness?

Morrone My heart's. God demands much but He leaves it to us to choose the means by which we reach perfection. No one can decide your life for you, not even God.

Gaetani Then your conjuring apparitions were nothing.

Morrone They were the questions not the answers. My soul is a battleground and in the midst of battle, it's difficult to know who's friend, who's enemy, who's winning, who's losing, till the victory bell tolls. Remember, during our journey here, Your Eminence, I asked you to join me in the carriage but there wasn't enough room. I said, 'Just let us be close friends and there'll be room enough.' We did and there was. Answer me now in truth, as a canonical lawyer, can I abdicate and return to the holy life if I should wish?

Gaetani No self-respecting lawyer likes to give a direct answer to any question. But I will try for friendship's sake, Holy Father. No Pope has ever handed back ring and mitre. Canon Law makes no provision. You have no superior, so into whose hands would you resign your sacred office? Yet other clerics can lay down their burden. I believe it lawful for you to do the same. The Pope being the voice of God on earth cannot recognise a superior on earth: if you resign, no one on earth can say no.

Morrone You answer in truth like a learned lawyer. Now look into my eyes and answer in truth, like a close friend, should I resign?

Gaetani Man reduced to his own resources is too wicked to be free. He must be governed. The indispensable check can only be found in Papal authority. But if that authority doubts its own authority, then respect disappears, Church and worlds slide to ruin. In defence of our Mother Church, Holy Father, there can be only one truthful answer to your question.

Morrone I weep. I weep for Jerusalem . . . If I go, I mean to go to Jerusalem. I try to imagine Jerusalem but it soars so beyond imagining and I can only imagine someone who's been to Jerusalem.

He kisses **Gaetani** *who trembles.*

Gaetani
   I'm not shaking.

It is the ground that's shaking under
    my feet.
I'm scorched, shriven by the black.
Stay, Holy Father! Stay Supreme Pontiff!
That's not what I should say, meant
    to say.
Father, if you leave us,
We remain bound, doomed to falsehood
    and decay,
The Universe will imblast itself,
All things will lose coherence,
Leaving nothing between a man and his
    face.
That is not what I should say, meant
    to say.
But I am blinded by your soul's light,
Fiercer than any visible light.
I am blinded by its pure fire
It is the light that shone once on a
    bank in Egypt
And from a manger in Bethlehem
I cannot lose that light, that holy
    light.
The dark, Father! Stay and save me from
    the dark!

Morrone *embraces him and exits upstage centre.* **Gaetani** *collapses onto his knees.*

Scene Twelve

Jacopone *enters the throne room downstage right with a bandaged* **Sophia**.

Sophia (*singing*) 'Angels, don't talk to me of angels./They just make me sigh./It's no great trick being an angel up there in the sky./Angels, don't talk to me of angels./Let them come down here./And try to live with misery and fear./Raising kids and making money./Isn't funny./Don't talk to me of angels, of angels./Let them deal with sickness and old age./On a weekly wage./Then they can soar./But not before./Don't talk to me of angels.'

Jacopone Whaaa haappee, Yoo Emmineence?

Gaetani (*rising*) I failed myself, Jacopone. The words weren't mine. Who gave me the wrong words? The Holy Father asked me what he should do. I told him to stay Pope. Seduced by his terrible goodness, Jacopone. Now we are lost.

Sophia Now it's 'we'. Before it was 'I'. So I fought the other Gabriel for nothing. You remain Cardinal, Jacopone and me stay servant and whore respectively.

Jacopone Eeee . . . eeeee . . . eeeee . . .

As **Jacopone** *lets out long keening laments, bright festive banners in red and gold are lowered from the flies.* **Charles II** *and* **Queen Maria,** *limping with her arm in a sling, enter upstage centre. As* **Jacopone** *bows and* **Sophia** *curtsies,* **Charles II** *throws coloured ribbons at them.*

Charles Rejoice, the new French Cardinals have been reported entering the city. I've sent word to His Holiness. 'Tis unbecoming of kings to crow, but on this occasion . . . *Cock-a-doodle-do, cock-a-doodle-do.* I win, Your Eminence, I win! More than my father ever won! I flick him off – *ugh.*

Sophia *and* **Maria** *are staring at each other's bandages.*

Sophia Your Majesty seems in distress.

Maria And you, Mistress – have an accident?

Sophia No, I'm trying to give them up.

Jacopone Yooo Maajeees thiiiiss isss Missstreee Soophiaaa Alldesssscaaa.

Charles For some reason I can't understand him, Your Eminence. He never seems able to get his tongue round the words.

Gaetani Because he hasn't got one. He was introducing Mistress Sophia Aldesca to Your Majesties.

Maria Mistress Sophia? A name I've heard whispered in back corridors and stairwells. What is it we know of her?

Gaetani You know enough knowing she is under my strict protection.

Charles Soon it won't be enough. The protection of an Italian Cardinal will mean less when the French join the Sacred College and you sink under their weight.

Trumpets sound a triumphant fanfare. Drumbeats as Cardinals **Orsini, Colonna, Malabranca** *enter solemnly upstage centre in full ceremonial robes, followed by* **Sala** *and* **Montefelto.**

Orsini The Snail-Eaters're upon us.

Colonna We didn't act, now only God can act for us.

Gaetani He won't.

Malabranca I need at least twenty-four hours sleep a day but I must wake from this everlasting dream-stuff.

Trumpets sound another fanfare. A choir sings 'Gloria In Excelsis'. All kneel facing the throne as **Morrone** *enters upstage centre, dressed in his magnificent pontificals: robes, mitre and ring. The choir stops singing as he takes his place on the throne.*

Morrone My brethren, I took the chair of St Peter with sorrow but look at my joy now. For by the Blood of Christ and by his Holy Mother, I herewith, on this Feastday of St Lucy, 13th December, in the year of Our Lord 1294, do resign the honour of the Papacy.

Maria *screams. All scramble to their feet.*

Charles No, no, that's not what we're here for!

Sala Holy Father, do not abandon us, think of the Celestine Order!

Gaetani Holy Father, have you considered this . . . ?

He clamps both hands over his mouth to stop himself speaking.

Morrone By the Blood of Christ and by his Holy Mother, I herewith, on this Feastday of St Lucy, 13th December, in the year of Our Lord 1294, do resign the honour of the Papacy.

Maria Charles, do something – pretend to be a king.

Charles Where are the new Cardinals? Quick, help me find 'em.

He and **Maria** *rush out upstage centre.*

Colonna Holy Father, the earth spins away.

Orsini Are you set true on this course?

Sala It cannot be, Holy Father. You are the hope of the world. I'll tell the people. They won't let you!

He rushes out upstage centre.

Morrone By the Blood of Christ and by the Holy Mother, I herewith, on this Feastday of St Lucy, 13th December, in the year of Our Lord 1294, do resign the honour of the Papacy. And the Sacred College must assemble and confirm it. The rest go pray for us.

Jacopone *and* **Sophia** *exit, bowing and curtseying upstage centre.*

Montefelto You make the great renouncement out of cowardice, utter the great refusal out of littleness of spirit. Not large enough to burn, Peter de Morrone, you are condemned to the icy ante-chamber of Hell.

As he exits, **Colonna** *and* **Orsini** *close the large doors upstage centre behind him.*

Morrone Condemned to ice? Then so be it. My former life, old age, habit, ignorance, state of my soul and the world's are reasons enough for the renouncing. It's not my unworldliness but the knowledge of my unworthiness that compels me.

Malabranca Ah . . . I tremble . . . Nothing weighs. What do I say next? Help me, I can't remember what I say next . . .

As **Morrone** *begins to strip, a crowd is heard, chanting off, faint at first but growing louder . . . 'Celestine . . . Celestine . . . Celestine . . .'*

Morrone I renounce the mantle of office. (*He takes off the robe and lays it down on the throne.*) I renounce St Peter's robes and mitre . . .

As he places the mitre on top of the robes, the chanting grows louder.

Colonna Holy Father, show yourself at the window. Calm them.

Dressed in a coarse smock, **Morrone** *comes downstage centre, faces the audience and holds up his hands. The chanting immediately dies down.*

Morrone Brethren, I am Pope Celestine the Fifth, soon to be plain Peter de Morrone the First again. An old man who wants to die as he lived, at peace. But I will stay Pope if just one of you stands up and shouts 'I believe in goodness and virtue. I believe in truth, purity, justice and mercy!' Shout and believe it . . . Ahhh. Instead of the believing shout, the disbelieving silence. Another Pope will do as well.

A woman cries. As **Morrone** *turns back upstage to the throne there is the crack of Japanese wood blocks. The* **Cardinals** *kneel.* **Morrone** *raises his hand and slowly removes the ring and places it on top of the robes. It begins to snow.*

Morrone I stand naked but still not completely Peter de Morrone till you elect my successor.

A troop of men are heard hurrying towards the throne room doors upstage centre. The **Cardinals** *scramble up.*

Gaetani The French Cardinals're coming!

Orsini They'll elect one of their number over us!

Colonna We must do it first! Quick!

Morrone (*picking up the ring*) I raise this ring to place on the finger of the man most fitted, the man who begged me to stay Pope. His begging convinced me I should go for 'twas done in friendship's name not Christ's. Your Eminences, for his strength, knowledge, greatness of heart, devotion to the Holy See, what say you to Cardinal Gaetani as Supreme Pontiff?

Orsini   ⎤ In the name of the Father and the Son and
Colonna   ⎬ the Holy Ghost, we elect Cardinal Benedict
Malabranca ⎦ Gaetani, ruler of the Church of God.

The banging continues upstage centre and the unseen crowd starts rhythmically chanting downstage as **Gaetani** *steps forward and* **Morrone** *gives him the mitre and drapes the robes round his shoulders.* **Morrone** *picks up St Peter's ring. The banging and chanting die down and it stops snowing in the throne room as* **Morrone** *carefully places the ring on* **Gaetani**'s *finger.*

Gaetani I take the name Pope Boniface VIII.

The banging on the doors resumes and the rhythmical chanting of the crowd turns to 'Boniface! Boniface! Boniface!' **Gaetani** *sits on the throne,* **Morrone** *kneels before him. As the others follow suit, the doors upstage centre burst open. The doorway is crammed with* **Maria, Charles II** *and the new* **French Cardinals.** **Charles II** *lets out a* *piercing cry of despair at the sight of* **Orsini, Malabranca, Colonna** *and* **Morrone** *kneeling before the enthroned* **Gaetani.**

Malabranca I'm awake! I'm no longer dreaming my life. I'm awake!

Gaetani *turns and looks at* **Charles II, Maria** *and the* **Cardinals** *in the doorway. They slowly fall on their knees as the unseen crowd roars, 'Boniface! Boniface! Boniface!' and the lights fade out.*

Act Two

Darkness. Spot up with a long drawn out cry which grows louder till it turns into an animal roar and the spot is full up to reveal **Gaetani** *stage centre in white robes. He reads a Papal document accompanied by the sound of a huge drum.*

Gaetani I declare the Bull Sanctum, which establishes the singular oneness of the Holy Church and its absolute necessity for salvation. To those who argue they are not subject to the authority of the One Church and its ruler we proclaim they do not belong to Christ's flock. But the One Church has two swords, two powers, spiritual and secular, but the secular power is subordinate to the spiritual power of the clergy which is not human but Divine. We declare, determine, proclaim, pronounce that henceforth every human being is subject absolutely to our authority, the authority of the Roman Pontiff, absolute.

Scene Two

Lights up on the throne-room of the Castel Nuovo. **Orsini, Colonna** *and* **Malabranca** *kneel in front of* **Gaetani.**

Gaetani Pope Celestine worked miracles. I will work wonders. But first I declare all his acts null and void, all his clerical appointments cancelled; his Celestine Order curtailed; his Papal household reformed. More important, I have created twenty-four new *Italian* Cardinals. They'll easily outvote the French ones left waiting in the ante-chamber.

The others nod approval. As **Gaetani** *gestures for them to rise,* **Jacopone** *hurries in stage right with documents.*

Jacopone Haa Faa, yoo reeceivee aaa messaa ooo coongraatulaaa aaa obeediee froo Kii Eddwaa oof Englaann.

Gaetani Congratulations and obedience from King Edward of England. Nothing less was expected. The English're born to obedience. They make a useful race of servants. But what of Philip of France?

Jacopone Noothii.

Gaetani You hear, Your Eminences? No word of obedience from Philip and his lawyers. Don't stand there like dumb stones. If you wish to thrive in my company, you must understand my new Master of Protocol, Master Jacopone. To get to me you will go through him. You'd be wise to learn tongueless talk. Master Jacopone . . .

Jacopone Hoo Faa.

Gaetani Say it, Your Eminences.

Orsini
Colonna } Hoo Faa.
Malabranca

Jacopone Aaan aappointee foo auuddiee wii thh Hoo Faa, muuss fiirss bee aapproo byy meee.

Orsini
Colonna } Aaan aappointee foo auuddiee wii thh Hoo Faa, muuss fiirss bee aapproo byy mee.
Malabranca

Jacopone Ooonce mooo wii feeliii.

Gaetani Yes, once more with feeling.

Orsini
Colonna } Ooonce moo wiii . . .
Malabranca

Trumpets sound and **Charles II** *and* **Queen Maria** *enter upstage centre. They kneel before* **Gaetani,** *who holds out his hand and they kiss his ring. He gestures and they rise.*

Charles Holy Father, hearing Celestine was no longer Pope, James of Aragon once more claims Sicily for himself.

Gaetani The Holy See gave your father and his heirs Sicily. We will continue to support you.

Charles Your support wasn't expected, Holy Father.

Gaetani Why? 'Cause of our former enmity? Sicily affects our authority and leaves no room for likes and dislikes. We will talk further in Rome.

Maria You've grown weary of our hospitality, Holy Father.

Gaetani Very. We miss the Holy City and the necessary apparatus of power. We move on immediately – if not before.

Jacopone *whispers to him as the* **Guard** *and* **Mistress Maifreda,** *in chains, enter downstage left. The* **Guard** *kneels before him and kisses his ring.*

Gaetani This is a matter I've yet to dispose of. No change, Mistress Maifreda?

Guard But there is, Holy Father. No longer content to be nameless, I resolved to serve the rich and toady to the great, *honk-honk*. So I wrestled with her hard, arguing there was only one true Pope, showed her a mirror to confront her with her own sad visage. But I pressed her day and sleepless night, argued like St Thomas Aquinas that just as two angels could not be found in the same cloud at the same time, so two Popes could not sit on the same throne at the same time. So I weakened her will, till one glorious dawn she saw her face and the truth.

Maifreda Saw the light; not the light shining round the tomb of our Lady Guiglielma making me Pope Maifreda. Saw the true light, the holy light round Pope Celestine.

Malabranca You had that dream too, poor fool?

Maifreda Saw the light, the holy light but like Apostle Peter, I denied him. Condemn me – fire, rope, axe, hot irons.

She collapses on her knees.

Gaetani From your kneeling position I conclude you are a Christian again. You are to be congratulated, Master Sogoni.

Guard That's my name – *honk-honk, honk-honk*!

Gaetani And you are released to go thy ways in peace, Mistress Maifreda.

Orsini Holy Father, is this wise? She is condemned for heresy.

Gaetani We serve a God both visible and sensible who can tolerate a little local heresy. She poses no threat to me. Release her.

Maifreda Only the Pope I foreswore can release me, condemn me to life. Only sweet Celestine, the blessed Peter can pass sentence. I claimed to be Pope and am condemned for it. Now

this false Father, this two balled sack of white, does likewise.
As you condemn me, Your Eminences, condemn him.

Gaetani Guard, stop her mouth. (*The* **Guard** *whips out a strangling cord.*) Not here. Outside.

The **Guard** *drags* **Maifreda** *upstage.*

Guard Once I was Master Sogoni, now I'm thrown back to plain 'Guard' again, *honk-honk*. I had a part to play as a great crawler, toady, lick-spittle, arse-kisser extraordinaire, but you betrayed me, Mistress: oblivion waits me.

Maifreda I have one bad ear but I can still see what's being done, Your Eminences. Satan reigns. The sea burns . . . (*They exit upstage centre but* **Maifreda** *continues speaking.*) Holy Father, forgive them in thy mercy. When I was young, I came in like starlight, I go out like *arrgg* . . .

There is a dying gurgle as **Maifreda** *is strangled and her body is heard slumping to the floor and being dragged away. All applaud as a darkness slowly spreads from upstage centre.*

Colonna Swift and decisive justice, Holy Father.

Charles It shows greatness of soul to recognise a mistake and reverse it.

Gaetani It was necessary.

Jacopone Tiimm ooo leeaveee, Hoo Faa.

Gaetani What did he say, Your Eminences?

Orsini
Colonna } Time to leave, Holy Father.
Malabranca

Gaetani The blessed Peter de Morrone will accompany us to Rome. I need his holy presence near me always. We'll take the coast road, Your Eminences. The stars shine brightest on winter nights like this . . . shine . . . shine on for me . . .

As he points, the stars shine in the darkness above them as they exit upstage centre and right.

Scene Three

Distant sound of the sea and an outline of tents against the night sky, upstage. Two soldiers of **Charles II**'s *army,* **Nicoli Lucera** *and* **Simon Roffred,** *warm themselves by a burning brazier stage centre.*

Roffred
   Is that the sound of the sea,
   Waves on the shore,
   Or a thousand rebellious mouths whispering
   'Pope Celestine, Pope Celestine, Pope Celestine'?
   No, it's just a trick of the stars and the night.
   You've gone broody, Nicoli
   What are you thinking of?

Lucera
   Who traced the circles of a man's eyes, Simon,
   Pierced the orifices of nostrils and
        ears?
   Made the openings of the mouth?
   Who stretched out the sinews and tied
        them fast?
   Dug the channels of the veins, made
        the loins hard, covered with
            flesh?
   Who separated the fingers, gouged the
        tear ducts?
   Hollowed the cavities of the lungs,
        created the spleen long, the
            belly large?
   Who shaped the heart, Simon?
   Oh, what a wonder man is.

Roffred
   But his nature's corrupt
   Just as rust forms on metal, dew on
        grass, dirt on bodies,
   So evil collects in our souls, and corrodes
        them.
   The fault lies in the nature of the
        thing called man.
   Jesu, you've got me babbling now.

Lucera And in verse too.

Gaetani, *his face hidden by his fur hood, enters upstage and joins them by the fire.*

Lucera It's guarding the sainted Peter de Morrone that makes me babble. He prays in silence, day-long, says nothing so eloquently that he pierces to the heart and makes me too wonder at the wonder of life.

Roffred He stays silent with great fire, but we shouldn't listen to him.

Lucera He's a good man whatever good means. And now Boniface thinks to take his place. I knew Boniface when he was plain Gaetani and bum-boy to Pope Nicholas.

Gaetani You support the former Pope Celestine against this new Boniface then, friends?

Lucera Never. Celestine gave the world the prospect of universal love and peace. We're Genoese crossbowmen, trained and bred for hate and war. We're paid to kill at long range, torture at short. What we do are virtues in war, crimes in peace.

Roffred We've risen to be respected Captains in Charles' army because of past and future wars.

Lucera This Boniface could turn out to be another Clement IV who declared a Crusade against the Emperor Frederick. Crusades against fellow Christians are the best -- well paid in booty, with full remissions of sins and no travelling to foreign parts. Another home-Crusade and Roffred and me could retire to our farm outside Genoa. We'll not end on stale bread and begging bowls.

Roffred It's time for us to settle. War's changing; they're starting to use the terrible, black exploding powder in 'pots-de-fer'.

Gaetani The Pope will ban its use.

Lucera A Pope banned the crossbow and we've made a handsome living from it all our lives.

Roffred We plan to marry country wenches, make love and raise families, tell tales in front of warm fires: we've earned our peace.

Jacopone and **Montefelto** *hurry in stage right.*

Jacopone Hoo Faa, Pee dee Mooroonee haaa flee!

Montefelto He's escaped with Brother Sala.

Gaetani Captains Roffred and Lucera, find Peter de Morrone and bring him to me in Rome.

Roffred We are in the service of Charles of Naples.

Gaetani (*throwing back his hood*) You are in the service of Pope Boniface VIII. (**Roffred** *and* **Lucera** *start to kneel.*) No time for ceremony, kneel later. His Majesty will transfer you to Papal Command and I will double your stipend.

Lucera We're yours, Holy Father, we're easily bought.

Gaetani Count Montefelto, take charge of the expedition to bring Peter de Morrone back to us.

Jacopone Heee's goon too JJJeeesusss.

Montefelto I don't care where he's gone. I am of the Celestine Order, Holy Father. My true concern is prayer and fasting.

Gaetani Your true concern is war and violence, axe and fist.

Montefelto That Montefelto's dead, the demon is in my pocket, I submit to the sweet yoke of Christ.

Gaetani The blessed Peter promised you that the meek would inherit more than six metres of earth. But he renounced his calling and the reign of salvation never began.

Montefelto I'll not let the red come again – not on me.

Gaetani But I see it suckering on your forehead. It swells as it feeds. The Celestine Order's doomed at the root by the blessed Peter who nominated me to take his place and left you to face life alone. We cheated you!

Montefelto (*wiping his forehead and leaving it stained red*) Rats with sharpened teeth gnaw my toes but the hate-demon's gone from me!

Gaetani (*laughing*) Nothing's changed, you Ass-Head – you were tricked.

Montefelto Torment of the cross tear my hands, feet, knees . . . pain like a cawing bird . . . I'm humble . . . I'm meek . . . Anti-Christ!

He hits **Gaetani** *who crashes to the floor.* **Lucera, Roffred** *and* **Jacopone** *grab* **Montefelto.** *But* **Gaetani** *gets up still laughing and rips open* **Montefelto**'s *monk's habit to show he has armour on underneath.*

Gaetani God's berserker you've come prepared. (*Making the sign of the cross over him.*) You fight in the service of Mother Church who remits all thy sins.

Montefelto *still struggles.*

Roffred In the battle of Kessenbrum, I felled an enemy soldier and knelt on his chest to cut his throat. But he spat in my face so I let him go, I didn't want to kill him in a rage. When we kill, we should try to kill cold, pure in the sight of God.

Montefelto *stops struggling.*

Montefelto We start at once, Peter de Morrone will not be easy to find. He has friends.

Gaetani They are my enemies.

Lucera If he does not wish to come?

Gaetani Tell him the Pope commands it.

Montefelto, Roffred and **Lucera** *bow and exit quickly stage right.*

Gaetani The Pope commands it. I eat the Universe, ride the rack of this night sky in joy! (*He plunges his hands into the brazier.*) I am the whirlwind. I cannot command the worms out of my bowels but I reward and punish men here and hereafter. It scalds my soul, creeps into every corner of me, my heart's lighter than a sparrow, brighter than gold-dust, moon-dust. (*He takes his hands out of the brazier.*) I am happy. I sleep the sleep of contentment. Jacopone, put out the lights.

He exits upstage.

Jacopone Yeee Hoo Faa, nooo Hoo Faa, threee baaggss fuuu Hoo Faa. (*He shows the rings on his fingers.*) IIII haaa rii ooon mmm fiiingeeesss. (*Pointing to his nose.*) Aaann ooon throoo mmm noooss. (*Laughing.*) III'mmm riiishhh. I haa iiit aall, whooo neeeedsss aaa toonguee, sooo III'll juuuu puuuut ooout thhh liii . . . (*He points up at the flies.*) Ooout . . . ooout . . . ooout.

One by one, the stars go out and **Jacopone** *exits stage right with the brazier.*

Scene Four

Morrone *and* **Sala** *are heard in the darkness.*

Morrone's Voice (*singing*) 'Jesus was a poor man/He wore a poor man's hat/It was not made of taffeta/He was too poor for that.'

Sala's Voice (*singing*) 'Jesus was a meek man/As meek as he could be/He was meek in everything/But strong in ecstasy.'

Morrone's & Sala's Voices (*singing*) 'Jesus was a good man/A good man sweet and true/If you find your love in Jesus/Then Jesus will love you and you – and you.'

Lights up on **Morrone** *and* **Sala** *entering stage left in a raging storm. They battle against the wind.*

Morrone Rainbows, haloes and glories, serve the Lord with gladness and come before Him singing. Blow, wind, blow. (*There is a lightning flash.*) Light the sky with joy. (*The sound of thunder.*) The heavens greet us, Brother Sala. We travel live roads again.

Sala Rain, wind, cold. Days past, I would've asked what rain? What wind? What cold? But palace airs have softened me. Now rain, wind, cold, bite and I shiver.

Morrone Do you regret, Brother Sala?

Sala I've stayed in poverty, wealth, now poverty again. Nothing's changed 'cept the circumstances. We've played with power but I prefer these spiteful spouts, this wrathful sky and the flowers whispering of the life everlasting.

Morrone Yes, the middle of the road is for horses, the right royal way is very high, very low, one foot in heaven, the other in the abyss, dancing on the dagger's edge. Still, could it be we've done it all wrong, old friend?

Sala Most would think so.

They laugh, embrace and sing, 'Jesus was a poor man/He wore a poor man's hat . . .' as an apothecary's wagon is dragged on through the storm stage right by **Zachery** *and* **Isobella Bartol.** *Their son,* **Benvenuto,** *rides on top.*

Bartol Look, they're singing and dancing in the rain. Fathers, come buy my elixir, the Elixir Bartol, sovereign remedy for starved spirits, humid flux, malignant humours, wet or dry. One drop in the nostrils for catarrh, likewise ears for deafness. It cures rheums, hernia ventosa, torsion of the gut, stomach gripe, convulsions, paralysis, epilepsy, melancholia, yellowing molars, dandruff and liver slugs.

Isobella Zachery, the middle of a storm is no place to be trading.

Bartol A tradesman trades wherever, whatever, my love.

Isobella These two damp starlings look bare-bummed and groatless – not even worth robbing.

Bartol Father, I confess when trading's bad we turn to robbing defenceless travellers. I'm a big man, so's my wife. Muscles everywhere; it comes of drinking Bartol's Elixir. We're not gentlefolk, when we move into a town noses go up and values go down. The name's Zachery Bartol and my good wife Isobella and son Benvenuto.

Morrone He has the face of an angel.

Bartol That's because he's an idiot. 'Tis no more possible to get sense from him than a fart from a dead donkey. His wits're long gone.

Benvenuto Da-da-da-da.

Benvenuto *climbs down to the others sheltering from the storm by the wagon. He smiles and* **Morrone** *takes his hand.*

Sala I am Brother Sala and this is the blessed saint Peter de Morrone.

Isobella If you're a saint, give us a miracle.

Morrone I'm no saint but miracles come easy. In the name of Jesus Christ, do you want to be struck blind, deaf, dumb? Do you want carbuncles?

Isobella No.

Morrone Then I'll perform no miracles for you, Madam. And I refuse to hurt anyone else just to convince you I can if I wish.

Bartol (*laughing*) The wife and me appreciate the coney-catching side of that, Father. (*He hands* **Morrone** *a bottle.*) A drink. Aside from its miraculous remedicinal properties, Elixir Bartol warms the inner man. It's one part sassafras, cuckoo flowers and mugwood, and three parts wood alcohol. Drink it quick so it doesn't touch anything on the way down.

Morrone *drinks and shudders. He passes the bottle to* **Sala** *who eyes it suspiciously but finally drinks. He gasps and twitches convulsively.*

Isobella Are you true priests? I've never seen true priests go beggar-naked, sharing cold and rain with the likes of us before.

Sala I'm Brother Sala, Hermit Extraordinaire, and this is Peter de Morrone – the Peter de Morrone who was the Holy Father, Pope Celestine V.

Bartol *and* **Isobella** *roar with laughter. As* **Benvenuto** *joins in,* **Morrone** *smiles at him, and strokes his head.*

Bartol And I'm the Emperor Barbarosa, fallen on hard times.

Isobella If you were Pope, why aren't you Pope now? No man forgoes living in palaces, sleeping on silk cushions, eating fresh peacocks' tongues less he's touched like my son. Why did you give up being Pope then?

Sala It was not worthy of him.

Morrone In truth there's no true answer. 'Twas God's will and His will is inscrutable. Do you know where God lives, friends? – where He's allowed to enter. And if He enters us, we can enter the gates of heaven in joy.

Isobella Come, Father, since the day of our exile from Eden all the gates of heaven have been closed 'cept the gates of tears. I know, I've seen five children die. Strong sons, fair daughters and Benvenuto lives with not enough wit to imitate a deaf mute and beg outside churches. We pray and are punished.

Bartol Come, my love, you are too melancholic. Those sons and daughters remaining do us credit. Cesare is Chief Executioner in

Sienna, Giacomio a well-paid informer in Tuscany and Anna, lovely Anna, isn't she Head Abbess of the most respected whorehouse in Florence? And she deserves to be, she had your looks and wit, my love.

Isobella Zachery, Zachery, you old fool, old fool.

Bartol Father, you may not have been Pope, but give us thy blessing.

Bartol *and* **Isobella** *kneel, pulling* **Benvenuto** *down beside them.*

Morrone I bless you in the name of the Father, and of the Son and of the Holy Ghost.

He makes the sign of the cross over them. It thunders as they rise.

Sala Despite the storm we've miles yet to travel, Brother.

Morrone Let us embrace, friends, for the kindness I have felt.

He embraces **Bartol, Isobella** *and* **Benvenuto.**

Benvenuto Da-da-da-da.

Morrone Sweet boy, your sweet wits're lost but not your sweet innocence.

Bartol Fathers, do not forget to extol the wonders of Bartol's Wonder Elixir.

Morrone *and* **Sala** *wave as they exit upstage centre.*

Isobella Zachery, I believe that good old one spoke truth.

Bartol We should give thanks to God for meeting a saintly man.

As he takes a drink, **Benvenuto** *jumps up and down excitedly.*

Benvenuto Da-da-da-da-da!

He shows **Isobella** *a small bible and rosary.*

Isobella Where did you get them?

Benvenuto *mimes being embraced and then picking a pocket; it is obvious he has stolen them from* **Morrone.**

Isobella Zachery, I believe our son has stolen this bible and rosary from our passing saint.

Bartol (*examining the bible and rosary*) Is it true? Yes . . . It's stolen. What've you done, Benvenuto? Mother, you know what this means?

Isobella *and* **Bartol** *embrace* **Benvenuto.**

Isobella It's a miracle.

Benvenuto Da-da-da.

Bartol Sweet boy, with your fair looks and golden locks you'll pass through crowds picking pockets with ease. Your mother and me'll die happy knowing you'll never starve.

Isobella Good times ahead, Zachery. Good times!

Another clap of thunder. They start to drag the wagon off when **Montefelto, Lucera** *and* **Roffred** *enter stage left, with stiff Papacy flags on poles strapped to their backs.*

Bartol More customers, 'tis our lucky day. Gentles, come buy my Elixir Bartol, the sovereign cure for starved spirits, humid flux . . .

Montefelto We look for an old priest, Peter de Morrone.

Isobella To do him ill. We've known too much evil, not to smell it hanging in the air.

Bartol It's none of our concern, we sell potions. But we've passed no stranger, seen no priests today, friends.

Lucera These baubles betray you, friends.

Lucera *has noticed the bible and rosary* **Benvenuto** *has been playing with and takes them from him.*

Isobella Our son's wits're addled. We give him such trinkets to keep him happy.

Montefelto *takes the bible and opens it.*

Montefelto Yet it has the name, Peter de Morrone inscribed here on the page.

Bartol What's that to us? We can't read.

Isobella *screams as* **Montefelto** *pins* **Bartol** *against the wagon and* **Roffred** *and* **Lucera** *draw their swords.*

Montefelto Which way did the old man go?

Isobella He's a saint. Our souls, our souls're endangered.

Roffred So are your lives. There's four gold pieces if you tell us.

Bartol Four gold ones . . . I betrayed my own mother for less. I've stolen teeth from blind men and gone back for the gums . . . Four gold ones eh? I can't betray the habits of a lifetime, of course I'll betray him. I only met the old man for a moment so it's easy . . . But I looked into his eyes. This is madness. One moment of honour in a lifetime of lies. (*Lightning flash.*) I won't tell you.

Montefelto Beshat scutzbag, he's corrupted you too. You were an honest knave before he fouled you with his goodness like he did me. Which way?!

Benvenuto Da-da-da-ahhh.

Roaring with rage, **Montefelto** *turns and stabs* **Benvenuto.**
Isobella *screams and points stage right.*

Isobella For Jesus' sake, he went that way.

Montefelto (*sheathing his sword*) My sword blade's stained. It's the suckering red demon here – on my forehead here – that made me strike down your son. Not me, Madam, not me.

He throws four coins on the ground beside **Benvenuto**'s *body and moves off.*

Lucera Mighty convenient for him to have a little demon to blame for his sins.

Roffred He must be watched, else his little demon does for us.

They exit stage right as a weeping **Isobella** *and* **Bartol** *examine* **Benvenuto.**

Isobella Oh my lost boy, my last, lost boy.

The sound of rain as they gently carry **Benvenuto** *onto the wagon.* **Isobella** *climbs up beside him, whilst* **Bartol** *picks up the money.*

Bartol Four gold ones. A pretty price for a pretty son, even brain-gone. Cheaters, may they age quick and die slow. Lucky you sent 'em the wrong way, Mother, there's some satisfaction there: the biters bit. Four gold ones just when he was proving himself. He could've been an asset; a big earner. But when death creeps softly in, all chances are gone forever . . . We'll take him down, Mother, down to the water's edge and do our weeping by the shore.

He gets between the shafts of the wagon and begins to pull it off stage left as it grows darker.

Isobella (*singing*) 'The night, her silent sable wore/And glooming was the skies./Oh glittering stars appear no more./For death has closed his eyes./Now at the heavenly gate he'll knock/Where others too have been./Clad only in a simple smock/Oh Father, Father, let him in . . .'

Bartol (*singing*) 'Oh let him in/Let him in . . .'

Scene Five

Tumultuous cheers in the darkness. A white carpet is unrolled from upstage as lights up on the top of Mount Majella. There is a bucket of water and bread stage right. The cheers and shouts come from the unseen crowd below the edge of the mountain top upstage. **Morrone** *and* **Sala** *appear upstage centre, panting and gasping and carrying the life-size cross.* **Sala** *turns back to wave to the crowd below and almost loses his balance. An icy wind blows as they shiver violently and put the cross upright in exactly the same position as before, upstage.*

Morrone It's good to be home.

Sala A triumph for you, Brother M. They came to greet you in thousands, camping on the mountain, believing it sacred because it is where you abide. See the bread and water they've left and your hut below the rim is full of gifts.

Morrone I never received gifts like that when I was Pope; then the gifts had strings. 'Twill be hard to leave this place again.

Sala We must in the spring, when the rivers melt and the sea winds blow fair and we can take a ship to the Holy Land. Jerusalem, friend.

Morrone Jerusalem.

Sala I've a taste to travel the wild, wide world so's when I meet the Lord I can say I've seen some of the wonder of His creation.

They drink water.

Morrone Salonika, Tripoli, Aleppo, Acre. The Saracens will let us through to the Holy City. Though they are Infidels, they respect holy fools like us.

Sala What preaching we'll do, what times we'll have.

Sharp drum beats and the figures of **Montefelto, Roffred** *and* **Lucera** *appear upstage gasping and staggering from the effort of climbing the mountain. As they shamble forward,* **Lucera** *lurches straight into the cross, and knocks himself out.* **Roffred** *and* **Montefelto** *fall on their knees in exhaustion.*

Roffred We . . . we . . . we were sent . . . the wrong way . . . Otherwise we'd have . . . stopped . . . you . . . long before . . . you got to the . . . top . . . of . . . this accursed . . . mountain.

Montefelto Don't . . . look into . . . his . . . eyes . . . Father Morrone's eyes . . . or he'll turn . . . you . . . weak.

Montefelto *and* **Roffred** *try to avoid looking straight at* **Morrone.**

Sala Brother Montefelto, your task was to stay in Corruption City and guide and protect the Celestine Order.

Montefelto I've . . . thrown off the chains . . . of office. As Father Morrone . . . threw them off. Now in the service of . . . Pope Boniface.

Sala You deserted your post.

Montefelto So did he! (*He gets up and turns his back on them.*) Mustn't look into his eyes, makes hard stone go soft.

Lucera (*groaning*) Water.

Morrone *picks up the bucket of water and pours it over him.* **Lucera** *yells and jumps up.*

Lucera Genoese bowmen at the ready!

Roffred (*getting up*) Keep your eyes down, Nicoli, according to the Count, he has powers. Father Peter de Morrone, we come to take you back to Rome.

Sala They'll shackle you. Free, you are a danger to them.

Morrone How? I pray in silence, preach no word.

Sala You yourself are the word.

Lucera *and* **Roffred** *unhitch the crossbows from their belts, level them at* **Morrone** *but still look down.*

Roffred We don't have to take aim to hit the target.

Morrone Force has no validity at this height, gentles.

Lucera (*producing a rope*) We mean to bind you and carry you down.

Sala You will have to kill me first.

Roffred Yes. Of course.

Morrone It's foolishness, friends. There is no way down for you. Thousands of my followers are encamped below. They will tear you to pieces if they find I'm being forced.

Sala And once they notice I'm dead, they'll do far worse.

Roffred I see the logic. It would take an army to remove you, Father.

Lucera We two are the best but we never make the mistake of overestimating ourselves, hard as that is.

They put away their crossbows.

Montefelto (*shielding his eyes*) You need no armies, Captains, when you have Count Montefelto.

Lucera No, we cannot bring him to Rome, though the Holy Father commands it.

Morrone The Holy Father commands it? Let me pray.

He falls to his knees.

Montefelto You betrayed us, Father, showed us Eden, brightest hope, first and last chance of the world, lance-thrust in my side, pain my forehead, grasping I'm a giant dungheap in Hell, erto erto eeesses this is Lucifer!

Raging, he unsheaths his sword to kill **Morrone** *but is grabbed by* **Roffred** *and* **Lucera**. **Montefelto** *roars as they struggle until* **Sala** *finally knocks him unconscious with the empty water bucket.* **Morrone** *prays, unconcerned.*

Lucera (*taking out the rope*) Bind him before he does us all a mischief.

They tie **Montefelto**'s *arms and legs.*

Roffred We couldn't let him kill you, Father Morrone. Turning a saint into a martyr wouldn't please our paymaster.

As they finish tying **Montefelto, Morrone** *rises.*

Morrone I thought that rope was for me. I prayed and heard voices . . . I'll come with you to Rome.

Sala Father, you escaped them once, never again. You'll stay in darkness: lose all.

Morrone I lose all to gain eternity. Short goodbyes are best. No one had a truer friend. You will see Jerusalem first.

Sala I will see them burn, Brother, burn.

They embrace.

Morrone I'll lead you down.

Roffred *and* **Lucera** *hoist the bound* **Montefelto** *on their shoulders and move upstage with* **Morrone** *who turns and makes the sign of the cross over* **Sala***. The three exit upstage, down the mountain. They are greeted with the cheers of the unseen crowd. These fade out as they descend.*

Sala Now I go to weep in Jerusalem, for Jerusalem; weep as one only weeps in Jerusalem. I hunger to begin the last journey that will make me worthy of the stories they'll tell of me. (*The lights blaze down, the carpet has turned sandy-yellow as tambourines beat rhythmically.*) Carrying the cross before me, I'll journey on through the great desert alone. Angels will fly above me, bells heard around me as I walk towards Jerusalem. (*He picks up the life-size cross.*) Trackless in the sand, my footprints vanish, I haze, merge with the sun, walking out of history and into legend . . . You won't see it, of course, but oh what a magnificent story my life will be from now on.

He exits upstage centre, down the mountainside.

Scene Six

The carpet with the bucket and loaves is pulled upstage as the tambourines change to the sound of a church organ and thick steam fills the stage. We are in the Vatican Steam Room. **Gaetani,** *naked except for a towel, enters, sweating, upstage centre.*

Gaetani Rome pleases me 'cept she leaves no place private. Every wall, roof and floor has ears. The place is honeycombed with spies spying through holes in the air. Most are mine but enemies have 'em too. (*He suddenly points to a shadowy figure stage left.*) Pestilential peeper – this is a holy steam room. Is no place sacred? (*He spots another figure through the steam stage right.*) Gangs of 'em! You, on pain of death and mutilation – go!

Spy's Voice You hired me, Holy Father!

Gaetani Then you're supposed to be spying for me not on me, Copperhead. All of you – out! (*The figures scurry out.*) I'm surrounded by disobedience. The Cardinals, Philip of France and Peter de Morrone conspire. Why can't people just obey without question? I have their interests at heart. I'll fill their bellies, empty their minds of choice. Life can be a garden of delight under One Church, one ruler. But quick, it must be quick; every day more of me dies.

There is the sound of tiny bells and the figure of **Morrone** *emerges through the steam upstage centre, sweating in a loin-cloth.*

Morrone Bells sustain the Universe – without the sound of bells, it would all collapse.

Gaetani You look like Morrone, you sound like Morrone, but you can't be the real Morrone who's roaming Italy stirring up discontent, not here steaming.

Morrone You asked, I came. God commanded, I obeyed.

Gaetani I did leave strict instructions that the holy Father Morrone was to be brought to me alone wherever I was. But you could be just a figment with dimensions, not the real Holy Father.

Morrone I'm Peter de Morrone, a child lost in creation, tired with blue veins between my fingers. We grow old, very old, and then we die.

Gaetani Why did you leave me?

Morrone I was journeying to Jerusalem where Christ was crucified.

Gaetani He's crucified here, there, everywhere daily. Your virtue is contagion which will destroy Mother Church. You cannot roam free.

Morrone Then I'll stay. The Lord is here as well as in Jerusalem.

Gaetani Father, you must speak out in praise of me, your successor.

Morrone What belongs to God in Zion is not praise but sweet silence.

Gaetani Then let your silence speak for me.

Morrone It will, for you are the Lord's true anointed.

Gaetani I am and more. For I am truly the successor to St Peter, the Vicar of Christ, the Doctor and Teacher of the Faithful, the Visible Heart of the Church, the Patriarch of the West, the Bishop of Rome, the Supreme Pontiff, Boniface VIII and not e'en the gates of Hell shall stand against me. (*He kneels.*) Bless me, Father, for I am nothing and I have sinned.

Morrone (*making the sign of the cross over him*) I bless thee Holy Father in the name of the Father and of the Son and of the Holy Ghost.

Roffred *and* **Lucera** *in armour enter through the steam upstage centre. They stand either side of* **Morrone** *as* **Gaetani** *gets up.*

Gaetani Convey him to a safe place and watch him close, he is most precious to me.

As **Roffred** *and* **Lucera** *escort* **Morrone** *out upstage centre, a prison door is heard clanging shut.*

Scene Seven

The steam clears to reveal a Vatican ante-room with purple banners with gold crosses hanging down from the flies. **Jacopone** *enters downstage right with white robes and helps* **Gaetani** *on with them whilst whispering to him. A bejewelled* **Sophia** *enters upstage left and kisses* **Gaetani**'s *ring.*

Sophia Holy Father, Rome has a thousand ears and they all know I've gained yours. I've also gained a family. They suddenly crawled out into the light: aunts, uncles, nieces, cousins, not to mention two bastard sons who seemed to have slipped my mind. All want a share of my share – whatever it is.

Gaetani Families do that.

Sophia So I've come for the promised husband.

Gaetani You can trust me, Mistress. But, tell me, who can I trust?

Sophia No one.

Gaetani Sweet daughter, I need your womanly view of the world. I have decisions to make.

He claps his hands. Drumbeats and **Montefelto** *in a black cloak and armour enters upstage centre. Kneeling, he kisses* **Gaetani**'s *ring.*

Gaetani Up, up, up, Sir. You are high in my favour, bringing the denuded Morrone back to us. Rise, you are no longer a penny-poor aristo. The land between Lago and Aquapendente called the Tuscan Patrimony, is now bequeathed to you, Count Montefelto, on your wedding.

Montefelto (*rising*) Wedding? Am I marrying someone I know, Holy Father?

Gaetani Mistress Sophia Aldesca brings with her, besides the Tuscan Patrimony, a large dowry, my blessing and the influence my blessing brings.

Jacopone Maaa yoouur maaaraaa beee haappeee aaa frruuuttffuu.

Gaetani Prepare yourselves.

He exits with **Jacopone** *downstage right.*

Montefelto I cannot marry a notorious Madam. Never.

Sophia There's no marriage 'twix an ex-whore and current madman. Never.

But **Montefelto** *turns his black cloak round to show it is gold on the reverse side and she pulls off her gown to reveal a white one underneath. They both take out a handful of seed corn and throw it over each other like confetti.*

An organ plays the 'Wedding March' as **Malabranca** *enters upstage centre, in full regalia and carrying a prayer book.* **Sophia** *and* **Montefelto** *walk solemnly upstage together and kneel before him as lights go down to a spot on them.*

Malabranca Wheat and sweet music can't stop me dreaming. I thought I woke when I made Pope Boniface, Pope, but that too was dream. I'm gathered here on the church porch to join this man and this woman as the Holy Father asked. My brain clouds over in holy matrimony . . . vos in matrimonium in nomine Patris . . .

The spot fades out to wedding bells playing amid the raucous sounds of eating, drinking and laughter. It stops abruptly.

Scene Eight

Charles II *and* **Queen Maria** *in the ante-chamber in dawn's half-light.*

Charles My friend Morrone, Pope Celestine, still lives, just. It's your fault, Madame, if I hadn't listened to you, I'd've been a truer friend to a friend and he'd've repaid my friendship now.

Maria It's your fault, Sir. You do the right thing too late and the wrong thing too soon.

Lights full up on the ante-chamber and **Gaetani** *hurrying in upstage centre with* **Jacopone** *carrying a large bag.* **Orsini,** *his right leg bandaged, hobbles in after them.*

Orsini Holy Father, you gave the Tuscan Patrimony to Count Montefelto – so-called. My leg may be infected but not my brain. I remember Pope Nicholas promised that land to the Orsini.

Gaetani The Orsini will be favoured in other ways, Your Eminence.

Charles II *and* **Maria** *cross to them.* **Charles II** *kneels and kisses* **Gaetani**'s *ring.*

Charles Holy Father, you promised us a Crusade against the Sicilians.

Maria (*kneeling to kiss* **Gaetani**'s *ring*) Instead we wait, w-a-i-t.

Gaetani *Ahhh!*

Orsini What is it, Holy Father?

Gaetani My finger!

Jacopone Fiiii?

Charles Finger?

Gaetani Your wife is biting it!

Charles II, Jacopone *and* **Orsini** *react and drag* **Maria** *off.*

Maria I can't wait, wait, wait!

Charles Forgive her, Holy Father.

Maria Don't ask forgiveness, you're a king, turnip-head!

Jacopone *rubs* **Gaetani**'s *bitten finger.*

Gaetani 'Tisn't broken or bleeding, is it? A woman's bite can send a man raving quicker than a mad dog's.

Jacopone 'Ttiiiss buuu bruuuss. Heeer Majjess neeedss aaa reesss.

Maria I need no rest. I need action this day.

Charles Come, our physician will give you a quick restorative. With your permission, Holy Father.

He starts to lead **Maria** *off.*

Maria Don't ask permission. Be a king.

They exit downstage right.

Jacopone Nooot fiiiitiiing beeehaaa foo aaa Queee.

Gaetani I understand Her Majesty. Before, when I was kept waiting, I longed to bite into bare skin and bone. But we are not hound or hawk. God lets us control wolfish urges. 'Tis what marks us from mere animals.

Colonna *hurries in upstage centre, a black patch over his left eye. He is about to kneel and kiss* **Gaetani**'s *ring when* **Gaetani** *hastily pulls away his hand.*

Colonna (*rising*) I cannot see out of my left eye, Holy Father, but I see a poor Ghibelline is not permitted to kiss St Peter's ring which explains why the Tuscany bequest was given to Montefelto when it was promised to the Ghibellines by Pope Celestine.

Gaetani Pope Celestine? I acknowledge no Pope Celestine. Who was Pope Celestine?

Colonna Father Peter de Morrone, who now is in prison without the sanction of the College of Cardinals.

Gaetani You filthy puses use that good man as rotting bait to hook in the weak and disaffected 'gainst me. You all conspire.

Colonna We Ghibellines have justified grievances, but we'd never conspire against you, Holy Father. We are concerned with the strength and well-being of the Church. It's why Father Morrone was removed.

Orsini Whatever he may be to the Ghibellines, Father Morrone remains an enemy to all Guelphs. His weakness invites revolution.

Gaetani You limp lobcocks long for him. I tire of your pinking eyes, scat-suckers! Run! Run!

Colonna *and* **Orsini** *bow and exit upstage centre.*

Jacopone Reeesst, Hoo Faa.

He opens his bag and takes out a bow and musical saw and starts to play it. The haunting sound hangs in the air as the lights slowly fade.

Gaetani Xerxes' army, they say, drank whole rivers dry, and Hannibal ate through the Alps with vinegar, and the mighty cities of Tarsus and Archiale were built in a day, but what feats could I perform if there was no Father Morrone? The light fades, why doesn't Morrone fade with the light? So much death, paper boats are more durable than we are . . . so why doesn't he fade gently with the fading light? . . . Why doesn't he? . . . Ahh, Jacopone . . .

Darkness. The music continues till it too fades into silence.

Scene Nine

Frantic whispering in the darkness. Lights half-up on a small prison cell. **Morrone,** *his eyes closed, stands stage centre with the demon* **Verrier** *and the prophet* **Elijah** *on either side of him.*

Verrier List, list to Verrier, your old friend.

Elijah Elijah is by your side.

Verrier Learn to hate your enemies.

Elijah No, love them.

Verrier Recover your place, become Supreme Pontiff again.

Elijah Do not thirst after the power and the glory. You've tasted God's love.

There is the sound of a bolt being drawn back, upstage centre. **Morrone** *opens his eyes and* **Verrier** *and* **Elijah** *hurry backwards and exit through the cell walls stage left and right. The lights come up full to show a single barred window to the right of the low door upstage centre which opens and* **Lucera** *and* **Roffred** *enter.*

Lucera We heard no sound, Father, so we became concerned. You were praying?

Morrone Praying and listening. This is the hour when devouts like me are visited by saints and demons. They come believing I'd be filled with envy and hate.

Lucera Most would be. You were Pope, a ruler of this world and the next. Now, your kingdom's these few dark feet of earth.

Morrone It's vast and has no boundaries. I began a young penitent in a cell little bigger than this. After years of devotion and sacrifice, I return and the circle closes. I had Peter's chair, ring, Empire. Now, I have all this.

Roffred }
Lucera } *(looking slowly round)* All what?

Morrone All Paradise.

Roffred We've only known the abyss. As a boy I saw wounded men lying in heaps along the roads, groaning like abandoned dogs.

Lucera We did our share; a woman, her skull, axed open, pink brain raw, lying in the stubble.

Roffred We know when to kill and fight and when to run. A good soldier soon learns when to run. Now it's your turn,

Father. Don't you see the walls moving in? Your space gets smaller. It's time to run.

Lucera Only this time you'll run to safety 'cause we'll help.

Roffred We've been corrupted. The bloody code of chivalry holds no meaning for us. Our code is simple and inflexible: always sell yourself to the highest bidder. But you're no high bidder, we're giving you our services free. Count Montefelto warned us not to look into your eyes.

Lucera You should've escaped long since, Father. We left the cell door open nightly: you only closed it. We dropped the keys for you and you gave them back. We were too subtle. This time there will be no mistake.

Roffred It's our one virtuous act and we'll pay more dearly for it than all our days of infamy.

Lucera The world darkens as we talk. You have to leave now, Father.

Morrone What do I have to fear? I am nothing and have nothing worth taking.

Roffred Nothing 'cept your life. Failures have no rights and the dead no friends.

Morrone *bends and picks up some of the grains of wheat scattered in Scene Seven.*

Morrone Corn grains gleam in my hand like gold. These seeds contain the secret of eternal life and truth and become the loaf that nourishes. These seeds of Babylon, Troy and Christ can lie a thousand years till they germinate in their time. But only if they die first. Unless a seed dies it will not bear fruit. If it dies then this cell will sprout a field of golden wheat, which will girdle the earth.

Lucera Words – we only listen to force.

They pick him up to carry him out when **Montefelto** *enters upstage centre.*

Montefelto Ah, caught trying to escape. The Supreme Pontiff will hear of this, Father. Good work, my Captains. (**Lucera** *and* **Roffred** *drop* **Morrone** *in surprise.*) So you can't win by giving us the good eye, Father. Captains Roffred and Lucera are men forged steel-hard in Mars' foundry and I have my protection too. (*To shield his eyes, he flicks down a peak attached to his helmet.*) If he tries to escape again, Captains, you have my permission to use maximum force.

Roffred He'll not try to escape again. His chance has gone.

Lucera But we'd like to go. We're expensive Genoese cross-bowmen wasted set guarding one old man.

Montefelto Who can turn the world underside up. He did me, showed me another world and left me beached.

Malabranca *appears in the doorway stage centre and enters gasping.*

Malabranca Broo . . . Broo . . .

Montefelto Ah, His Eminence, Cardinal Malabranca has been given permission to see the prisoner.

Morrone I do not complain but this cell is becoming more crowded than St Peter's Square on Feast Days.

Montefelto One of us will be outside at all times listening, noting, so speak freely and say nothing.

Montefelto, Lucera *and* **Roffred** *exit upstage centre, closing the door behind them.*

Malabranca (*gasping*) The climb up here . . . too hard . . . at my age, Brother Peter. The Holy Father asked me to come . . . Wants you to forswear all intrigue against him . . . me to persuade you . . . I'm dying, Brother Peter, I know the signs. I suddenly can't breathe and I don't know what to do with my hands. Where's the snow, Brother? Where's the snow? . . . I came to warn you . . . I forget . . .

Morrone Before we are born, an angel teaches us the art of forgetting, because life would be unbearable if we remembered everything. Isn't that strange?

Malabranca Give me your hand!

He clasps **Morrone**'s *hand tightly and they walk slowly downstage.*

Morrone Rest, rest, in the blue pastures of heaven, Latinus.

Malabranca Is that my name? Why do you live so high up, Brother? It's time to go down. We'll go down together. I don't want to go alone.

He stumbles. **Morrone** *gently lowers him to the floor.*

Morrone Be not afraid, Brother. Let God enter.

Malabranca It's another dream. But it's so real. I am on a mountain or on my bed, the heavenly musicians of light are coming and I'm slowly turning, becoming a wingbeat, a sigh, sunlight on water, lighter than sunlight. (*His eyes close.*) Here I am . . . there I was . . . (*He opens his eyes.*) Ah, I see I'm in your cell, Brother, not dying on a mountain top. It was all a dream.

He dies. Lights fade down. An organ plays the 'Dies Irae' quietly as **Elijah** *and* **Verrier** *enter through the cell walls stage right and left. They pick up* **Malabranca**'s *body and slowly carry it out on their shoulders through the wall stage right, whilst* **Morrone** *prays.*

Morrone His dreaming's done, now let him wake, Lord.

The organ music dies away in the darkness.

Scene Ten

Lights up on **Montefelto**'s *bedroom in the Vatican apartments.* **Sophia** *and* **Montefelto** *face each other kneeling on the bed upstage centre.*

Montefelto
> Let other men die for a flag
> I'll play the bold warrior and kiss
>   thy honey-sweet lips
> And kiss and kiss.

Sophia
> Five thousand kisses make and more
> So our kisses grow thicker than fields
>   of Egyptian wheat.

They kiss.

Montefelto
> Let your kisses snuff out my rage
> I've seen in a world filled with hate
> Love is not enough; rage is needed.

Sophia
> My heart will help cool it
> It's cold enough; iron not gold.

I will freeze your hot rage
And you thaw my arctic heart.
Fused, we make one whole being,
Bright and magnificent.

They embrace as the door bursts open stage left. **Montefelto** *and*
Sophia *whip out a sword and dagger from under their respective*
pillows but it is **Gaetani** *who rushes in, followed by* **Jacopone,**
both in long white nightdresses.

Gaetani No time for ceremony, Cardinal Malabranca's dead.
He's gone, taking his white hairs and dysentery with him.
Captains Lucera and Roffred found him.

Montefelto *pulls on his breeches.*

Montefelto Loyal Captains both.

Gaetani Malabranca was loyal, then turned traitor and died
on me, and left a vacancy in the College of Cardinals. All will
expect me to nominate one of their number and the people
will shout 'Celestine! Celestine!' And so my larger vision's
thwarted whilst I have to concern myself with minor matters.
Malabranca dies but Brother Morrone doesn't.

Montefelto Last time you sent a friend to him, Holy Father.
Send an enemy. I'll go.

He slashes a pillow with his sword.

Gaetani Go then. But you have no orders. I love to give orders
but you have none. There is at most a glance, a half smile,
an unfinished gesture. But no orders. You heard me give no
orders did you, Jacopone?

Jacopone Nooo oorrrdd, Hoo Faa.

Sophia No orders come expensive, Holy Father, being the
most dangerous to carry out. The Tuscany estate relieved of
all taxation, plus a payment of five thousand in gold, would
suffice for fulfilling no orders.

Gaetani You've acquired a caring wife, Count Montefelto;
cleave to her.

He exits stage left.

Jacopone Thhh Hoo Faa haaas assk Caapptaa Lucee and
Caapptaa Fooffree too assttenn yooo.

He exits stage left after **Gaetani.**

Sophia Sweet, do not act in rage, this is policy. Do not act out of hate for Father Morrone but love for me and our union.

Montefelto We'll rise by this, join the best families of Europe, who grew out of blood and filth. But will he pay?

Sophia He needs us, so he'll pay – till he finds a better assassin. But there's none better than you, my sweet.

Montefelto Or you, my dove.

They embrace. There is a knock on the door stage left.

Sophia Your Captains. I'll go to my chamber and dress. Remember, chuck, the night is full of demons.

Montefelto I'll be protected by your love. Come, Captains!

Sophia *exits stage right as* **Lucera** *and* **Roffred** *enter stage left.*

Lucera We've orders from the Holy Father to report to you for orders, Sire.

Montefelto (*strapping on armour and sword*) And I've no orders from him to see Father Morrone.

Roffred No orders are too dangerous: they give no protection.

Montefelto What protection can a soldier have 'cept his own right arm?

Lucera Look on his face, Roffred. It's the full dead-man's face. We've seen it enough times before.

Montefelto Yes, the men and women we've slaughtered cannot be computed: sword, knife, axe or rope, no differences – they fall. They are like grass. But grass and men grow again.

Lucera Father Morrone isn't grass. A man who despises the things other men and women sweat, kill and die for is a man precious. Cut down, he cannot be replaced.

Montefelto Bumfodder, he's not worth one drop of water from my crouch-bag. He betrayed me. You have your orders.

Lucera No, we have no orders.

Montefelto Serking shit-sacks, *arrrhh!*

In a sudden rage, he grabs a pillow, tears it apart. A cloud of feathers engulfs **Lucera** *who shrieks in pain and staggers out of it, his slashed face and throat covered with blood. He collapses amid the feathers.* **Roffred** *rushes over to him as* **Montefelto** *sits on the edge of the bed, staring at his bloodstained sword.*

Lucera Feathers . . . death by feathers, that's a rich one. A good death defending a good man, that's richer . . . Friend, friend, remember the times we had, the nuns we raped at Celure . . . we cuckold Christ then by enjoying his brides . . . Now I pay . . . You'll have to tend our land alone . . . count the herds, offer up ears of corn for a good harvest . . . I can't see, the sky's dark with feathers . . . Roffred, Roffred, is this dying?

He dies.

Montefelto 'Twasn't me. I promised there'd be no hot rage in me. It's Satan's red demon – here. (*He points to his forehead.*) Father Morrone cured me – then it came back. Can't you see it, Roffred?

Roffred Yes, Sire, I see it. It's a red scaly devil sitting in the middle of your forehead. I'll pick it off – there!

He takes out his dagger and stabs **Montefelto** *between the eyes.* **Montefelto** *rises, the dagger handle protruding from his forehead.*

Montefelto It's gone . . . Sophia . . .

He crashes to the floor amid a cloud of feathers. **Roffred** *crosses back to* **Lucera.**

Roffred You won't see God in splendour but perhaps Father Morrone will intercede – he's in good standing. No time for further laments, friend. I'm not afraid, but my feet aren't going to stand here and see my body abused. I'll survive to keep our friendship green.

The sound of footsteps stage right and he exits quickly stage left. **Sophia** *enters stage right, fully dressed. She stops, whips out a knife, makes sure no one else is in the room then kneels beside* **Montefelto.** *Taking a handful of feathers, she throws them gently into the air so they fall over his face.*

Sophia You promised but you fell in scalding rage, now you lie cold. You betrayed us. We should've died wrapt together in a bundle of time. Now we go separate and Heaven becomes Hell because you're not there. Though I blocked every entrance to my heart, love took me by ambush. I'll not be caught unguarded again. Fool! Fool! (*She beats* **Montefelto***'s chest.*) I'll try to forget you; my sorrow I'll not keep raw. I'll not wash my clothes in the waters of my tears. I'll dress and put a merry face on it. But I know the good seasons have slipped away like shadows. Now the nights will be endless and the gates of mercy closed. (*Singing as the lights fade down.*) 'Strew his grave with roses./Plant a yew tree at his head/And the bay leaves scatter/For my love is dead, oh my love is dead.'

Lights out.

Scene Eleven

Charles II *and* **Maria** *wander out of the darkness downstage right, fully dressed but in carpet slippers.*

Maria You're indistinguishable in this bad light, which is the light I always see you in now, flip-flop. Hear our slippers go flip-flop.

Charles I keep my head when everyone else about me is losing theirs.

Maria That's because you're too stupid to understand the problem.

Charles And you know more and more about less and less, until you know everything about nothing. God won't deny me success after a lifetime of begging.

Maria He will. He has. We're no longer at the centre. Pope Boniface ignores us and sends us home. We play our last scene in poor light, pushed to the margin, flip-flop.

Charles I didn't ask much. I had a simple dream, of ruling the world. Where was I wrong? I betrayed Father Morrone and Judas hanged himself in a potter's field for it, but kings betray their subjects daily and thrive, flip-flop.

Maria We shrink; I feel myself shrinking, the squeaking consort of a minor princeling in the wet fish trade. Perhaps, if you asked Father Morrone's forgiveness?

Charles No. True rulers can't ask forgiveness. Forgiveness is against their calling. Forgiveness is catching. If I looked into Father Morrone's eye, I might forgive my father.

Maria Keep him in darkness, then. He makes us feel unworthy.

Charles Keep him in chains. It's his fault and his fault and their fault but not my fault, flip-flop, flip . . .

Maria Flop, flop.

They shuffle off in the darkness stage left as lights blaze up on the Vatican throne-room. The entrance is upstage right. A series of magnificent banners with gold crosses hang from the flies. **Orsini** *and* **Colonna,** *in cardinal's robes and formally carrying the Guelph and Ghibelline banners, kneel before* **Gaetani,** *in white robes, seated on the golden throne upstage centre, illuminated by two spot lights. A bejewelled* **Sophia** *and* **Jacopone** *kneel either side of him. They all rise.*

Orsini Both my feet now eaten away but I stand upright and say before God and the Holy Father, the next Cardinal to replace Cardinal Malabranca must be a Guelph.

Colonna My one good eye's clouding o'er but anyone with half an eye can see the new Cardinal must be a Ghibelline.

Jacopone Yoouu Emminenceeess, thh Hoo Faa grieevess, Couuntt Monteefeel tooo iss deaa.

Colonna Couuunntt Monteefeel deaa?

Orsini Hoo diii hee diii?

Sophia Vioolentleee.

Colonna Thii couurtt haa beecoo viollenttt.

Sophia This court is no more violent than most.

Jacopone Ann Goo dooeees noo tuurn aaawaa ffroom blooo.

Orsini No, God does not turn away from blood.

Sophia Yet the court air turns sick.

Colonna Perhaps we are being punished for our sins.

Jacopone Whaa paarticulaa siiinnss, Youu Emmineeencee?

Orsini Father Morrone . . .

Colonna Father Morrone . . .

They sigh.

Gaetani Who will rid me of this holy man? He does nothing and blocks me. Your sighs tear me down. Father Morrone listened to your small ambitions; they are beneath me. Morrone's the Saviour for you. I'm having him brought here for judgement. If you want him back, take him. (*The light builds in the doorway upstage right.*) Poor, humble, despised, his powers increase by abstinence and suffering. To cleanse others he has cleansed himself complete, to give light he is become all light.

The light in the doorway is blinding. All eyes except **Gaetani** *shield their eyes as* **Morrone,** *in torn jerkin, enters through the light upstage right, smiling.*

Colonna Do not smile, Father.

Orsini We cannot brook your smile.

Gaetani When I smile the strong stop breathing but no one says don't smile.

Orsini Father Morrone, forgive us. Show us Christ's mercy and forgive us.

Colonna We raised you high, and plucked you down. All done for Mother Church. Forgive us, Father.

Orsini Why do you still smile?

Colonna My optics blur. Do you still smile?

Orsini Is it because God's crushed my extremities and I move like a turtle in mud? My legs stiffen, feet dead . . . (**Morrone** *makes the sign of the cross over him.*) . . . But . . . but . . . You make signs, smile and I feel 'em. They stir, they stir. My beautiful legs stir. By jigs and hornpipes they stir. I caper!

He leaps into the air. **Morrone** *makes the sign of the cross over* **Colonna.**

Colonna You look absurd dancing in the shining light . . . Wait . . . wait . . . my eyes . . . By God's light and powers optical I see colours clear again.

They whirl round together.

Orsini It's a miracle!

Colonna It's a miracle!

They stop dancing round and make the sign of the cross over **Morrone.**

Orsini I tremble.

Colonna We are afraid together. The world is governed by laws. When it hails, the field of the just man cannot be miraculously spared, for that just man may sin after the harvest and then his grain would have to rot miraculously in his barn.

Orsini Each action would need another miracle to counter the last, so miracles would be the ordinary order of things and the exception the rule, and disorder, order. Don't give us miracles.

Colonna We want no part of 'em. We were right to vote you out.

Orsini You are a man of chaos.

Colonna Fling him back into the pit! Have mercy, Father.

Orsini Lock him and lose him! Have mercy, Father.

They kneel and pray.

Jacopone You heaarrd, Hoo Faa. SSStriiikee hiii dooownn ffoo hiiiss duumbb inssooolencee. (**Morrone** *makes the sign of the cross over him.*) Arrrrhh. I – I – I – Icccurse heaven for letting you live, may your blood eat away the decaying fabric of the earth, and Hell consume you. You've taken Jacopone from Jacopone. Hoo Faa, whoo aaa III nooo? That was Jacopone, the only speechless courtier in Christendom and the most powerful. Others had to learn to speak without tongues. Sweet music hearing 'em pay homage. Now I'm just another talking toady with the daily larding of butter for the great. If I say, 'Go feed upon the bare trees of Hell', it's mere words. But, 'Gooo feee upooo thhh baa trees ooo Heee' – that's something more. You've stolen my poetry and I'm lost. Go die in darkness, Father Morrone.

Sophia I've no need of miracles. (**Morrone** *makes the sign of the cross over her.*) Make no sign over me, Father, I have all my senses intact . . . (*She cries.*) Is that why I weep? These are real tears, I taste the salt in them. I'm a woman hardened against sorrow. And now I weep for Eden lost. For what is Eden to me now? There's no love there. Hell, I consider you excellent, for you house my lover there. I cry for him, my soul, my heart, my grief and joy gone forever . . . Father, you made me feel my sorrow and now I'm fit for nothing. This man is dangerous.

There is the sound of a crowd approaching as **Orsini** *and* **Colonna** *rise and* **Sophia** *and* **Jacopone** *back away from* **Morrone.**

Jacopone Father, you gave us choice.

Colonna You turn our world.

Orsini All we want is a fireside and an overstuffed chair.

Sophia You make us all feel guilty.

The approaching crowd chant 'Guilty!' as the lights fade down and **Sophia** *and* **Jacopone** *exit downstage right and* **Orsini** *and* **Colonna** *downstage left, the banners are pulled up and the throne off and the prison cell walls descend from the flies stage left, right and centre with a reverberating clang.*

Scene Twelve

Morrone *and* **Gaetani** *stand facing each other in the centre of the prison cell. There is a shaft of light from the barred windows upstage right.*

Gaetani They rejected you. I knew they would, that's why I brought you before them for final judgement.

Morrone A man doesn't lower himself by failure but by the excuses he makes for it. They were right to reject me. I don't even live in the Holy Land.

Gaetani *You* are the Holy Land, Father, and this cell is Jerusalem. And still they rejected you for the key to the true nature of man is imbecility.

Morrone But God looked over the world and found it good.

Gaetani He should've been more demanding. He created the world in six days and just look at it.

Morrone Would you've done better?

Gaetani Yes.

Morrone Then start work. Why do you wait?

Gaetani I need you to move over before I can begin to fight this suffering, this despair.

Morrone I don't fight it, I turn it into ecstasy shouting 'Lord, Lord, is this the way to rule your world? It's time to have love and have mercy on your children.'

Gaetani According to the Gospel of Peter, Jesus didn't say on the cross 'My God, My God, why hast thou forsaken me!' but 'My power, power, thou hast forsaken me!' He knew power, not love, saturates the earth. And it flows to the strongest. Think of the power coiled in Attila's skull. For what is the Christian Church?

Morrone The river of life.

Gaetani It is a centralized, coherent and structured movement with objectives and rules, disciplines and prerogatives. It cannot be governed by saints. Its lower orders may be made up of good men but it can only flourish in the world by installing Judas as chief steward. Poisons have their place in curative medicine, so human malignants are needed to rule Christ's Church.

Morrone I do not rule. I am naked, alone, imprisoned. What more can I do, Father?

Gaetani Die.

Morrone The Angel of Death rarely comes when called.

Gaetani If he does not come, I'll take his place. I have the instruments – knife and rope. (*He produces a knife and thin rope.*) But these hands can suffice.

Morrone I prefer hands. Steel and hemp are too cold. Warm hands have the touch of life about them even when they take it. But you will be damned, Holy Father; even you. Impaled forever on the mill-wheel of Hell.

Gaetani Hell is here, now. To pull mankind up out of the mud you must step into the mud yourself.

Morrone I'll try to help, Holy Father. If I turn my back to you, it should be easier.

He turns round.

Gaetani My thanks, Father Morrone. Hands will do it.

Morrone I'll expose my neck, so. It's scrawny enough for you to get your hands right round it.

Gaetani *has moved quietly forward. His hands come up slowly and are almost round* **Morrone***'s neck when he suddenly stops.*

Gaetani I'm not fit to be Supreme Pontiff. I cannot find it in me to touch you. Such niceties of scruple unman me and I cannot play my role. I've failed and plant the seeds of destruction of the one true Church.

Morrone The answer is still in your hands, Holy Father. You are Christ's Vicar on earth. Command me to die and I will submit.

Gaetani You will submit?

Morrone For God, and in such circumstances the Angel of Death will oblige I'm certain. For I suddenly grow weary. My soul longs for home.

Gaetani You will submit?

Morrone Souls, they say, change to birds.

Gaetani You will fly to Heaven – if not higher.

Morrone I prefer Hell. For who are in Heaven? – only the good and the pious and they don't need me.

Gaetani Then we'll meet in Hell's fourth zone, the place for souls consumed with arrogance and envy. But I'll weep, for you will have seen God's face.

Morrone If you wish to see Him just think of the sun, and think again.

Gaetani I've no time. The God I serve is the God who created this whirling world where the strong must slay the weak and I am soaked.

Morrone There's only one thing more terrible than despair – resignation. God is love and nothing but love.

Gaetani I, Pope Boniface VIII, pronounce and declare, proclaim and command that Father Peter de Morrone, being subject to the absolute authority of the Roman Pontiff and for the good and glory of the Father, Son and Holy Ghost, cease breathing: die and release your soul.

A flute plays.

Morrone Each man is born with his death inside him and needs to die his death. (*He sinks down stage centre.*) I see the spheres turn like the potter's wheel and the earth suspended from the cords of Christ's love. I pray for you, Holy Father. You live and win and lose by winning. I die and lose and win by losing. In due time I will come to harvest. What I plant will grow and the world will change and the day will come when the stars will be as fair as they are now in Eden, the sun as bright, the sea as pure and the earth without those miseries which destroy its peace and beauty and mankind will be without the briars and thorns of pride, greed and violence. Evil will be blown away – mere chaff and stubble – and the sky, Benedict, oh, the sky. But others must gather in these fruits, these fruits of love.

He dies. **Gaetani** *prays on his knees upstage left as the lights grow brighter.*

Gaetani Died gentle as he lived, quiet as a mouse. Accept him, Lord, he is the best we have to offer. Honour him, Lord, for I must wrap him in oblivion. His everlasting lot will be wordless; blot out his example and his name, else men and women will know how near they came to Paradise. Hide him in darkness.

As the light becomes brighter and hotter, rows of wheat sprout up from the prison floor, hiding **Morrone**'s *body from view. The cell is a golden wheat field. The cell walls are taken up to reveal behind them, on every side, more wheat. It is a harvest stretching into the distance.*

Gaetani (*rising*) Send in the reapers!

The lights begin to fade down as three reapers with scythes enter upstage left, dressed in black, their faces completely wrapped in black silk. As they move forward and rhythmically cut down the wheat, a column of black smoke rises upstage; the field is being burnt.

The lights begin to fade down.

Epilogue

As flames mingle with the smoke upstage a single spotlight picks out **Gaetani,** *now white-haired and bent, his robes dirty and torn.*

Gaetani Seven years since Saint Celestine died. Seven years trying to defend the unity of the Church, to bring peace to Europe and happiness to its people. I used force, Pope Celestine love, Pope Nicholas force and love. We all failed – but I get the best notices. I made a mess of it but my mess had muscle. So I'm remembered with respect. Pope Celestine's deep in oblivion's pit. The Church condemns him for incompetence as if that had ever been a bar to high office. They're ashamed of him because he shamed them. But there hasn't been a moment in these seven haunted years after, I've not thought of him. Now, on my death day, I stand on this mountain and look out over a Universe robbed of salvation where human beings are so ugly they've stopped hating each other and hate themselves. (*He kneels.*) Men and women can no longer bear it. Do you hear us, Lord? Do you hear us?

A cold wind blows as the spotlight becomes smaller and smaller until it vanishes.

Bye Bye Columbus

Bye Bye Columbus was a Greenpoint production for BBC Television. It was televised on 3 February 1992. The cast was as follows:

Columbus	Daniel Massey
Frair Marchena	Simon Callow
Louis de Santangel	John Turner
Beatriz de Bobadilla	Dilys Laye
Cardinal Mendoza	Peter Bayliss
Queen Isabella	Harriet Walter
King Ferdinand	Alex Jennings
Torquemada	James Laurenson
First Seaman	Shaun Prendergast
Second Seaman	Barry Stanton
Martin Pinzon	Timothy West
Rodrigo	Nicholas Farrell
Father Nervo	Timothy Bateson
Roldan	Christopher Ettridge
Parrot's Voice & Singer	Jack Shepherd
Beatriz Enriquez de Arana	Christie Horn
Director	Peter Barnes
Producer	Ann Scott
Music by	Stephen Deutsch
Designer	Luciana Arrighi

Heroic music. Lights up on an expanse of untouched sand and blue sky.

A longboat crunches up on to the beach Stage Right and **Columbus** *and a crew of Spaniards, holding aloft the royal red and gold banner of Castille clamber ashore;* **Columbus** *making sure he is the first.*

As they fall on their knees, **Columbus** *unsheathes his sword and holds it high, handle first, to form a cross.*

Columbus At sunrise, October 12th, in the Year of Our Lord 1492, I, Christopher Columbus, Colon, or even Colombo, as Admiral of the Oceanic Sea, do solemnly take possession of this new land, in the name of King Ferdinand and Queen Isabella of Castille, bathed in the glory of God . . .

As he looks ecstatically up to the heavens, the Others, unable to wait, scramble up agitatedly, rush Upstage, pull down their soiled pantaloons and hose and crouch in a line.

Lights fade down on a row of white bottoms ready to pollute the virgin sand.

A ballad is sung in the darkness.

Singer Columbus was counting his money
        And knew he had to have more
        When the parrot had a suggestion
        Get three ships from the Queen
                    and explore

Spot up Stage Left on **Columbus** *lying on a bed. There are legal documents scattered on the floor around the bed, and a* **Parrot** *on a perch.*

White haired and arthritic, **Columbus** *suddenly sits up.*

Columbus Gold! Oh, most excellent gold. Who has gold gets what he wants, imposes his will on the world and even helps souls in paradise . . . (*He gets up and addresses the* **Parrot**.) When the Lords of Panama die, Polly, they bury their gold with the corpses. There are tons still there. I'm fifty-three and my hair's white and I've passed too much water but all I need is the word to dig it up. Give me the word!

Parrot Dig it up, dig it up!

Columbus Ten per cent of all that gold's mine. Legal documents signed by King Ferdinand and Queen Isabella give me ten per cent. It's here, here, here, in black and white . . . (*Holds up documents.*) I was cheated!

Parrot Lawyers! It's the lawyers!

Columbus Black-coated, hellspawn! The Devil visited a lawyer I knew and said he'd give him riches, fame and a long life in return for his eternal soul and the souls of his mother, father, wife and children. The lawyer said, 'Good, but what's the catch?' . . . That's the kind of men I'm dealing with. They swindled me out of the fruits of my genius. I told them I knew a quick way to the East. And I proved it. But they denied me as Christ was denied . . . You hear my story, Polly, and give me your verdict. One thing I know, Pol, I've been fighting blind prejudice and heaven-high ignorance all my life. Everything else is confused . . . Born in Genoa, wasn't I, Polly? That's true, I think. Trouble is, I've peddled so many stories about myself – I'm a peddler by trade – it's difficult to remember the truth.

Parrot You're the son of Domenico Colombo of Genoa who was jailed for owing money to a cheese merchant.

Columbus That's right, but not so loud, Polly. I'm either an Italian from a Spanish family or a Spaniard from an Italian or even a converted Jew. I look back and ask what is life, Polly?

Parrot Why don't you ask what is a carrot?

Columbus Life is business, Polly. I know, I was a travelling salesman in dry goods for the firm of Di Negro and Spinola for years. One of the best. They were sorry to see me go. But I had a dream. Not just the normal one of fame, money, power. But for something else, above and beyond. I had to prove I was right and everybody else was wrong. I studied and sailed from Thule – that's Iceland, Polly – to Guinea. I sought out scholars and map-makers but they didn't know the truth. Only I knew the truth. I found it in the Priory of La Rabida, kneeling before the Lord: I heard Him speak.

Parrot I know what He said! I know what He said!

Spot out. Organ music.

Spot up Stage Right on a large crucifix with the young **Columbus** *kneeling before it in a golden light from the stained glass window.*

Parrot's Voice You are God's instrument. Carry my name to new lands and make them submit. The way to the East is West. India is only a few days' sailing distance away. Repeat and repeat!

Columbus The way to the East is West. India is only a few days' sailing distance away.

Parrot's Voice Now go find it. Be rich and give me back Jerusalem!

The golden light from the stained glass fades. **Columbus** *gets up as* **Antonio de Marchena** *joins him with an armful of maps.*

Columbus Friar Marchena, God spoke to me and confirmed what I already knew in my heart.

Friar Marchena He usually does.

Columbus He told me the shortest way to the riches of the East lay due West.

Friar Marchena *spreads the maps on the floor.*

Friar Marchena I've long felt that too. But you won't find confirmation in any of these and as the best map-maker in Spain I have the biggest collection in the country. The only map that would confirm the western route was made by Paolo Toscanelli of Florence based on Marco Polo's travels. It is now in the possession of the King of Portugal.

Columbus I must see it!

He starts to move away but **Friar Marchena** *pulls him back by his coat.*

Friar Marchena Now you must do nothing on impulse. You seek fame and fortune. The Franciscan Order will help. But remember nothing comes free.

Columbus I'll do anything for everything.

Friar Marchena *gives him a Franciscan habit, lying folded on a bench.* **Columbus** *puts it on.*

Friar Marchena With this robe and girdle you are now a lay member of the Order of St Francis. This uniform, like all uniforms, will give you unearned authority. But you must be transformed, remade . . . Your hair . . . Turn it grey . . . (**Columbus** *passes a hand over his hair, turning it grey.*) Good. Now your walk. Make it sure, deliberate. (*He walks gravely up and down and* **Columbus** *copies him.*) Good. Now standing . . . Be rock-still. Feet slightly apart, eyes never turned away . . . (**Columbus** *copies his look and stance.*) Good. Now speech . . . No pauses, no hesitations, no humour . . . 'I speak of gold, pearls, precious stones and Jerusalem and Mount Zion rebuilt by Christians with treasure from the East.'

Columbus 'I speak of gold, pearls, precious stones and Jerusalem and Mount Zion rebuilt by Christians with treasure from the East.'

Friar Marchena More important than speech is silence, the silence that hangs in the air, the silence that crushes, the silence of one who *knows.*

Columbus But I do.

Friar Marchena Think long, not in days, weeks, months but in years. You've worlds to conquer and that takes time. Remember you're the son of a weaver who went into cheese so in this, the Year of Our Lord 1485, the whole system is against you.

Columbus What do I do?

Friar Marchena Outface your betters, the Lords, Dukes and minor Princes. After all, they're only the descendants of the louse-ridden thugs of Charlemagne. But they've hedged themselves round with high sounding names and titles. Do you the same. In order to succeed you must reinvent yourself.

Columbus That's easy. I've always known I'm the bastard son of Count Colombo.

Friar Marchena Good. Lies carry their own truth.

Columbus But it is true. Anything I say three times I believe is true. Often twice is enough.

Friar Marchena Two final pieces of advice. Only deal with the rich and powerful – those that can help your God-given mission – the rest of humanity don't count, much less read. And get married. It will engender sympathy from your fellow-sufferers.

Spot out Stage Right. Music.

Spot up on the bedroom Stage Left where **Columbus** *is pouring himself some wine.*

Columbus A wedding is a funeral where you smell your own flowers . . . who did I marry, Polly, I forget?

Parrot Filipa Moniz Perestrello, daughter of the Governor of Porto Santo. What happened to her?

Columbus She died after giving me a son, Diego. But it was a good marriage, her father had a marvellous library and two sisters who were the mistresses of the

Archbishop of Lisbon. So I met the right people.

Spot up Stage Right on a huge fifteenth-century wall-map of the known world.

Cardinal Mendoza, *the financier* **Louis de Santangel** *and the notorious mistress of kings,* **Beatriz de Bobadilla**, *sit on three ornate chairs in front of it.*

In the shifting shadows they look more like potential conspirators than potential investors.

Columbus *enters from the darkness and stands in front of them.*

Columbus This meeting is honoured by the attendance of the greatest names in the Spanish Court – Cardinal Mendoza, Louis de Santangel, and Beatriz de Bobadilla. We meet at night because I have the secret of untold riches and the fewer people know it, the larger our share. Since Pope Pius II announced the world is round we can obviously reach the East by sailing West. As everything comes in threes, Father, Son and Holy Ghost, so there are three continents, Europe, Africa and Asia. There is nothing to stop a ship sailing West thus . . . (*He disappears round the back of the European end of the map and reappears at the other end beside Asia.*) . . . and reaching India and China. By my calculations it's only a few days' good sailing.

Santangel How do you know?

Columbus The great authors confirm it: Marco Polo, Aristotle and de Mandeville! And the signs and portents are there too. Asian driftwood found on the Venetian coast, two Chinamen washed up in Galway – they say they were Laps but I saw their slitty Chinese eyes. . . . And what of the dying pilot, Alonzo Sanchez, who told me with his last breath of a land beyond Madeira and the secret maps of the West kept by the Portuguese and Italian trading houses? The world will fall into their hands 'less we act.

Santangel And Spain will go down. But if it's only a few days' sailing distance, why hasn't anyone else done it before?

Columbus Because the Universe is filled with limp lobcocks. I'm nailed on the cross of their disbelief! But there's another reason they won't make the journey West, they're cowards all. They never sail out of sight of land except with a homebound wind, whilst I will launch out into the unknown – unknown to all except me. I expect to meet dangers of course: the Sirens that tempted Ulysses, the fiery wall guarding the Earthly Paradise, dogfaced men and vegetable lambs. There will be many souls to save for Christ, before we reach those fabulous cities tiled with gold.

Cardinal Mendoza By your own admission, you're a man who does not believe what others believe: you're a heretic, a rebel, a revolutionary.

Columbus Never! All heretics should be staked and revolutionaries garrotted. I'm for King, Country and the Papacy now and for ever. My desire is to make the rich richer, including myself. My only heresy is finding the way to the gold.

Cardinal Mendoza How do you get it?

Columbus We take it. There will be uncharted islands, lands unknown on the way. When natives are warlike, with a leader like the Great Khan – as in China – we trade. When they're weak, docile or divided against themselves, as in India, we take the gold, by force in the name of Christ.

Cardinal Mendoza That seems fair enough.

Columbus We must do it for Spain as well as ourselves. The prize we reach for is nothing less than the salvation – and domination – of our World.

Santangel You'll need at least three ships. That'll cost more than two million maravedis.

Columbus *picks up his papers from the floor.*

Columbus I understand, gentlemen. Like any man marked out for greatness I accept rejection. I'm prepared to battle long years if need be. Just as Christ suffered, so I will suffer to fulfil my destiny.

He starts to leave.

Santangel Two million is very little risk capital considering the rewards.

Cardinal Mendoza The Church will see to it that potential investors are persuaded to contribute.

Columbus What?! You mean I don't have to struggle, starve, face ridicule and neglect? I'll have the finance?

Santangel Congratulations.

Cardinal Mendoza *and* **Santangel** *cross to* **Columbus** *to congratulate him.*

Columbus I'm a little disconcerted. Frankly, gentlemen, I didn't expect it to be this easy.

de Bobadilla It shouldn't be . . . (*The others turn back to her.*) If we're talking business, we must talk plain. I'm Beatriz de Bobadilla, mistress of the highest, lay and cleric. I made my money, gentlemen, on my back. It was earned hard and I'm not spending it easy. I've learned when men are asking for money not to listen to what they say but watch what their hands are doing. Yours were twitchy, Signor Colombo, Colon, Columbus or whatever.

Columbus I must remedy that.

He hides his hands behind his back as **de Bobadilla** *gets up.*

de Bobadilla I never listen to my heart only my head and it's rarely fooled. Making Spain great and buying souls for Jesus are commendable objectives, gentlemen, but not with my money. When I invest I invest for profit not glory. And I want to know all the facts in order to make a judgement.

Columbus I'll tell you everything.

de Bobadilla I know you went to King Joao II of Portugal with this same scheme two years ago. He's into exploration in a big way. The Portuguese have discovered the island of Cape Verde and the gold of Guinea and Bartholomew Díaz has already rounded the Cape of Good Hope so why did he turn you down? Didn't he like the scheme?

Columbus Yes he did. He even agreed to finance the whole expedition except he wouldn't meet my terms.

de Bobadilla Terms? What are your terms?

Columbus My terms for leading the Westward expedition were, are and ever shall be, as follows: one, I am to be given the title of the Grand Admiral of the Oceanic Sea; two, I am to be made Viceroy and have the right to nominate all governors of all the lands I discover; and three, I am to take ten per cent of all commerce from such lands in perpetuity.

They all whistle in astonishment.

Santangel You asked King Joao for that much?

Columbus I'm worth that much.

Cardinal Mendoza Nobody in the history of exploration is worth that much.

Columbus I am.

Santangel Such greed.

de Bobadilla Wonderful! I wasn't impressed before but I am now, seeing you put such a price on yourself.

Santangel However impressed we are by your demands they do change the situation. Only royals have the power to give you your titles. We mere subjects cannot make you a Grand Admiral.

Cardinal Mendoza Without these terms you can sail West within the month. If you insist on them, you must negotiate with Queen Isabella and King Ferdinand, and that can take years.

Columbus I insist on my terms!

Spot out.

Spot slowly up Stage Left on the bedroom with **Columbus** *gesturing furiously with a legal document.*

Columbus And they were not negotiable! That's what they didn't understand. Even when it was all that stood in way of my expedition, even when I was in despair, even when all my friends begged me to be flexible, I never changed the terms, not one jot or tittle. Greed too has its heroes. But it was more than greed. My demands put my expedition out of the reach of the most powerful sea-powers in Europe: they couldn't afford it. That made it even more desirable. I've learned never to sell cheap.

Parrot Never sell cheap, never sell cheap! What else did you learn?

Columbus Never to reveal the circumstances of my birth, never to explain my plans, and never to reduce my demands, not even to Queen Isabella and King Ferdinand, dual Monarchs of Castille and Aragon, devout Christians who devoted themselves to the extermination of heresy and the exaltation of the Catholic Faith.

Spot up Stage Right on the Spanish throne room: two thrones and a large iron crown suspended over them.

King Ferdinand *in shabby black,* **Isabella** *in a dark dress and high lace collar, and the Inquisitor-General,* **Torquemada,** *are arguing fiercely.*

Isabella I had the Holy Father resurrect the Holy Inquisition and you've burnt, garrotted, and imprisoned over ten thousand Jews, and assorted heretics over the last year. Not enough and too expensive.

Ferdinand Yes, where's our profit? The goods and property of every man and woman convicted by the Holy Inquisition are forfeit. By some art of creative accountancy we haven't seen a half-groat.

Torquamada I have expenses, Your Highnesses. Top class clerks, confessors, torturers and executioners cost money; then there's kindling wood and garrotting rope. Purifying the race comes expensive.

Ferdinand Economise. My fanatical spouse may be interested in purification but I'm only interested in money. It's your fault, Madame. You had your idiot Confessor, Signor Torquemada here, made Inquisitor-General and he's cheating us.

Isabella Aragonese clodpole! This is God's work even when it isn't profitable.

Ferdinand Castilian windbag, everything has to be profitable!

A fanfare off and **Isabella** *and* **Ferdinand** *immediately dash back to their thrones.* **Torquamada** *stands between them, forming a dignified regal picture.*

Herald Your Highnesses, Signor Christopher Colon, Colombo or Columbus, craves audience.

Columbus *enters carrying a small gold-embossed case, and kneels before the throne.* **Isabella** *gestures and he rises.*

Isabella Cardinal Mendoza and others have told us of your proposed enterprise to find a quick way East. Convince us you know how.

Columbus *opens the case, takes out a small globe of the world and holds it up.*

Columbus This is a globe of our world . . . (*He spins the globe on his forefinger.*) It is divided into three hundred and sixty degrees. According to my calculations the circumference of the world at the equator is some 20,000 miles.

Torquemada As Inquisitor-General I'm a symbol of benighted fanaticism and brain-numbing ignorance but I know that a degree measures 60 nautical miles, that the circumference of the globe at the equator is 25,000 miles and so this the true size of the world.

A title appears on the screen behind them which reads: 'Torquemada is right. The world is at least one quarter bigger than Columbus claims.'

All read the title, but **Columbus** *shakes his head as one who knows better and spins the globe on his forefinger in the opposite direction.*

Columbus According to my true calculations by sailing due West on the latitude of the Canaries, Japan is only some 2,400 miles away.

Torquemada Surely it's nearer 10,000? And no ship can carry supplies for that distance.

A title appears reading: 'Torquemada is right again.'

They all read the title which **Columbus** *dismisses with a wave of his hand.*

Columbus These are mere facts! I'm concerned with visions . . . Beyond Japan lies China and India, and lands unknown except in legend, gold-wide, gold-deep, peopled not with pestilential Jews and Moors but heathens ripe for conversion – millions of 'em. With sword and fire, rack and iron boot, we'll bring them the benefits of Spanish civilisation and the Catholic Faith; we'll bring souls to Paradise and show them Christ in glory. I'm talking of a new Crusade which will spread your names across a new world, and Queen Isabella and King Ferdinand and Thomas Torquemada will live for ever and for ever with the Saints! And all for three ships.

Fascinated, **Isabella** *and* **Ferdinand** *have risen and moved closer to him with* **Torquemada.**

Torquemada Cheap at the price!

Isabella For new souls, new glory!

Ferdinand What are you asking for this new glory?

Columbus The title of Grand Admiral of the Oceanic Sea, to be made Viceroy and have the right to nominate all governors of the lands I discover, and to take ten per cent of all commerce from such lands in perpetuity.

Ferdinand You're mad! If you were successful your power would rival ours.

Columbus Like Elijah who could light fires by snapping his fingers, I will be successful – God wills it. And when I am, you'll be so rich no person or State could rival you.

Ferdinand A beautiful dream but we can't afford the price of three ships.

Isabella Not whilst all monies are pledged for the war against the Moors. We must root out their accursed tolerance from the soil of Spain. When Granada is free we'll have money.

Ferdinand That may take years.

Columbus I can wait till Hell freezes over – and longer.

Ferdinand *and* **Isabella** *gesture together and* **Columbus** *bows low and retires backwards into the darkness.*

Torquemada That man is a fanatic.

Ferdinand Worse, he's a foreigner who thinks he knows best.

Isabella But God is with him. I can tell by his eyes.

Torquemada You noticed them too. Rather like mine.

Isabella And mine now I come to think on it.

Ferdinand You like him, Madame, because I don't.

Isabella That's a big plus in his favour. I propose to give him a small pension.

Ferdinand With your monies, Madame, not mine.

Isabella He'll be on hand should we need him.

Ferdinand We won't. He's a man who brightens a room just by leaving it. Let him fade.

Spot out Stage Right.

Spot up Stage Left on the bedroom where **Columbus** *is haranguing the* **Parrot**.

Columbus But I didn't fade. I'm not a fading person though I often felt myself fading. Instead I waited. For seven years I waited, waited till the cows came home. Seven years of waiting, seven years of pain and humiliation, when I was rebuffed by stupid kings, ignorant nobles, jealous courtiers.

Spot out.

Soft organ music. Spot up Stage Right on **Isabella** *praying beneath the shadow of a great cross, as a figure sidles up beside her. It is* **Columbus**. **Isabella** *starts in surprise.*

Isabella Not now, not now!

Spot out.

Spot up Downstage Right on **Ferdinand** *squatting on the toilet seat in a privy, reading a book, when* **Columbus'** *face appears out of the darkness behind him and whispers in his ear.*

Ferdinand Not now, not now!

Spot out.

Sound of cannons and men fighting and dying.

Lights up on thick smoke and piles of empty bloodstained armour whilst rows of the crescent banners of Islam burn furiously.

A great drumroll as **Isabella** *and* **Ferdinand** *appear triumphant in bright armour out of the smoke.*

They acknowledge the cries and screams from the darkness with nods and smiles as if they were applause.

There is a loud fanfare.

Ferdinand Rejoice, rejoice, carnage maketh the man. Granada, the last citadel of the Moors in Spain, has fallen on this cold January in the Year of Our Lord 1492.

Isabella Christ said forgive your enemies, but now we have none, we've butchered them all. So give thanks on this deliverance, when the Spanish soil is at last cleansed with blood and we ride to glory.

Columbus *emerges from the smoke with a petition in his hand.*

Columbus Your Majesties, on this day when God's will is finally done, I come to reclaim a pledge. Remember my enterprise and the gold and silver waiting for you.

Ferdinand Not now, not now!

Columbus If not now, when? If not when, never? The King of France has asked to see me.

Isabella France is interested? You catch us on a good day. Now Granada has fallen we look on your enterprise with favour. Find the ships and men and we'll find the monies.

Columbus Your Highnesses!

He retreats joyfully backwards into the smoke.

Ferdinand You'll find monies where, Madame?

Isabella Italian bankers, and the loot from Granada. Anything's worth it to catch up with our rivals in the race to the Indies.

Ferdinand You're doing it to spite me, to cloud my joy on this joyous day.

Isabella Of course.

Lights out.

Spot up on a massive ornate mirror hanging Stage Left.

Naked to the waist, **Beatriz Enriquez de Arana** *admires herself in it, her long black hair cascading over her shoulders.*

Columbus' Voice There were distractions, but they were only personal . . . Beatriz Enriquez de Arana who judged with her body not her mind. She cost me dear. The Church wouldn't make me a Saint because of her, but that's another story . . .

Columbus *comes up behind* **Beatriz** *and nuzzles her neck. She smiles languidly. He stares fixedly at her breasts.*

Columbus Those breasts, those sister-swelling breasts. They are the real size and shape of the world. Fools say the glove is the size of a melon but it's truly the size of your breasts . . . Why can't they see what I can see? (*He fondles them.*) Hemispheres of perfection . . . the hope and comfort of mankind . . . I can explore the real world as easily as I explore your breasts . . . (*He covers her breasts with his hands.*) See how I cover them, squeeze them dry . . . (*She cries out.*) They're mine!

They kiss passionately.

Spot up Stage Right on a smoky tavern atmosphere with **Columbus** *seated at a table, trying to hire* **Two** *weather-beaten* **Seamen** *for his crew.*

Columbus I'm paying one thousand maravedis a month. Plus shares in all spoils taken and found including gold, silver and precious gems for a few days' sailing West . . . Who'll sign? . . . No one? . . . I know you're frightened . . . It's sailing West into the unknown isn't it?

First Seaman No . . . At a time when gentlemen like you are winning fame and fortune exploring the oceans, we fishermen of Rouen and St Malo are making two voyages a year to the banks of Newfoundland with the fog rolling in and the souls of dead seals honking soft in the distance. We stay at sea for months of fishing without ever taking shelter on land. Anything you discover we've seen first. But that won't be noted in the records, not remembered by future generations because it's all in a day's work, and we're only first seamen, and second seamen, men without names. We're unknown so how can we be frightened of the unknown?

Columbus What are you frightened of, then?

Second Seaman You, Signor Colon, Colombo or Columbus or whatever you call yourself. I'm an old sea-dog and I'll cock my leg up anywhere but I wouldn't sail with you to the next port let alone into the unknown.

Columbus Why?

Second Seaman You can't use a quadrant, can't calculate latitude, and you've never captained a ship before. We're not putting our lives into the hands of a glib-tongued blowhard like you.

First Seaman We won't sail for you unless you take on a partner who knows ships and the sea.

Columbus I don't need one. I'll never share my gold or my glory.

Second Seaman Then you'll have no crew.

Columbus I won't be forced – never! Who did you have in mind as my partner?

First & Second Seamen Martin Pinzon and his brothers.

Columbus No.

First & Second Seamen Yes.

Columbus No!

First & Second Seamen Yes!

Columbus Never!

Spot up on the throne room Stage Centre with **Martin Pinzon** *standing in front of* **Isabella** *and* **Ferdinand** *seated on their thrones.*

Isabella Ah, Martin Pinzon.

Columbus *joins* **Pinzon**.

Isabella I'm glad to see you've taken on our loyal subject Martin Pinzon as your partner in this venture.

Pinzon *bows again,* **Columbus** *scowls.*

Columbus No sacrifice is too much for the good of the enterprise, Your Highnesses.

Ferdinand With Pinzon aboard we lessen the risk to our capital. You've behaved more sensibly than I thought possible . . . (*He hands* **Columbus** *a document.*) Lawyers have spent weeks drawing up this contract. No, no, don't bother to read it! It's against my better judgement but my wife is much taken with you, so we've agreed to all your exorbitant terms, including that obnoxious ten per cent, Admiral.

As **Columbus** *backs away into the darkness with* **Pinzon**, **Ferdinand** *and* **Isabella** *exchange sly looks.*

Spot up Stage Left on the bedroom where **Columbus** *gestures at the* **Parrot**.

Columbus Cheated – the contract was false-bottomed! I'd waited seven years, I should've waited another seven. I was too eager to be gone. But the ships were waiting.

Parrot The 'Pinta', 'Nina' and 'Santa Maria'.

Columbus Oh Pol, I can still see it, smell it. Friday the 3rd of August, in the Year of Our Lord 1492, we upped anchor and sailed down the river Tinto and away, away . . . My plan was simple, like all plans of genius. We set course for the Canaries, and then on the 6th of September we sailed from Gomera. Two days later we lost sight of land and began to enter the unknown sea.

Lights fade down.

Light on screen hanging Upstage to show film of the sea at night and one shooting star curving across the sky.

Columbus' Voice Admiral's Log. 11th September. 'At the beginning of this night, we saw falling from heaven, four or five leagues off our ships, a marvellous branch of fire . . .'

The image on the screen dissolves to a calm sunlit seascape.

Columbus' Voice Admiral's Log. 20th September. 'The air was sweet and very pleasant; only lacked the song of the nightingales; and the sea was as smooth as a river . . .'

The image on the screen dissolves to a blood red sunset.

Columbus' Voice Admiral's Log. 8th October. 'All night we heard birds flying over . . .'

The image on the screen dissolves to a dawn sky and the first indistinct outline of a tongue of land in the far distance.

Columbus' Voice Admiral's Log. 12th October . . .

Spot up Stage Right on the lookout, **Rodrigo**, *clinging to a topmast. He points excitedly and yells.*

Rodrigo Land! . . .

Spot up Stage Left on the bedroom and **Columbus** *pointing dramatically.*

Columbus Land! . . . I was proved right! Journey's end . . . We landed next day on a small island we called San Salvadore. The native Arawaks behaved very properly, greeted us as gods, and cried out in delight when we gave them worthless beads and trinkets. We'd reached Japan – the gold-tiled palaces were on the other side of the hill. But when Cuba and Haiti were discovered, I realised we were actually off the coast of India. But I had problems, they wouldn't tell me where the gold was and I didn't trust my partner Martin Pinzon. He'd made me wreck the 'Santa Maria' so he could get back to Spain first with the news and steal my glory. But I transferred to the 'Nina'. God was with me as always, Polly. I fought storms and tempests all the way home and reached safe harbour first whilst Judas Pinzon lay down dying, weak, weak as water.

Parrot God was with you!

Columbus I arrived in Palos, 15th March '93 and organised a triumphant march to Barcelona to greet their Highnesses and give thanks to Holy Mother Church!

Spot out.

A great **Choir** *thunders* Gloria In Excelsis, *in the darkness.*

Spot up Stage Centre to reveal the magnificent figure of **Columbus** *in golden costume, cloak and plumes.*

Golden confetti rains down as he waves majestically to acknowledge the exultant cries of an **Unseen Crowd**.

Spot out.

Spot up Stage Right on a ship's hold where **Pinzon** *lays dying, with the lookout,* **Rodrigo**, *beside him.*

Pinzon We arrived too late. He's already in Barcelona, eating up our fame. We're left to die forgotten but it was my triumph too. That incompetent couldn't sail a boat in a bathtub. Wrecked the 'Santa Maria' with his stupidity. His crew were ready to mutiny. I stopped 'em just in time. Now he'll grow fat on it. Fame's a fickle whore.

Rodrigo And what of the money? The first man to spy land was to be given a life-pension of 10,000 mauvides. That's mine. 'Land! Land!' Everybody heard me shout 'Land! Land!' But he's stolen that from me. The Admiral of the Oceanic Sea has claimed the reward and given it to his mistress, Beatriz Enriquez – that's all she'll ever get from him but it's left us both bone-dry. You without your fortune and your fame, me without my pension. There's no justice nowhere when that Christ-Bearing snot-bag, Columbus, gets it all . . . I'm going to Morocco and turn Mahometan.

Pinzon I'd go too if I wasn't dying. Martin Pinzon, who made it all happen, left to rot in oblivion's pit. Wrong-time, wrong-place Pinzon. Cain-marked and damned, never entered into the records. See, see, now the shadows lengthen and my name fades with yours, friend. We're not forgotten – we'll never be remembered. History's a bitch, no sense of right and wrong. Let's try and roll back the night, make one last cry and perhaps they'll remember us . . . The name's Martin Pinzon!

Rodrigo Land! Land!

Pinzon Martin Pinzon! Martin Pinzon!

Rodrigo Land! Land!

Pinzon Martin Pinzon! Martin Pinzon!

The spot fades out.

Lights up Stage Centre on the throne room where **Isabella** *and* **Ferdinand** *are taking inventory of various*

*items, screeching green parrots in cages, rolls of cloth,
bamboo poles, stuffed alligators.*

Ferdinand This, Madame, is the return on your
glorious expedition – twenty parrots, a few swarthy
natives, some gold nose-rings, thirty bamboo canes, five
rolls of coarse cloth which we make better in Seville and
two badly stuffed alligators.

Isabella We have new territories to rule, thanks to the
Admiral.

Ferdinand Where? That idiot doesn't even know
where he's been. First he says Japan, then China, now
it's India.

Isabella He should've taken a map-maker with him.
But he's come back with thousands of souls to save in
Haiti alone. There's work for Christ and the Church
there, to say nothing of all the cheap labour. The
Inquisitor-General and the Holy Father are delighted.

Ferdinand I'm not so easily pleased. Where's the gold?
That's the reason he was sent. Gold is the only measure
of success.

Isabella Next time. He'll get it for us next time.

Lights out Stage Centre.

Spot up Stage Left on the bedroom as **Columbus** *jabs a
finger at the* **Parrot**.

Columbus That's the thanks I got. They gave me a
coat of arms which meant I didn't have to mix with riff-
raff but for the rest it was all carping. In the end you
must love yourself, Pol, it's the only affection you can
depend on. I never got what I deserved. Naturally it
was easier to raise money for the next expedition. This
time we went with a fleet, fifteen hundred men, 25th
September in the Year of Our Lord 1493 . . . I was in
charge of course.

Spot out.

Spot up Stage Right where **Columbus** *and* **Father Nervo** *are interrogatting a* **Native Chief** *to the sound of chattering monkeys and screeching parrots.*

Columbus Gold . . . Do you understand . . . It's yellow metal . . . (*He draws his sword, the* **Chief** *jumps back.*) Metal like this . . . only yellow . . .

Nervo Yellow . . . Yellow! . . . My son . . . (*He starts to spell it.*) Y-E-L-L- . . .

Columbus It's no good spelling it if they don't understand the language . . . (*He takes out a thin yellow bracelet.*) See . . . see . . . this . . . this!

The **Chief** *looks at the bracelet again and starts pointing.*

First Native Whoaa . . . oooh . . .

Columbus I knew it! It's outside . . . Lead us to the gold!

Spot out.

Columbus' Voice The gold was there, but always on the other side of the mountain. So we had to find other sources of income.

Lights up Stage Centre on a cracked and peeling high, white wall, lit by burning torches and a brazier.

Hanging on the wall are chains, manacles, ankle-irons and man-traps.

The sound of a whip cracking over. And the groans of **Men** *and* **Women** *marching in chains as* **Columbus** *enters and starts to take down the instruments of torture.*

Columbus' Voice We couldn't get our hands on yellow gold so it had to be black. Slaves always bring a profit. I should know, I'd been a slave-trader all my life.

Father Nervo *enters.*

Nervo Is this Christian, Admiral? We're here to convert the heathen not necessarily to enslave him.

Columbus We're here for profit.

Nervo Won't it cost too much to ship them home, Admiral? How are you going to feed 'em on the voyage?

Columbus We ship cannibal slaves. They can eat each other on the journey and cost us nothing.

Nervo Queen Isabella won't approve. She's for conversion. Technically the natives are Spaniards now and under her protection. She might take it amiss that you're enslaving her people.

Columbus I know Queen Isabella's mind better than you. We'll ship five hundred on the first boatload. Help me down with this.

Nervo *helps* **Columbus** *take down from the wall a vicious looking man-trap and then dumps all the instruments on to the* **Priest** *who staggers off with them.*

Columbus' Voice But the Priest was right for once. Queen Isabella didn't want her subjects made into slaves. Besides they died off too quickly to be good workers. They weren't robust. A generation after we landed, the whole population of Haiti had been wiped out. A weak people, they couldn't survive the onslaught of civilisation.

Blood pours down the wall.

Columbus This place is gutted. We move on to Cuba. We'll find gold there.

He crosses Stage Right where **Nervo** *is crouched over a map of Cuba spread out on the ground.* **Columbus** *looks down at it.*

Columbus What is it?

Nervo It's a map of Cuba.

Columbus But you've drawn it as an island.

Nervo It is an island. Our ships have voyaged round it.

Columbus Of course it isn't an island! How many times do I have to tell you? It's part of the continent of India.

Nervo India? This isn't India!

Columbus You may be a Priest and royal map-maker but I know better than you because I'm an Admiral and God's instrument. So I am promulgating a law which requires all Europeans to sign a solemn statement that Cuba is part of the continent of India. (*He forces the* **Priest**'s *mouth open and grabs his tongue.*) Anyone going back on his word will have his tongue torn out. Agreed?

Nervo *Arrrrr . . .*

Columbus I thought you would. Now remember, Father, we haven't come here to settle but to trade for gold – that is, to loot. There's no other way of getting it except by force, cruelty and terror.

Nervo Yes . . . yes . . . but what about *that!*

He points to a **Spaniard** *crossing Upstage with his arm round a* **Native Woman**.

Nervo (*angry for the first time*) Vile lust! Sin and degeneracy!

Columbus I'm against it myself. I've no need to indulge when I swell in my mind at thoughts of fame and fortune.

Nervo God's curse will be branded for ever on the flesh of his accursed people!

Lights out.

Spot up Stage Left on mist and a row of white-faced dummies' heads on stakes with burnt-out holes for eyes.

Columbus' Voice Syphilis . . . The curse was a new disease called Syphilis or the Great Pox. When we sailed home in '95, we found Spain full of men who'd returned before us, rotting with disease.

Spot up Stage Centre to muffled drumbeats, on **Columbus**'s *gold jacket, cloak and gold hat with a plume hanging wet and dirty on butchers' hooks.*

Columbus' Voice I organised another procession but it wasn't a success.

Spot out.

Spot up Stage Left on **Columbus** *sitting slumped on the bed slowly tearing up legal documents.*

Columbus That was a bad homecoming, even my misery lacked grandeur. Next time it was worse. I went out to the Indies again in '98. I had arthritis and eye-trouble but we caught a north easterly and found another new land – Trinidad – and the delta to a great river – the Ganges.

Parrot The Ganges? The Ganges?

Columbus Listen, Polly, listen. This time I'd discovered nothing less than the entrance to the Garden of Eden. It was simple logic, you see, Polly. The four great rivers of the world, the Ganges, Nile, Tigris and Euphrates all spring from a well in the Garden of Eden. Now all I had to do was follow the river to its source and I was in Eden's Garden.

Parrot Did you find it? Did you find it?

Columbus Didn't have time. I had to go back to Haiti. You won't credit it, Polly, but I had a rebellion on my hands.

Spot out.

Spot up Stage Right on a bare room with one ornate chair, a table and the elegant **Francisco Roldan**, *waiting impatiently for* **Columbus** *who enters, furiously.*

Columbus As Viceroy I made you Chief Justice of this province and I find you're leading a conspiracy against me!

Roldan There's no conspiracy, Admiral. Only Spaniards demanding their rights.

Columbus Their right not to work, you mean. Every Spaniard with two pesos to rub together has an utter contempt for all forms of manual labour. Shipwrecked they won't even build a boat to save themselves.

Roldan We let our servants do that for us.

Columbus By Jesus, you have enough of them here. Three natives a piece. It's ruined the colony. I imposed a tribute of gold on every native. The quota's not being fulfilled because the wretches're too busy fetching and carrying for Spanish idlers and degenerates.

Roldan It's not being fulfilled because the quota is too high. There isn't enough gold, no matter how hard we flog 'em. That's why they're giving so much trouble.

Columbus They're giving us trouble because you're letting Spanish gentlemen go off prospecting for gold on their own account. That's my monopoly! It's more than a conspiracy, it's a rebellion!

Roldan If there is, it's because no one respects you . . . 'Admiral'.

Columbus No one what?

Roldan Respects you. How can they? You're no true Spaniard. You own no land or titles in Castille. You're a foreigner. You haven't the blood.

Columbus Beshat gutter-slush, I'm the son of Count Colombo, descendant of a Roman general and Gascon Admiral!

Roldan So you say, but true aristocrats know.

Columbus Know?! Know?! Know?!

Roldan You can't hide it, you stink of cheese, Admiral.

Columbus Rotting crotch-sack! Chief Justice! I'll show you Justice!

Spot out.

An image is projected on the screen Upstage: Six **Corpses** *with black bags over their heads, dangling from a gallows.*

Columbus' Voice They sent out a Royal Commissioner to seek out truth and apportion blame. The man was a complete idiot – he blamed *me*!

Lights up Stage Centre on **Isabella** *and* **Ferdinand** *on their thrones, looking at each other and sighing.*

Ferdinand Do we have to see him?

Isabella It's our duty, unfortunately.

There is a fanfare.

Herald's Voice Your Highnesses, the Admiral of the Oceanic Sea craves audience.

There is a loud rattling sound as **Columbus** *hops towards them, wrapped in chains. He attempts to bow and crashes over.* **Isabella** *and* **Ferdinand** *cross to him as he staggers up.*

Isabella Why're you still bound? We gave orders for you to be released.

Columbus I refused. I said only my dear Sovereign, Her Majesty, Queen Isabella can release me from this bondage.

Isabella *touches the chains and they fall from him.*

Isabella This is a sad business, Admiral.

Columbus I'm ill-used, Your Highnesses. Now it's routine to cross the Atlantic, but remember I was first! I brought this new world under your domination and Spain once reckoned poor will soon be rich.

Ferdinand How soon?

Columbus Within the next seven years set aside for the gold. Then we will ransom the Holy House of Jerusalem! For I am that messenger of the new heaven and new earth, revealed in the Book of the Apocalypse!

Ferdinand Quite so, quite so.

He takes out a yo-yo and plays with it, yawning.

Columbus You forget I've given the Indies to the Kingdom of Castille.

Ferdinand and Isabella Given?!

Ferdinand It's ours!

Isabella By right!

Columbus *falls on his knees, weeping.*

Columbus Of course, of course! Everything's yours, Your Majesties, no question. I'm an old man, the folds and edges are frayed. Now others reap what I sowed. And I'm left begging for what's mine. I'm the Christ-Bearer, I brought a million new souls to Jesus. I deserve something more.

Isabella Your reward will be in Heaven.

Columbus I want it down here too.

Ferdinand That could prove a little more difficult.

Columbus *cries loudly.* **Isabella** *helps him up imperceptibly and guides him out.*

Isabella Let me say solemnly before witnesses, that favours we've granted to you will be maintained in their entirety. And you and your children shall enjoy them as is right and just.

Ferdinand Absolutely. See our lawyers.

Columbus *bows fawningly.*

Columbus Thank you, Your Highnesses . . . Thank you, Your Highnesses.

Isabella *pushes him gently out of the light.*

Ferdinand What a fool.

Isabella I was right to back him but now he's become tiresome. He's served his purpose.

She returns to sit on her throne.

Ferdinand Time to move on. There are others waiting in the wings who'll prove more profitable.

Isabella Next!

Lights out.

Spot up on the bedroom Stage Left.

Columbus Never put your trust in princes, Polly. I was forbidden to set foot in Haiti, never made Governor or Viceroy again. As for my percentage I'm still fighting for it. After Isabella died I managed to gouge one-tenth of the royal fifth – that's two per cent – out of Ferdinand. So I won't die poor. I'm rich but not rich enough! Not as rich as I deserve to be. Made one last voyage . . . 11th of May in the Year of Our Lord 1502 . . . can't remember much . . . The voyage was all midnight, Pol . . . it seemed the Devil himself was against us . . . great seas and hurricanes . . . (*A wind blows through the room swirling some of the torn paper into the air.*) . . . We reached South China . . . It's all jimbles and jambles in the mind, Pol . . . But then one day in the storm and the night we found it . . . We found the gold! And a new dawn opened for civilisation.

The wind dies down as **Two Natives** *come out of the wind and darkness with gold masks over their faces and carrying golden spears.*

Columbus I was proved right again! . . . Sailed home rich and loaded but then the Devil smote us . . . water

spouts eighty feet high, skies the colour of blood . . .
our treasure ship sank . . . sank, Pol, and me with it.

The **Natives** *retreat back into the dark.*

Columbus And I'm here, Polly, and my bones ache
. . . Fifty years from now, Spain's Empire will stretch
from Mexico in the North to Chile in the South . . .
and later . . . (*The sound of a howling police siren is
heard.*) . . . much, much later . . .

*The extraordinary skyscraper image of New York, taken
from a helicopter, comes up on the screen Upstage Centre
to the accompaniment of the single police siren.*

Columbus' Voice Great cities will rise and rise and
rise and shadow the earth. Like the rest, it's all based
on blood and violence, cruelty and death, but what of
that?

The screen goes dark.

Columbus *sighs and crosses to the* **Parrot.**

Columbus I made it possible. I made it happen. I did
it for Christ and myself. Christ is happy but I'm
disappointed. I should be the richest man in Christendom . . . Instead . . . Anyway you've heard it all now.
So what's your verdict, Polly?

Parrot It's all a joke! God let the mild, gentle natives
be exterminated just because they were mild and gentle,
and chose an ignorant windbag like you for greatness,
whilst killing off a man with all the claims like Martin
Pinzon. If the Almighty was fair you would've ended up
with a small shop in Genoa, selling cheese, instead
they'll raise statues to you.

Columbus They will?! They will?!

Parrot They'll name cities, states, countries and even
holidays after you. You will be everybody's blue-eyed
hero – brave, honest and white: Columbus the Christ-
Bearer, Columbus the Great Explorer, Columbus

Founder of the Modern World. You conned 'em all,
from generation to generation, you conned 'em all!

Columbus *notices the* **Audience** *for the first time,
reacts, and then starts to cackle and point jeeringly at
them.*

As the Spot fades out **Columbus** *roars with laughter and
the final verse of the ballad is sung in the darkness.*

Singer This is the way it happened
       Forget the legend and song
       Some have heroic views of Columbus
       But we know who's right and who's wrong.

Lightning Source UK Ltd.
Milton Keynes UK
UKOW02f0429080415

249285UK00001B/37/P